CW00926264

WHERE THREE STREAMS MEET

Seán Ó Duinn, OSB

Where three streams meet
Celtic Spirituality

the columba press

First published in 2000 by
the columba press
55A Spruce Avenue, Stillorgan Industrial Park
Blackrock, Co Dublin

Cover by Bill Bolger
The gilt bronze figure of a bishop is used by courtesy of the
National Museum of Ireland.
Origination by The Columba Press
Printed in Ireland by Colour Books Ltd, Dublin
ISBN 1 85607 288 6

Acknowledgements
The author and publisher gratefully acknowledge the permission of the
following to use material in their copyright: The Royal Irish Academy for
quotations from *The Celtic Ethography of Posidonius* by J. Tierney;
Thames and Hudson Ltd for a quotation from *Myth and Symbol in
Ancient Egypt* by R. Rundle Clarke; Head of the Department of Irish
Folklore, University College Dublin for quotations from their manuscript
collection, especially from replies to a questionnaire entitled 'The Feast of
St Brigid' contained in IFC 899-907; The Irish Texts Society for quotations from *Lebor Gabála Érenn* by R. Macalister and from *The Poems of
Blathmac Son of Cú Brettan* by J. Carney; An Clóchomhar Teo for quot-
ations from *Caoineadh na dTrí Muire* by A. Partridge; Gabriel Rosenstock
for the use of his translation of Caoineadh na Maighdine; Mercier Press
for quotations from *Irish Wake Amusements* by Seán Ó Súilleabháin;
Foilseacháin Ábhar Spioradálta for quotations from *Ár bPaidreacha
Dúchais* by Diarmaid Ó Laoghaire; Scottish Academic Press for quotations from *Carmina Gadelica* by A. Carmichael; The Editor of *Monastic
Studies* for the quotation from Thomas Berry on page 189; The Editor of
Peritia for the quotation from D. J. Lewis on pages 124-6; Pueblo
Publishing Company for a quotation from *Prayers of the Eucharist Early
and Reformed* by R. Jaspar and G. Cuming; The Editor of *Celtica* for the
quotation from W. Gillies on pages 129-130; Veritas Publications who
previously published chapter thirteen as an essay in *Celtic Threads*, edited
by P. Clancy.

Contents

Introduction

Our purpose is to examine the traditional path to God which the Gaelic-speaking peoples of Ireland and Scotland evolved over the centuries. Remnants of this ancient heritage still remain and, when put into the wider context of the great family of the Celts, of which the Welsh and the Bretons form so important a part, we can arrive at some notion of a great spiritual heritage which, because of its special qualities, may speak to us today in a compelling manner.

Amidst the numerous works which have appeared over the past number of years on the various spiritual paths, a new emphasis was given to the Celtic way by Professor John Macquarrie in his book *Paths in Spirituality* (Oxford 1972). He drew attention to the Gaelic tradition of piety, which stressed the presence of God in the world, filling everything, invigorating everything, enfolding everything.

While safeguarding the transcendence of God – that is, God as being utterly different from us or anything we can imagine and being infinitely far away – the Gaelic-speaking peoples laid great stress on the immanence of God – the nearness of God to us and his involvement with nature and with the world – 'in him we live and move and have our being' (Acts 17:28).

Generally speaking, the church both in East and West has shown a tendency to stress the transcendence of God and emphasise his majesty and distance from us, with a consequent need to lay great stress on the means available in the church to

provide access to him. The transcendence of God is part of
Christian belief and was held by the Celts as with other
Christians, as the magnificent text from the Irish *Stowe Missal*
makes clear:

> It is truly meet and right, just and for our salvation, that we
> should here at all times and in all places give thanks unto
> thee, Holy Lord, almighty everlasting God, through Christ
> our Lord, who together with thine Only-begotten and the
> Holy Ghost art one and immortal God, incorruptible and
> immovable God, invisible and faithful God, wonderful and
> praiseworthy God, honourable and strong God, most high
> and magnificent God, living and true God, wise and power-
> ful God, holy and beautiful God, great and good God, terri-
> ble and peace-loving God, noble and upright God, not in the
> singleness of one person, but in the Trinity of one substance.
> We believe in thee, we bless thee, we worship thee, and we
> praise thy name ever world without end; through whom is the
> salvation of the world, through whom is the life of men,
> through whom is the resurrection of the dead. (West, 1938, 78)

One the other hand, as we shall see, native texts in Irish
rather than in Latin, tend to stress the immanence of God – *Rí
na nDúl* – the God of the Elements, earth, air, fire and water,
the God who surrounds us. There was no difference in belief in
this matter between the Celts and other Christians; both parties
held that God was both transcendent and immanent, as is necessary for orthodoxy, but the Celts tended to place particular
emphasis on the immanence of God. This tendency to emphasise the nearness of God and his association with nature and
with the events of everyday life had, naturally, repercussions on
the Celtic Way.

What was important was to build up an awareness of the
divine presence, to cultivate an intimacy with God who is nearer
to us than we are to ourselves, and this cultivation of awareness

gave rise to the *paidreacha dúchais* or folk-prayers which are such an important part of Gaelic spiritual tradition. There was a prayer for rising, for going to bed, for blessing the bed, for milking the cow, for seeing the moon, etc. – in other words, special prayers and rituals were used as a technique for building up an awareness of God. In this way one became united to God, which is the aim of all forms of spirituality.

Professor Macquarrie puts the matter very succinctly, bringing together the archaic past and the present:

> And I doubt whether the quest (for a vision of the world in a new wholeness and depth) can be fulfilled unless we can realise again the presence of a transcendent reality that is none the less that which is nearest of all; immanent in the world and in human life itself. It may be worth while recalling this vision of the world and sense of presence that were once common in the West and are still common in parts of the world ... The Celt was very much a God-intoxicated man whose life was embraced on all sides by the divine Being. But this presence was always mediated through some finite, this-worldly reality ... (1972, 122-123)

We can distinguish several ideas in this quotation which help to introduce the subject:

Firstly, the idea of quest for an understanding of one's place in the world – an integrated life; secondly, the idea of the divine presence immanent in the world and in human life; thirdly, the concept of the divine immanence as having been lost in the West but preserved in Celtic spirituality.

To lead into an account of the Celts, their origins and way of life, we may pause for a moment to consider that strange episode described in chapter 17 of the Acts of the Apostles, in which St Paul addresses the Athenians. While his speech was directed to the people of Athens, the religious ethos it ascribes to them comes remarkably close to that of the Celts. In the year

279 BC the Celts had actually launched an attack on the sacred shrine of Apollo at Delphi, not so far away from Athens.

So, Paul, standing in the middle of the Areopagus, said: 'Men of Athens, I perceive that in every way you are very religious. For as I passed along, and observed the objects of your worship, I found also an altar with this inscription, "To an unknown god." What therefore you worship as unknown, this I proclaim to you. The God who made the world and everything in it, being Lord of heaven and earth, does not live in shrines made by man, nor is he served by human hands, as though he needed anything, since he himself gives to all men life and breath and everything. And he made from one every nation of men to live on all the face of the earth, having determined allotted periods and the boundaries of their habitation, that they should seek God, in the hope that they might feel after him and find him, yet he is not far from each one of us, for "In him we live and move and have our being"; as even some of your poets have said, "For we are indeed his offspring". Being then God's offspring, we ought not to think that the Deity is like gold, or silver, or stone, a representation by the art and imagination of man.' (Acts 17:22-29)

St Paul remarks on the religious zeal of the Athenians with their many shrines and an altar to 'The Unknown God'. According to a legend, a pestilence had broken out in the city several centuries before and, to avert the supposed anger of the gods, a flock of black and white sheep were let loose on the streets. Each sheep that lay down and dozed off in the sun was sacrificed. (Barclay, 1955, 143)

St Paul remarks that the Athenians were very religious. Similarly, Caesar says of the Celts of Gaul: 'The Whole Gallic people is exceedingly given to religious superstition.' (Tierney, 1960, 272)

The gods and goddesses of Ireland are well known, the country itself being named after the goddess Éire while other goddesses' names are in common use – names such as Áine, Úna, Méadhbh, Clíona, Eithne. Lugh (from which is derived Lughnasa) is perhaps the best-known god while An Daghdha and Aonghus Óg are associated with Brú na Bóinne, the great megalithic site in Co Meath.

As regards the view that God, being the creator of the world and all that is in it, does not live in shrines made by man, the Celts may have been nearer to Paul's view than the Greeks to whom he was speaking, as it appears that the oak grove or clearing in a forest was the ideal setting for Celtic worship among the druids. It is significant that what remains of Celtic Christian ritual today tends to be outdoor, as at holy wells and mountain pilgrimages.

In the phrase, 'In him we live and move and have our being' we have a quotation, not from the Old Testament, but from the pagan poet Epimenides. (Lattey, 1936, ixvii) The phrase carries overtones of an archaic system of philosophy and is reminiscent of the 'immanence' which will be discussed later in association with Celtic thought.

The phrase, 'For we are indeed his offspring' is taken from the poet Aratus. (Lattey, 1936, ixvii) Whatever the original meaning may have been, it bears a remarkable resemblance to what Caesar said of the Celtic Gauls: 'The Gauls all assert their descent from Dis Pater and say that it is the Druidic belief.' (Tierney, 1960, 273)

Dis Pater was the Roman god of the dead and corresponds to the Irish god of the dead, Donn. His great sanctuary is at Tech nDoinn, a small rocky island off the coast of Kerry, and also at Cnoc Fírinne in Co Limerick: Co mba ésin a edacht adbul dia chlaind chétaig: 'Cucum dom thig tíssaid uili íar bar n-ésaib'. (…and this was his last noble bequest to his hundreds of descendants: 'to me, to my house ye shall all come after your death.') (*Béaloideas* 18, uimh.1-11, Meitheamh-Nodlaig 1948, 152)

The great megalithic site of Newgrange at Brú na Bóinne, Co Meath, is thought to have been constructed around the latter part of the fourth millennium BC (Shee Twohig, 1990, 50), thousands of years before the Celts came to Ireland. Nevertheless, it is the Celtic gods and goddesses which are associated with Brú na Bóinne in Irish literature – An Daghdha, Aonghus Óg, Manannán Mac Lir, Midhir, Bóand, Coirceog, Eithne. This Celtic pantheon has obviously taken over a sacred site of the neolithic age.

From what has been said it is clear that we are not dealing with one exclusive religious system but rather with a series of different religions and cultures which have influenced each other. This, of course, makes the subject vastly more complex than dealing with a homogenous system, but on the other hand, is far more interesting. It shows the progression and at the same time the stability of the human search for the divine, the person as eager to press onwards on the path to God using new insights and, in the case of Christianity, a new revelation, but reluctant to part company with the ancient gods and the old ways. The Catholic religion has been particularly blessed in adopting generously the ancient ways, thought-patterns and customs of diverse peoples. In this way, the continuity of tradition has been preserved, linking the insights of early races with those of their more technologically advanced successors. It may well be that primal societies living close to the earth may have had a more integrated view of life than we have today.

We now turn to the Celts themselves to see something of their origins, way of life and general characteristics. What distinguished them as a race will no doubt be reflected in their distinct type of Christianity.

PART ONE

Who were the Celts?

CHAPTER 1

The Celts

Very briefly, it is generally held that the Celts began as a distinct people with their own language, customs, political and social organisation and general culture, about 1000 BC in the areas we now associate with central and south Germany, the Hartz Mountains, Austria, Bavaria and Bohemia. It appears that a group from the local Indo-European population gradually began to separate itself from the main body and developed a distinct language and culture and this group became known to Greek writers as the *Keltoi*.

From an early period, the Celts were associated with the salt mine of Hallstatt, near Salzburg, and as salt was an extremely valuable product in those days, the Celts of Hallstatt became immensely wealthy and the area became a great artistic and iron-working site. The large number of graves with their grave-goods testify to the importance of the area.

At a later stage, La Téne in Switzerland became another great artistic centre and the delicate curvilinear type of decoration which can be seen in brooches, swords, spears, etc. in the museums, appears to be influenced by the La Téne School. (Cunliffe, 1992, 16-17)

At any rate, during the first few centuries BC, the Celts began to expand and, with their iron weapons and the use of the horse and war-chariot, set off to conquer new lands.

Gaul, modern France, became their second home and again luck favoured them as regards wealth, for Gaul was *Gallia aurifera* or gold-bearing Gaul, and the gold washed

down from the mountains became a source of great wealth to
the Celts. Another great source of wealth was the fees charged
to traders using the great rivers. One of our greatest indications of the wealth and prestige of the Celts of this period is
the grave of a Celtic princess in Vix in France (Côte d'Or).
She appears to have died around 480 BC at about the age of 35.
She was buried with her chariot and beside her body was an
immense bronze wine krater with ornamental cups for distributing the wine. She wore a necklace of large stone and
amber beads, bronze ankle rings, bracelets and a massive torque
or collar of pure gold. This is no isolated case, as similar graves
have been found elsewhere. (Eluére, 1993, 42-43)

The Celts penetrated into parts of Spain, into the British
Isles, into the Rhineland of Germany and, on the other side,
into north Italy, the Balkans and finally established a colony
in Galatia in Asia Minor. St Paul's Letter to the Galatians is
addressed to these Celts of Turkey. Generally speaking, words
such as Galatia, Galicia in Spain and in Poland, Gaul, Gallia,
Gael, Gaeilge – indicate the presence of the Celts.

For about 500 years, the Celts dominated Europe and it is
significant that a recent book on the Celts by Christiane Eluére
is entitled, *The Celts – First Masters Of Europe.*

On archaeological evidence, the arrival of the Celts in
Ireland is quite late – in a series of migrations taking place
during the first few centuries BC. (MacCana, 1970, 12) On the
other hand, if it is accepted that a Celtic dialect was already in
use among the bronze age inhabitants of Ireland, the date of
arrival would be pushed back perhaps over a thousand years.
Was the maker of a late bronze age ornament a speaker of
Proto-Celtic? There is as yet no certainty but several scholars
favour the earlier date.

At any rate, even if the earlier date is considered more ac-
ceptable, the Celts were still latecomers to the island of
Ireland. The first definite traces of man in Ireland date from

about 6000 BC. The first settlers would appear to have crossed over from Scotland to northern Ireland and then moved southwards and westwards. However, little remains from this early period and we have to wait for another 3000 years for the great influx of stone age people from Britain or from further afield. These newcomers were better equipped, with polished stone axes to hew down areas of forest and gradually turn it into fertile land for the growing of wheat and barley. Cattle, sheep and goats grazed on the cleared areas and, no doubt, the diet was supplemented by hunting, fishing and wild berries.

An excellent insight into the blending of the megalithic, bronze age, Celtic and Norman into each other can be gleaned from a visit to Lough Gur in Co Limerick, where much has been preserved from the remote and not so remote past. Here, extensive archaeological excavations have discovered the remains of the simple thatched houses used by stone age man at Lough Gur, and the Information Centre on the site is a reconstruction of this type of dwelling. The stone circles and megalithic graves surrounding the lake indicate a preoccupation with religious ritual. One of the most impressive stone circles in Ireland is at Grange beside Lough Gur. The remains of other circles, a standing stone, a megalithic tomb, in close proximity to the enormous circle, might suggest a whole religious complex in this area. Pottery from the late stone age and early bronze age (c. 2000-1500) was found inside the Grange circle, again suggesting a peaceful merging of eras and possibly the amalgamation of different religious ideas.

Radio carbon dating has shown that the great megalithic site at Newgrange is somewhat older than the Co Limerick site, having been constructed about 3300 BC. Again, when we consider the later Celtic mythology connecting Celtic deities such as An Daghdha and Aonghus Óg with Newgrange (Brú na Bóinne), the impression is given of one system seeming to

slip into another in quite a natural manner that seems oddly
at variance with our modern tendency towards rigorous categ-
orisation. This impression is rather strengthened by the seeming ease with which Christianity took root in Ireland, giving
rise to the tradition that there were no martyrs in the transition from paganism to Christianity. This rather strange impression of continuity and change, this absence of abrupt and
violent transitions, must be taken into account in our later
treatment of Celtic religion and ritual. It would be a mistake
to make the categories too rigorous and exclusive of one another. It would seem rather that a certain fluidity of thought
existed, making it possible to show some continuity and even
dependence between different religious systems.

The enormous expansion of the Celts from Ireland in the
West to Galatia (modern Turkey) in the East in the first few
centuries BC might have seemed the ideal situation for the
foundation of a great Celtic empire. Such, however, did not
occur.

The Celts seem to have lacked that sense of cohesion, of
common effort and the flair for centralised government necessary for the foundation and consolidation of a great empire
or commonwealth. They squandered resources through internal divisions and engaging as mercenaries in foreign armies.
This inability to plan ahead coldly and calculatingly, and to
pursue a united campaign, appears to have been a fatal defect
which dogged the Celts throughout their history and perhaps
nowhere so much as in Ireland. It was a weakness which her
enemies traded on to perfection.

Dr Anne Ross quotes a passage from the historian Polybius
which illustrates the impetuosity of the Celts in rushing into
battle without adequate planning:

> Such was the end of the war against the Celts, a war which,
> if we look to the desperation and daring of the combat-
> ants, and the numbers who took part and perished in the

battles, is second to no war in history, but is quite con-
temptible as regards the plan of campaigns, and the
judgement shown in executing it, not most steps but every
single step the Celts took being commended to them
rather by the heat of passion than by cool calculation.
(1972, 96)

Similarly, Strabo remarks: 'the whole race which is now
called Gallic or Galatic, is madly fond of war, high-spirited
and quick to battle, but otherwise straightforward and not of
evil character. And so when they are stirred up they assemble
in their bands for a battle, quite openly and without fore-
thought, so that they are easily handled by those who desire to
outwit them; for at any time or place and on whatever pretext
you stir them up, you will have them ready to face danger.'
(Tierney, 1960, 267)

Even after 2000 years, this record of impetuous action and
distaste for planning the strategy of warfare seems not to have
changed. We have a marvellous account of the battle of Sliabh
na mBan, near Clonmel, in the rebellion of 1798 which says in
Irish what had been said in Greek nearly 2000 years earlier:

Níor tháinig ár Major i dtús an lae chugainn,
is ní rabhamar féin ann i gcóir ná i gceart;
ach mar sheolfaí aoireacht bó gan aoire
ar thaobh na gréine de Shliabh na mBan.
(Our major did not come to us at the start of the day,
and we ourselves weren't there in proper order and formation,
but like a herd of cows let loose without a shepherd
at the sunny side of Sliabh na mBan.)

If this type of incompetent fumbling in practical matters
were a racial characteristic, it is no wonder that a Celtic empire never emerged. As we shall see, the classical authors leave
no doubt about the personal bravery of the Celts, as again in

the personal sphere of artistic metal work and poetry the precision and order is beyond question. The peculiar difficulty
seems to arise when a large number of individuals have to
submerge their own individuality in the pursuit of a common
cause.

In short, a Celtic empire in the political sense never emerged
and no great centre such as Rome or London ever developed
in the Celtic area.

After their sudden expansion and rise to power, the Celts
suffered a rapid decline. They were subjected to pressure from
all sides – Dacians in the east, Germans in the north and
Romans in the south. The lack of unity, the absence of a centre of administration and lines of communication, soon made
themselves felt. Above all, the Celts were no match for the co-
hesive power and discipline of the Roman empire. In the first
century BC, Gaul, which might at this time be considered as
the home *par excellence* of the Celts, had been conquered by
Caesar. By the fifth century AD the Celtic language of Gaul
had practically ceased to exist and, while the Roman Empire
had collapsed in its turn, it was the Roman language and culture which was to prevail throughout the coming centuries
rather than that of the Celts. (MacCana, 1970, 12)

In Britain the Celts were experiencing similar reversals and
were being pushed into the remoter western areas of Wales
and Cornwall by the Anglo-Saxon invaders. The case of
Ireland of course was different; the country was never invaded
by the Romans and enjoyed a full measure of freedom to pursue its own cultural and political course. It is unlikely that the
introduction of Christianity or the depredations of Vikings
and Danes altered to any great extent the evolution of society
according to a basic Celtic pattern until a new era began with
the coming of the Normans in the twelfth century. Even then,
Gaelic ways and language continued unabated for a long time

to come until the final collapse of the Gaelic order with the disastrous Battle of Kinsale and the flight of the earls in the seventeenth century.

The remains of this once great civilisation, which at its height could be felt as a presence in areas reaching from Ireland to Asia Minor, is now reduced to a tiny remnant in six areas of Western Europe – Brittany, Wales, Cornwall, Scotland, Isle of Mann, Ireland. The Celtic languages still linger on but only as a whisper. In view of the mighty power of Anglo-American culture, it is surprising that Irish and Welsh are still spoken even in such sadly reduced circumstances. It is surely a sign of their tenacity and vigour in the face of such appalling odds.

While death beckons menacingly at the once great civilisation, a lingering breath still remains which perhaps could be the breath of life for the jaded victims of the consumer society. For myth is the great strength of the Celts and myth is associated with the hidden powers of renewal.

CHAPTER TWO

Lifestyle and Customs

A great deal of our information on the continental Celts is derived from Posidonius (135-51 BC). His works have been lost but, luckily for us, much of what he wrote about the Celts was copied by others close to the beginning of the Christian era. Among these writers, Caesar holds an important place. In his account of the Gallic War in which he defeated the Celts of Gaul his description of the people must have been influenced by personal experience and political motivation as well as by the information supplied by Posidonius.

The other three outstanding writers on the Celts from this early period, and also dependent on Posidonius, are Athenaeus, Diodorus Siculus, and Strabo – all writing in Greek.

Previous to these, however, was the historian Polybius whose notes on the Celts are neatly summarised by Professor Tierney:

> Lastly, we come to Polybius, the most voluminous author so far on the Celts. The mass of his material, as is natural, concerns history and geography, but a few passages can be found of ethnographical interest. In a short passage on Celtic living conditions in Cisalpine Gaul, he mentions such points as their beds of straw, their meat eating, their pursuit of war and agriculture and simplicity of life and finally, their institution of Clientship, all of which points we shall meet again. In connection with the battle of Telamon (225 BC) we hear of the Celtic breeches and cloaks, their necklaces and bracelets, of their vanity and bravado in

fighting naked, their head-hunting, their use of trumpets, their reckless courage and self sacrifice in battle and their mass suicide on defeat. Later on we hear of the golden standards of a goddess, Athena, clearly a Celtic war-goddess, and of the fact that the Gauls are most fearful only in their first spirited attack. A most interesting passage describes a series of duels instituted by Hannibal among Celtic prisoners, on his arrival in Italy. The prize was royal panoply, a horse and cloak. His account of the universal desire to fight and the universal congratulation of the vanquished dead no less than the victor throws a brilliant light on Celtic psychology. (1960, 197)

Appearance

Diodorus Siculus gives an excellent account of the appearance of the Celts and seems much impressed by the long hair and the treatment of it. It is likely, however, that the blonde or reddish hair referred to was not universal, and among such a far-flung and diverse society there must have been many stocky, dark people:

> The Gauls are tall in stature and their flesh is very moist and white, while their hair is not only naturally blond, but they also use artificial means to increase this natural quality of colour. For they continually wash their hair with lime-wash and draw it back from the forehead to the crown and to the nape of the neck, with the result that their appearance resembles that of Satyrs or of Pans, for the hair is so thickened by this treatment that it differs in no way from a horse's mane. Some shave off the beard, while others cultivate a short beard; the nobles shave the cheeks but let the moustache grow freely. (Tierney, 1960, 249)

Diodorus Siculus again describes the colourful Celtic dress. The chief articles of a man's dress seem to have been a trousers (baggy or tight), a thigh-length tunic and over this, the great

brat or cloak fastened by a large brooch. The trousers seem to
have come to the Celts from the horse-riding Scythians with
whom they had been in contact and from whom they no
doubt learned their ability with horses:

> They wear a striking kind of clothing – tunics dyed and
> stained in various colours, and trousers, which they call by
> the name of *bracae;* and they wear striped cloaks, fastened
> with buckles, thick in winter and light in summer, picked
> out with a variegated small check pattern. (Tierney, 1960,
> 250-251)

The same author gives an interesting account of the wealth
of the Celts of Gaul derived from un-mined gold. Archaeological finds such as the grave of the Celtic princess at Vix,
France, with her massive torque of pure gold, confirm his remarks. (Eluére, 1993, 42-43)

The gold could be used as grave-goods for the dead, for ornaments for the living and for offerings to the divinities:

> On the whole, silver is not found throughout Gaul, but
> there is a great deal of gold which nature yields to the in-
> habitants without the difficulties of mining. For the rivers,
> as they course through their winding bends and dash
> against the banks of the mountains which lie alongside,
> break off large masses from them and become filled with
> gold-dust. Those who are engaged in the business gather
> this together and grind or pound the lumps which hold
> the dust and by repeated washings they rid it of the earthy
> element and hand it over to the furnaces for smelting. In
> this way they accumulate large quantities of gold and make
> use of it for personal adornment, not only the women but
> also the men. For they wear bracelets on wrists and arms,
> and round their necks thick rings of solid gold, and they
> wear also fine finger-rings and even golden tunics. The
> Celts of the hinterland have a strange and peculiar custom

in connection with the sanctuaries of the gods; for in the temples and sanctuaries, which are dedicated throughout the country, a large amount of gold is openly placed as a dedication to the gods, and of the native inhabitants none touch it because of religious veneration, although the Celts are unusually fond of money. (Tierney, 1960, 249)

Food and drink

Another Greek writer, Athenaeus, discusses the food and drink of the Celts:

The Celts sit on dried grass and have their meals served up on wooden tables raised above the earth. Their food consists of a small number of loaves of bread together with a large amount of meat, either boiled or roasted on charcoal or on spits. They partake of this in a cleanly but leonine fashion, raising up whole limbs in both hands and biting off the meat, while any part which is hard to tear off they cut through with a small dagger which hangs attached to their sword-sheath in its own scabbard. Those who live beside the rivers or near the Mediterranean or Atlantic eat fish in addition, baked fish, that is, with the addition of salt, vinegar and cummin. They also use cummin in their drinks. They do not use olive oil because of its scarcity, and because of its unfamiliarity it appears unpleasant to them. When a large number dine together they sit around in a circle with the most influential man in the centre, like the leader of the chorus, whether he surpass the others in warlike skill, or nobility of family, or wealth. Beside him sits the host and next on either side the others in order of distinction. Their shieldsmen stand behind them while their spearsmen are seated in a circle on the opposite side and feast in common like their lords. The servers bear around the drink in terracotta or silver jars like spouted cups. The trenchers on which they serve the food are also of these materials, while with others they are made of bronze, or are woven or wooden baskets. The drink of the wealthy classes is wine imported from Italy or from the territory of Marseilles. This in unadulterated, but sometimes a little water is added. The lower classes drink wheaten beer prepared with honey, but most people drink it plain. It is called *corma*. They use a common cup. Drinking a little at a time, not more than a mouthful, but they do it rather frequently. The slave serves the cup towards the right, (not) towards the left. That is the method of service. In the same way they do reverence to the gods, turning towards the right.

And in former times, when the hindquarters were served up, the bravest hero took the thigh piece, and if another man claimed it they stood up and fought in single combat to the death. (Tierney, 1960, 247)

The scene which he describes is obviously a great communal feast given by a king or great lord, such as we meet so frequently in ancient Irish stories such as *Scél mucci Maic Dáthó* and *Fled Bricrend*. What is remarkable in the account is the hierarchical layout of the assembly, with each person occupying his proper place according to his rank and distinction. The *Curadhmhír*, or 'hero's portion', forms part of the account and we have several descriptions of this custom at feasts in Irish literature. The best warrior present was allowed to cut the meat. He, naturally, gave the largest portions to himself and his friends, leaving little for the lesser folk. Often a fight started over this, and even before the division took place who was to decide who was the best warrior? The hilarious contention of the heroes for the privilege of cutting up the pig in the 'Tale of Mac Dá Thó's Pig' (*Scél mucci Maic Dáthó*) ends in a riot. The two accounts show the unity of custom prevailing among the continental and insular Celts.

Athenaeus makes a most interesting remark when he says

that the server takes the vessel of *corma* (Irish: *coirm,* ale) around the circle of seated participants right-handwise (clockwise) and he says further that the same method is followed in religious ritual: 'In the same way they do reverence to the gods, turning towards the right.' This is obviously the *iompú deiseal* of the holy wells and pilgrimage sites of Ireland in which the pilgrims go around the well or other sacred object, one after the other in single file, being careful to keep the well at their right-hand side – following the course of the sun. This ancient ritual is something we will examine in greater detail later, but what a supremely moving experience it is in the 20th century to see people encircling the holy wells 'turning to the right' as Athenaeus had said 2000 years earlier.

Domestic life

Further information on the domestic arrangements of the Gaulish Celts is given by Strabo and undoubtedly much of it would also apply to the Celts of Ireland:

I have already described the numbers of the Helvetii and of the Arverni and their allies, and all this shows the great size of the population, and moreover, a point which I have already mentioned, the excellence of their women in bearing and rearing children. They wear the *sagus,* let their hair grow long and wear baggy trousers; instead of the ordinary tunics they wear divided tunics with sleeves, reaching down as far as the private parts and the buttocks. Their wool is rough and thin at the ends, and from it they weave the thick *sagi* which they call *laenae.*

Even to the present day most people sleep on the ground and dine seated on a litter of straw. They have large quantities of food together with milk and all kinds of meat, especially fresh and salt pork. Their pigs are allowed to run wild and are noted for their height and pugnacity and swiftness. It is dangerous for a stranger to approach them, and also for a wolf. Their houses are large and circular, built of planks and wickerwork, the roof being a dome of heavy thatch. They have such enormous flocks of sheep and herds of swine that they afford a plenteous supply of *sagi* and of salt meat, not only to Rome, but to most parts of Italy. Most of their governments used to be aristocratic, and in ancient times they used to elect one leader annually, and in the same way one man was declared general by the people to lead in war. But now, for the most part, they are subject to the commands of Rome. (Tierney, 1960, 268)

Diodorus Siculus remarks on the cold climate of Gaul with its terrible storms which are sufficiently strong to tear the clothes off their wearers. He connects the harshness of the climate with the Celtic fondness for drink:

And since the qualities of the climate are spoiled by the excess of cold, the land bears neither wine nor oil, and therefore the Gauls, being deprived of these fruits, concoct a drink out of barley called *zythos* (beer), and they wash honeycombs and use the washings as a drink. They are exceedingly fond of wine and sate themselves with the unmixed wine imported by merchants; their desire makes them drink it greedily and when they become drunk they fall into a stupor or into a maniacal disposition. And therefore many Italian merchants, with their usual love of lucre, look on the Gallic love of wine as their treasure trove. They transport the wine by boat on the navigable rivers and by wagon through the plains and receive in return for it an incredibly large price; for one jar of wine they receive in return a slave, a servant in exchange for the drink. (Tierney, 1960, 249)

The Celts in battle

Diodorus Siculus gives a lucid and most comprehensive account of several important factors in Celtic life: the belief in the immortality of the soul with its effects on the conduct of funerals; the elaborate battle tactics; the custom of single combat well known in Ireland from stories such as *Táin Bó Chuailnge* and *Forbhais Droma Dámhgháire*. By allowing only chosen warriors to fight and die, the vast casualties of ordinary warfare were avoided. There was the noisy boasting of deeds of valour with the intention of intimidating the opponent and the custom of the 'severed head' – again well known from the *Táin* in the incident in which Cú Chulainn deals with Ferchú Loingsech and his twelve companions:

> Ferchú took counsel with his men. 'What better plan could we carry out', said he, 'than to go and attack yonder man who is checking and holding back the four great provinces of Ireland and to bring back with us his head in triumph to Ailill and Medb. Though we have done many wrongs and injuries to Ailill and to Medb, we shall obtain peace thereby if that man fall by us.' That is the plan they decided on. And they came forward to the place where Cú Chulainn was, and when they came, they did not grant him fair play or single combat but all twelve of them attacked him straightaway. However, Cú Chulainn fell upon them and forthwith struck off their twelve heads. And he planted twelve stones for them in the ground and put a head of each one of them on its stone and also put Ferchú Loingsech's head on its stone. So that the spot where Ferchú Loingsech left his head is called *Cinnit Ferchon* that is *Cennáit Ferchon* (the Headplace of Ferchú). (O'Rahilly, 1967, 209)

The severed head set up in front of homes and temples is a custom which seems to have some very profound meaning not fully understood. For the moment it is sufficient to recall that some of our ancient churches, notably Clonfert Cathedral, Co Galway, Dysart O'Dea, Co Clare, and several others display the severed head at the doorway. Diodorus Siculus gives a very early and clear account of these matters:

They also invite strangers to their banquets, and only after the meal do they ask who they are and of what they stand in need. At dinner they are wont to be moved by chance remarks to wordy disputes, and after a challenge, to fight in single combat, regarding their lives as naught; for the belief of Pythagoras is strong among them, that the souls of men are immortal, and that after a definite number of years they live a second life when the soul passes into another body. This is the reason given why some people at the burial of the dead cast upon the pyre letters written to their dead relatives, thinking that the dead will be able to read them.

For their journeys and in battle they use two-horse chariots, the chariot carrying both charioteer and chieftain. When they meet with cavalry in the battle they cast their javelins at the enemy and then, descending from the chariot, join battle with their swords. Some of them so far despise death that they descend to do battle, unclothed except for a girdle. They bring into battle as their attendants freemen chosen from among the poorer classes, whom they use as charioteers and shield-bearers in battle. When the armies are drawn up in battle-array they are wont to advance before the battle-line and to challenge the bravest of their opponents to single combat, at the same time brandishing before them their arms so as to terrify their foe. And when some one accepts their challenge to battle, they loudly recite the deeds of valour of their ancestors and proclaim their own valorous quality, at the same time abusing and making little of their opponent and generally attempting to rob him beforehand of his fighting spirit. They cut off the heads of enemies slain in battle and attach them to the necks of their horses. The blood-stained spoils they hand over to their attendants and carry off as booty, while striking up a paean and singing a song of victory, and they nail up these first fruits upon their houses just as do those who lay low wild animals in certain kinds of hunting. They embalm in cedar-oil the heads of the most distinguished enemies and preserve them carefully in a chest, and display them with pride to strangers, saying that for this head, one of their ancestors, or his father, or the man himself, refused the offer of a large sum of money. They say that some of them boast that they refused the weight of the head in gold. (Tierney, 1960, 250)

The same story is told of the Celts by Strabo in a different way:

To the frankness and high-spiritedness of their temperament must be added the traits of childish boastfulness and love of decoration. They wear ornaments of gold, torques on their necks, and bracelets on their arms and wrists, while people of high rank wear dyed garments besprinkled with gold. It is this vanity which makes them unbearable in victory and so completely downcast in defeat. In addition to their witlessness they possess a trait of barbarous savagery which is especially peculiar to the northern peoples, for when they are leaving the battlefield they fasten to the necks of their horses the heads of their enemies, and on arriving home they nail up this spectacle at the entrances to their houses. Posidonius says that he saw this sight in many places, and was at first disgusted by it, but afterwards, becoming used to it, could bear it with equanimity. But they embalmed the heads of distinguished enemies with cedar oil, and used to make a display of them to strangers, and were unwilling to let them be redeemed even for their weight in gold. (Tierney, 1960, 269)

Two marvellous statues, from Pergamum in Asia Minor (Turkey) and dating from the third century BC show the heroic Celts in battle. The first statue shows a defeated Celt looking over his shoulder at his pursuers. He is naked with carefully treated hair. Rather than be subjected to slavery he has killed his wife and supports her with his left hand as she sinks to the ground. With his right hand he plunges his sword into his own breast.

The second statue, often called 'The Dying Gaul', shows a naked warrior, with treated hair and moustache and a rich torque around his neck. Beside him is his sword and trumpet. (Eluére, 1993, 74-75)

Even though some of the Celts went into battle naked, Diodorus Siculus gives a description of the Celtic protective equipment:

> Their armour includes man-sized shields, decorated in individual fashion. Some of these have projecting bronze animals of fine workmanship which serve for defence as well as decoration. On their heads they wear bronze helmets which possess large projecting figures lending the appearance of enormous stature to the wearer; in some cases horns form one piece with the helmet, while in other cases it is relief figures of the foreparts of birds or quadrupeds. Their trumpets again are of a peculiar barbaric kind; they blow into them and produce a harsh sound, which suits the tumult of war. Some have iron breastplates of chain mail while others fight naked, and for them the breastplate given by nature suffices. Instead of the short sword they carry long swords held by iron or bronze chains and hanging along their right flank. (Tierney, 1960, 251)

CHAPTER THREE

Political Organisation

As regards the type of political organisation and territorial divisions, we are better informed in the case of Ireland than that of the Continent.

The political and administrative unit, in theory at least was the *tuath*. This was a small kingdom presided over by a petty king. In theory the *tuath* was an independent political unit but in practice it happened frequently that a number were joined together under one king who succeeded in acquiring neighbouring territory by right of conquest. As political and military fortunes changed, territorial divisions changed with them but in general the pattern emerges of a small compact territorial unit organised on the lines resembling the feudal system. The king *(rí tuaithe)* was surrounded by a number of *flatha* (nobles). They received lands and cattle from him and were required to pay him taxes. They in turn hired out land and cattle to *bó airí* – farmers and cultivators – who paid taxes to the *flatha*. It was not, however, a completely one-way arrangement. The *bó aire* for instance, as a client *(céile)* of his lord *(tiarna, flaith),* was bound by Brehon Law to pay his taxes, usually in kind – so much corn, pigs, cattle, beer, etc each year, and also perhaps such things as swords, brooches, cloaks, drinking horns – and also perhaps provide some entertainment and military service. But the *céile* or client had equally clear rights in Brehon Law. He was *faoi choimirce an fhlatha* – under the protection of the *taoiseach* or lord who was bound to protect him if his rights were endangered by his

neighbours or a lord of some nearby territory. The key to the
system was clientship *(céilsíne)* and an aristocrat's position in
society was judged by the number of his clients. Just as in
more recent times the wealth and prestige of a farmer was
often calculated by the number of cows he owned, the *flaith*'s
prestige was judged by the number of clients depending on
him.

In Ireland, the role of the king must not be seen in terms
of a great and powerful autocrat. The enormous body of
Brehon Law provided a fixed system of legislation for the government of society and the king's powers were chiefly used in
negotiating treaties with other kings and business involving
relations with another *tuath*. In times of peace at any rate, the
king's duties may not have been over burdensome. Conchúr
Mac Neasa of Ulster is described as spending his day in the
following manner: one third spent in watching the youths
play hurley on the field before the *dún* (fort); one third playing *fichille* (a board game perhaps somewhat like chess), and
the third part drinking *corma* (beer) and listening to storytelling until he fell asleep – quite a pleasant daily programme.

The Aonach

One of the national institutions which seems to have embraced both political and literacy elements was the *oenach,*
(Modern: *aonach*). This was much more than a fair or market
in the modern sense as it clear from an extant account of
Aenach Carman:

> Kalaind August cen ail,
> tiagait ind cech tres bliadhain;
> and luadit co dana ar daigh,
> cert cech cana ocus costaid.
> (O'Curry, 1873, 3, 542)
> (On the calends of August without fail,
> They repaired thither every third year;

There aloud with boldness they proclaimed
The rights of every law, and the restraints.

Leaving aside the controversial question of the location of *Aenach Carman* – near Wexford in *(Loch gGarmáin)* or with much greater probability near Knockaulin, once a royal seat of the kings of Leinster in the Curragh of Kildare, the verses indicate the wide variety of activities engaged in during the week the *aonach* lasted. The laws were proclaimed, and presumably new regulations and decisions affecting the local population promulgated. It must have been a very effective instrument of government in the hands of an effective ruler. But it was also a great social and cultural occasion. Musicians, poets, storytellers of all kinds gathered to entertain the crowds and the traditional list of thematic stories were recited – stories of cattle-raids, courtships, elopements, destructions and so forth. Horse racing was a notable part of the celebrations – seven races per day according to the prose account.

The other great provincial fairs brought together the tribes of the province to the neighbourhood of the chief stronghold of the king, and must have followed the same general pattern as that of Carman. These were *Oenach Tailten* in the kingdom of Uí Néill, *Oenach Enma* in the kingdom of the Ulaid, *Oenach Téite,* (Nenagh) in Mumu depending on Cashel, and *Oenach Cruachan* in Connacht.

At least in some cases, fairs were held near the sites of ancient burial grounds. This is made clear in the case of *Aonach Carman:*

Secht n-dumai cen taidliud de,
do cáiniud marb co mence;
secht maige, tarmain cen tech,
fo cluiche Carmain chaintech.
(O'Cury, 1873, 3, 546)
(Seven mounds without touching each other,
where the dead have often been lamented:

seven plains, sacred without a house,
for the funeral games of Carman.)

The same connection between *aonach* and burial mound is found in the case of *Aonach Tailteann* and *Cruachan*, and indeed it may well have been a universal feature originating in the funeral games of the ancestors. While the local *aonach* must have been a much more modest affair, it no doubt played a highly important part in the political, social and cultural life of the local community.

The *aonach* combined in one celebration many aspects of the life of the community. The political and legal aspect of it might be compared to the promulgation of the law in Manx Gaelic and English from Tynwald Hill in present day practice on the Isle of Man. Something of the cultural aspect of the great *aonach* can be seen in the Oireachtas in Ireland and especially in the National Eisteddfod of Wales. A modern race meeting, agricultural show and cattle mart would embrace other aspects of it. It can be readily understood why the assembly of Carman took two years to prepare – it was a highly sophisticated and complex assembly which brought together in microcosmic form the interwoven strands of Gaelic society.

Class in Celtic Ireland
As we have seen, in Celtic Ireland before the coming of the Normans, and indeed for a long time after in some areas, the political unit was the *tuath*, of which there may have been about one hundred. The number tended to vary with conquests and amalgamations by petty kings.

Society was divided into basically three classes:
Rí, flatha and *aos dána*. (King, aristocracy (large landowners) and the learned class – druids, *filí*, bards)
Laochra (Warriors)
Bó airí (Farmers) (cf. Ross, 1972, 42-47)

This system is in accordance with the Indo-European system and is quite reasonable in terms of the ordering of society. For any type of state, no matter how small it may be, some kind of governing body is required, then some kind of army is necessary to defend the territory, and finally farmers are required to provide food for the population.

A learned class – like the Brahmans in the Indian tradition – is proficient in all that pertains to legislature, religious matters, territorial divisions, medicine, genealogies and general culture.

Craftsmen, and especially the *gabha* or blacksmith, had a recognised and valued position in society, and even among the *Tuatha Dé Danann,* the Celtic deities, the blacksmith god Goibniu is prominent. It is he who forges the spears for the *Tuatha Dé Danann* army in their struggle against the dark gods – the *Fomhóraigh* – in *Cath Maighe Tuireadh.* Almost to our own day a certain mystique enveloped the *gabha.* He knew the mystery of ironwork, of how to mould the molten mass of metal brought to its new state over intense fire and plunged into water to retain its new form. He was the craftsman who held the secrets of transmutation.

The role of the laochra

As regards the *loachra,* or *equites* (knights) as Caesar called them, before his own arrival to conquer Gaul, 'it used to happen nearly every year that they either attacked another tribe or warded off the attacks of another tribe.' (Tierney, 1960, 272) This idea of annual warfare may be put in conjunction with the passage which follows in *De Bello Gallico,* where Caesar gives a description of the notorious 'Wicker Man Sacrifice':

> The whole Gallic people is exceedingly given to religious superstition. Therefore those who are suffering from serious illness or are in the midst of the dangers of battle, either

put to death human beings as sacrificial victims or take a vow to do so, and the Druids take part in these sacrifices; for they believe that unless one human life is given in exchange for another human life the power of the almighty gods cannot be appeased. Sacrifices of this kind are also traditionally offered for the needs of the state. Some tribes build enormous images with limbs of interwoven branches which they then fill with live men; the images are set alight and the men die in a sea of flame. They believe that the immortal gods delight more in the slaughter of those taken in theft or brigandage or some crime, but when the supply of that kind runs short they descend even to the sacrifice of the innocent. (Tierney, 1960, 272)

Diodorus Siculus also discusses this type of human sacrifice in which the victims were burned:

They keep evildoers in custody for five years and then impale them in honour of their gods. They construct enormous pyres and then devote them together with many other first-fruits. They also use prisoners of war as sacrificial victims in paying honour to their gods. (Tierney, 1960, 252)

Putting together Caesar's account of the annual war and Diodorus Siculus' account of using prisoners of war as sacrificial victims, we might well wonder if one of the purposes of war among the Celts was to secure victims to be sacrificed for the welfare of the state and society. In other words, was war among the Celts considered to be a religious act carried out by the *laochra* on an annual basis for the purpose of obtaining suitable material to be sacrificed to the gods, who in return would bring fertility to the land and stability to the state?

The accounts of the sacrificial rituals of the Celts appear to bear some resemblance to those of the Aztecs:

They reasoned that for man to survive, the gods who permit his existence must also live and wax strong. These gods, however, received their best nutriment from the most precious of offerings, the hearts of men. Thus a vicious circle became established which led to sacrifice on an increasing scale. The gods manifested their favour and their strength to the Aztecs by letting them prosper, but the Aztecs, on their part, had to sacrifice hearts to the gods to maintain their good will ... war captives were the most esteemed offering. (Vaillant, 1953, 199-200)

The Aztec victim was held down, an incision was made in his chest with a stone knife and the still beating heart plucked out and offered to the god. War among the Aztecs, then, could be regarded as in the light of a cosmic sacrifice. By killing or being killed one paid one's debt to nature to whom one owed one's life.

A similar interpretation is given by Sylvie Muller in her research on the Wren Ritual in Ireland. On St Stephen's Day, the period of the winter solstice, the wren is caught and killed and taken from house to house by a company of masked figures – *An Dreoilín* – the wren boys. The wren stands for man and the wren has to die to pay back its debt to nature. Death is the price he had to pay for the gift of life. (*Béaloideas,* 1996-1997, 147-149)

Vaillant sums up neatly the concept of human sacrifice: Thus instances of human sacrifices keep cropping up in the world's religious systems, and we preserve in our own culture the concept of martyrdom, achieved by voluntary or involuntary means, as an act of virtue. The very beautiful example of the Saviour transmutes to the highest spiritual plane this idea of sacrifice for the good of humanity. (1953, 199)

It may be, then, that among the Celts war had a religious function in providing materials for sacrifice and so maintaining the order of the universe, the rising of the sun and moon, the cyclic succession of the seasons, the appropriate measure of sunshine and rain to produce abundant harvests. If so, the *laochra* played a vital part in society as entrusted with the functioning of the cosmos. All this is indicative of the integral part which the individual played in the universe which was kept in motion by his contribution to it, along and in harmony with the other members of society.

There is another unexpected element to be seen in the *laoch*. He often needs the support of a *spreagaire,* or inciter, to urge him on in the thick of the fight, to upbraid him or praise him as the case may be. The hero often needs the support of others when he is in danger of losing heart. We find an excellent example of this in *Táin Bó Chuailnge*. Cú Chulainn is watching Fer Diad, his formidable opponent, practising his marvellous feats and he tells his charioteer Laegh that today all these feats of skill will be employed against himself with deadly effect. Then Cú Chulainn tells Laegh what to do: '… you must incite me and revile me and speak evil of me so that my ire and anger shall rise the higher thereby. But if it be I who inflict defeat, you must exhort me and praise me and speak well of me that thereby my courage rise higher.' 'It shall be done indeed, little Cú', said Laegh.

The opportunity arrives soon enough, for Cú Chulainn is being buffeted unmercifully by Fer Diad. Laegh shouts out: 'Alas, your opponent has chastised you as a fond mother chastises her child. He has belaboured you as flax is beaten in a pond. He has pierced you as a tool pierces an oak. He has attacked you as a hawk attacks little birds, so that never again will you have a claim or right or title to valour or feats of arms, you distorted little sprite.'

Cú Chulainn is incensed by these insults. His *riastradh,* or battle distortions, transform him into a deadly monster and he makes short work of Fer Diad. (O'Rahilly, 1967, 226-229)

Similarly in the story *Forbhais Droma Dámhghaire* (The Siege of Knocklong) Cairbre Lifeachar acts as *spreagaire* or inciter to Colpa, the Leinster hero, as he fights against Ceann Mór of Munster. (Ó Duinn, 1992, 74)

It does seem that the great fighter needs to some extent the support of his friends acting in praise or derision, in much the same way as sportspeople and showpeople are dependant to a degree on their followers.

But, perhaps, this concept was applied also to the great hero – God – who has to defend and keep intact the order of creation, the cosmos, against the constant attacks of the forces of disintegration and chaos. While God, of course, has supreme power, it does seem that he expects the support of his followers in prayer and supplication, in this never-ending conflict of cosmos and chaos.

There is the incident of Israel's battle with her foes to illustrate the point. Israel is dependent on God's power to give them victory and he is perfectly capable of doing so on his own, but while the battle rages Moses keeps his arms raised in prayer and while he holds them thus in the ancient *orante* position, still used by the priests during the Eucharistic Prayer of the Mass, all goes well with the Israelites. But it is difficult to sustain this uncomfortable gesture for very long and Moses' arms began to grow tried and droop. Each time this happened, the Israelites suffered a set back. Then Moses had his arms held up by helpers at each side so that Israel recovered and won the battle. (Exodus 17)

It does seem that here we have a basis for the continuous prayer and ascetic practices of the Celtic Christian traditions. Just as in many ancient religious systems the gods had to be kept well fed with sacrifices so that they would have the energy to keep the ordered cycles of the cosmos intact and stave off the forces of disorder and disintegration, so it would seem that God in the Christian system demands continual sacrifice in prayer and devotion. In other words, God is associating us with his own function of keeping the universe in existence – preserving it from dissolution into chaos.

We have a marvellous example of this in *Tuireamh na hÉireann,* a seventeenth century political poem in which the poet, Seán Ó Conaill, recounts the terrible disasters which have occurred and left the country in a state of misery and disintegration. While all this may have been a punishment for sin, at the same time there is a certain lack of conviction that this is entirely the case and the poet hurls a few insults at God for allowing this terrible catastrophe. God's seeming indifference and inactivity hardly conforms to the promises to St Patrick:

A Dhia do dhealbhaig ré is réalta,
do chúm flaitheas is talamh is spéire,
do bhí agus tá is bhias gan traocha,
aoin Dia amháin tú is ní trí déithe.
An bhfuil tú bodhar nó cá bhfuile ag féachaint?
Nach tú do leag na hathaig led sméide?
Cá beag duit 'fhaid ataoi ag éisdeacht?
D'imig ár gcreideamh, ní mhaireann acht spré dhe.
An é so do gheallais do Phádraig Naofa
ar chnuc Hermon chionn teacht go hÉirinn
nó ar an gCruaich tar éis a thréannais,
Guígse is guím Dia na ndéithe,
an t-Athair 's Mac 's an Spiorad naofa,
ár bpeacaí uile do mhaitheamh i n-aonacht
's a gcreideamh 's a gceart d'aiseag ar Ghaeulaibh.
(O'Rahilly, 1977, 79-81)
(O God, you formed the moon and the stars; you made heaven and earth and sky; you were and you are and you will be without weariness. You are one God and not three Gods. Are you deaf or where are you looking? Isn't it you that knocked down the giants with a wink? Isn't it enough

for you the time you have been listening? Our religion disappeared, only a spark of it remains. Is that what you promised to St Patrick on Mount Hermon before he came to Ireland or on the Reek (Croagh Patrick) after fasting? Pray, and I pray myself to God of the gods, the Father, Son and Holy Spirit to forgive all our sins and to restore their religion and their rights to the Irish.)

The Role of the Irish King

The three major orders of society then, among the Celts, were closely allied to the Indo-European system. This tripartite division of ruling and learned class, warriors and farmers may be compared to the divisions of the human body, the head representing the kingship, the breast and arms representing the warrior class and the part of the body from the waist down representing the *bó airí,* the class concerned with the reproduction. The very name by which a special type of defensive prayer is called in the Irish tradition – the *lúireach* – is a Gaelicisation of the Latin *lorica* – the warrior's metal breastplate. It is difficult to know if the severed head had some connection with kingship, or the *Síle na Gig* with the *bó airí.*

At any rate, it is the special position of the king in Irish tradition which introduces us to the mystical quality of the land.

Despite the fact of having one hundred or more kings reigning at the same time we have no native word for 'coronation'. The phrase used to describe the coronation or inauguration of a king throughout the centuries was *bainis Rí,* 'the wedding of the king' or 'the king's woman-sleeping'. This was the sacral kingship in which the king was symbolically married to the goddess of the land. The purpose of the marriage was to produce a child and the child, of course, was the harvest, the *ith agus blicht* of ancient Irish tradition, the corn and the milk.

The wedding ritual of the 'bainis Rí' evidently comprised

two main elements, a libation offered by the bride to her partner and the coition. The sovereignty of Ireland appears to Conn of the Hundred Battles seated on a crystal throne and with a vat of red liquor beside her from which she serves him (and his successor) with a drink in a golden goblet, and the same essential function is implied in the name of the goddess Medhbh, 'The Intoxicating One'. (MacCana, 1970, 120)

Perhaps a pun was employed in the ritual. The woman representing the goddess of the land gave the goblet of liquor, ale or wine or mead or water to the candidate for kingship.

The word for 'liquor' is *laith* and the word for 'kingdom' is *flaith,* so that when the goddess gave the king the *laith* she gave him the *flaith* – and the *flaith* was herself, she was the land of Ireland. (*Ériu,* 1975, 11)

In the marvellous story *Echtra Mac Echach Muigmedoin* (*Revue Celtique* 24 (1903) 191ff.) the five sons of Eochaidh Muigmedoin are very thirsty after a deer hunt. One after another goes to a well which is guarded by a *cailleach* or dreadful-looking hag who refuses to give any water until the man kisses her. Each refuses until the last, Niall, kisses her without hesitation and immediately she is transformed into the most beautiful woman in the world. She declares, *'Mise an flaitheas',* 'I am the sovereignty', and she gives him the water. He becomes the great king Niall Naoi nGiallach, the progenitor of the O'Neills. Only the suitable candidate for kingship had the faith to see behind the disguise and the goddess herself, having met her rightful spouse, is transformed from hag to young woman, from winter to summer, from barrenness to fertility.

Here, then, is the mystique of ancient government in Ireland, in which a human, mortal king representing the human community is married to a divine woman to guarantee the fertility of the land. Perhaps this strange mystical quality is behind Meadhbh's boasting of having many lovers, 'each man in another man's shadow' – the kings to whom Meadhbh was symbolically married in the *bainis Rí,* or *Hieros Gamos* as it was called in Greece, came and went, while she, as the immortal goddess, remained forever.

In a remarkable study of Early Celtic traditions (*Ériu* 26, (1975) 1ff.), Professor Wagner traces links between the *bainis Rí* and the ancient customs of Mesopotamia. The festival of the *Hieros Gamos (bainis Rí)* between the earth-goddess Inanna and the king, marked the beginning of the New Year. *Bealtaine* (Mayday) is the equivalent in Ireland, the beginning of the year of growth, marked by fertility rites even to fairly recent times. What is more remarkable is the reference to the giving of the liquor to the king by the goddess: 'a lukur-priestess, being thought as representative of Baba, the earth-goddess, while the king himself appears as Tammuz or related male deity.' (1975, 15)

The *bainis Rí* tradition and the Cult of the Bull *(Tain Bó Chuailnge)* may both have made their way to the Celtic regions at a very early period indeed via Massilia or through Asia Minor and Thrace; 'ancient Mesopotamian belief, shaped in the third millennium, were carried deep into the first millennium, BC'. (1975, 16) This is the same Mesopotamia, the land between the two rivers, Tigris and Euphrates whose peoples contributed so much to biblical Israel. The Celts and the Bible were drawing from the same source.

Very high standards of integrity were expected from the Irish king. The *fír flatha* or honesty/justice/fairness of the king was of paramount importance to his reign. If he were a good king, ruling his people with justice and integrity, the goddess would smile on him and there would be peace and prosperity on the land. He had also to be *fial* or generous, lavish in entertaining and giving presents. By these qualities he maintained cosmic order.

If these qualities are not found in the king, his reign will collapse and his kingdom will become a wasteland. The tragic results of a mistake in administering justice is dramatically portrayed in the story of Conaire Mór, *Togail Bruidne Da Derga.*

The ten year reign of the Fir Bolg king Eochaidh Mac Eirc is described in glowing terms in *Leabhar Gabhála Éireann:*

There was no wetting in that time (but only dew). There was not a year without harvest. By him was falsehood expelled from Ireland. By him was the law of justice established first in Ireland. (Macalister, 1941, Part IV, 45)

The passage is strangely reminiscent of Christ's kingship in the Preface for the Feast of Christ the King:

… a kingdom of truth and life,

a kingdom of holiness and grace,

a kingdom of justice, love and peace.

CHAPTER FOUR

The Cult of the Ancestors,
then and since

The Aonach, the reunion of the tribe, at a sacred place containing the graves of the ancestors may well have been full of significance. Here the clan, in its periodical assembly, returned to the source of its existence and prosperity. The megalithic tomb is often perched on the side of a hill as if power flowed from it down to the agricultural plain and dwelling houses below.

The renowned Egyptologist, R. T. Rundle Clark, describes the attitude of ancient peoples to the ancestors:

The early agricultural peoples combined fertility rites with the cult of the dead. They were, in fact, two aspects of one religion – expressions of the hopes and anxieties of the community. The world seemed full of power, everywhere would be found signs of the life force, manifest in all living creatures, both animal and vegetable – in the heavens, in the waters and in the mysterious events of disease, death and decay. These forces could be temporarily localised in some person or place, but ancient men were not sufficiently self-conscious to think of them as residing in individuals as such. The community was not merely composed of the living but of the ancestors as well. Life on earth was a temporary exile from the true, undifferentiated, group-life somewhere beyond. The ancestors, the custodians of the source of life, were the reservoir of power and the vitality, the source whence flowed all the forces of vigour, sustenance and growth. Hence, they were not only departed souls but still active, the keepers of life and fortune. Whatever happened, whether for good or evil, ultimately derived from them. The sprouting of the corn, the increase of the herds, potency in men, success in hunting or war, were all manifestation of their power and approval. Hence the place where the ancestors dwelt was the most holy spot in the world. From it flowed the well being of the group. Without the tomb or the cemetery, life on earth would be miserable, perhaps impossible. The ancestors were not particularised. They were a collective concept without individual names. (1959, 119)

The cult of the ancestors among African peoples has been taken into account in the Liturgy of the Mass in the Zaire rite:

Brothers and sisters, we who are living on earth are not the only followers of Christ; many have already left this world and are now with God. But together with them, we make up one great family. Let us join ourselves to them, and especially to the saints, so that this sacrifice may gather us all together into one body. And you our ancestors, be with us, you who have served God with a good conscience be with us. Here is our prayer. (Thurian and Wainwright, 1983, 205)

The inclusion of a Christianised form of intercession in this modern adaptation of the *Ordo Missae* to suit African conditions has seemed to some to be an innovation. But is it really so? In the First Eucharistic Prayer we have the text:

For ourselves, too, we ask some share in the fellowship of your apostles and martyrs, with John the Baptist, Stephen, Matthias, Barnabas, (Ignatius, Alexander, Marcellinus, Peter, Felicity, Perpetua, Agatha, Lucy, Agnes, Cecilia, Anastasia) and all the saints.

Here, the faithful followers of Christ who have died and the saints in heaven are the ancestors – like Abraham 'our father in faith', as the Roman Canon has it.

The obvious place to look for some Christian equivalents or adaptations of the pre-historic cult of the ancestors is, of course, the feast of All Saints (1st November).

This feast, as we shall see later, seems to owe much to the great Celtic feast of *Samhain* in which the barriers between the divine world of the *Tuatha Dé Danann* and the human population were broken down with a consequent intermingling of the two races. But the distinction between the dead – the ancestors and the *Tuatha Dé Danann* or goddesses and gods of Ireland – is a fine one as indeed is hinted in the feast of All Souls on the 2nd November, for purgatory in the Catholic tradition is another department of the otherworld like hell and heaven.

In the Magnificat Antiphon for All Saints (Tridentine Breviary) the angels and saints are bound together in one mighty concourse of supernatural beings making intercession for us:

O you Angels and Archangels, Thrones and Dominations, Principalities and Powers, Virtues of heaven, Cherubim and Seraphim; (these are the nine choirs of angels, the 'natural' inhabitants of heaven who surround the throne of God as described in the Reading for the Mass and now comes a list of the various categories of saints who have joined them in the otherworld). O you Patriarchs and Prophets, holy Doctors of the Law, Apostles, All Martyrs of Christ, holy Confessors, Virgins of the Lord, Hermits and all Saints; intercede for us.

God is the ultimate power but, nevertheless, the saints around his throne are powerful intermediaries.

Another point regarding the cult of the ancestors in relation to the liturgy is the little-known rite for the consecration of a church. In the old form of the ritual in the *Pontificale Romanum,* the relics of the saints were kept in a building apart from the church to be consecrated. On the night before the consecration took place, a vigil was held in honour of the saints. Next day, when the 'sepulchre', or little cavity in the altar of the new church, was ready, the relics were brought from their place to the new altar and buried in the 'sepulchre'. A solemn procession was organised and the relics, enclosed in an ornamental bier, were carried on the shoulders of four priests in a circular tour of the new church on the outside, followed by the bishop and the faithful, who sang *Kyrie eleison*, over and over again.

In the first part of the translation of the relics from the building to the church the following antiphon was sung:

Surgite, Sancti Dei, de mansionibus vestris, loca sanctificate, plebem benedicite, et nos homines peccatores in pace custodite. (Arise, O Saints of God, from your dwelling place, bless these places, bless the population and preserve us sinners in peace.)

Here again, the close relationship between the blessed dead and the living faithful is expressed. It is they who will bring prosperity and peace to the locality, as presumably the ancestors in the megalithic tomb were considered as the benefactors of the local community.

When the bishop had inserted the relics in the altar and closed up the cavity, the following antiphon was sung:

Sub altare Dei sedes accepitis Sancti Dei; intercedite pro nobis ad Dominum Jesum Christum. (O saints of God, you have accepted a dwelling place under the altar of God; intercede for us with our Lord Jesus Christ.)

Then is added: 'Corpora Sanctorum in pace sepulta sunt: et vivent nomina eorum in aeternum.' (The bodies of the saints are buried in peace and their memory will last for ever.)

In the early church, the custom began of building churches on the burial sites of the martyrs. Then, as Christianity spread to areas where there were no martyrs, it became customary to collect pieces of the bones of the martyrs and insert them in the altar of the local church.

One wonders if the cremated remains in the stone circles at Drombeg, Bohonagh, Reanascreena, in Co Cork, as well as Cashelkeelty in Co Kerry, were dedications in the same manner. (Ó Nuallain, 1984, 8-9)

It is noticed also in the excavated stone circles of Reanascreena and Bohonagh, that they contained soil-filled pits. Was this a sample of rich soil – a sample of the kind of rich fertile land the worshippers wanted to provide abundant harvests and fat healthy cattle? In other words, the ancestors were in the stone circle to help the people, and the soil sample beside them was a gentle reminder of this, in much the same way as the Christians reminded the saints whose relics were in the altar that they were not there to go to sleep but to sanctify the place, to bless the people and to intercede for them with Our Lord Jesus Christ.

What we are suggesting is an unbroken stream of tradition coming down to us in the Catholic Church from neolithic times. When the Protestant reformers threw out the altars in favour of the communion table, were they cutting themselves off from that stream of human experience lodged in the collective psyche of mankind?

Here in Ireland, in some ways we have suffered much religious impoverishment through the vicissitudes of history. Many ancient graveyards are to be seen throughout the Irish countryside. Often they are enclosed by a circular wall of earth or stone and the heaping up of the soil towards the centre suggests the innumerable burials which have taken place during the centuries. In the centre, the ruins of a medieval church – no doubt often replacing an earlier structure – may be seen. This was the ideal situation. On an important occasion, the Sunday liturgy, the barriers between the living and the dead were seen to be broken down and the living and the dead formed one united community, as we have suggested happened at the great Celtic festivals of *Lughnasa* and *Samhain,* when celebrated at the tombs of the ancestors. Often, nowadays, the church stands several miles away from the graveyard, so that this sense of unity with the dead ancestors is forgotten.

'The druids preferred yew for wand making over their other favourite woods, apple and oak.' (MacKillop, 1998, 380) The yew tree is extremely long-lived and when cut down can arise again as the snake sloughs his skin and emerges as a reborn snake. In some cases we might well wonder if the yews in our ancient graveyards were first planted by druids.

In all of this, I am pointing to the landscape of Ireland. In that landscape, with its megalithic tombs, its stone circles, its rows of standing stones and single pillars, its earthen raths and *liosanna,* natural formations given a religious significance such as *Dhá Chíoch Dhanann* (The Paps) near Killarney, its sacred lakes, rivers, wells and trees, Christian monuments such as monasteries, churches, graveyards, places of pilgrimage – in all this vast array of phenomena we see the lingering footmarks of man's quest for the divine from the most remote past to the present day. The Catholic Church, to its credit, has tried to embrace this vast religious experience of mankind within its liturgy. This of course is not well understood and many Christians tend to look down on what they call 'paganism', forgetting that for the overwhelming extent of their life on earth people have been 'pagans'.

With this type of mentality, perhaps Jesus himself could be accused of being a pagan. As known from the gospels, he could read and write – practices invented by the pagans long before the incarnation. He also wore clothes – a practice made possible by the invention of weaving and the manufacture of cloth from the wool of sheep. This also was the invention of the pagans. Jesus visited the synagogue and Temple – but architecture was also the invention of the pagans. In short, Jesus made use of much of what was the common heritage of the surrounding culture as it had evolved over thousands of years.

CHAPTER FIVE

Goddesses and Gods of Ireland

The sacral kingship among the Celts was concerned with the fertility of the land, with peace and prosperity and with preserving the order of the universe. In the case of Eochaidh Mac Eirc he was married to the goddess Tailte from which we get Tailteann in Co Meath, but whatever her local name might be, the king was married essentially to Éire.

The goddess Éire, who gives her name to the country, is the land of Ireland. She is the Great Mother who makes the grass grow, the corn ripen, who puts apples on the trees, fish in the rivers – the nourishing mother of her people.

According to the legend in *Leabhar Gabhála Éireann*, Clann Mhíle on entering the country first met the goddess Banbha of the mystic race of the Tuatha Dé Danann. They spoke to her and she agreed that they could take possession of the land if it were called by her name. They agreed and in bardic poetry the country is frequently referred to as 'Banbha'. From Sliabh Mis in Kerry, where they had met Banbha, they journeyed on until they came to Sliabh Eibhleann (Slieve Phelim) on the borders of Limerick and Tipperary. There they met the second of the three goddesses – Fodhla. Again, she agreed to let them have the country if it were known by her name. They agreed and likewise in bardic poetry the island is known as Fodhla.

Finally, they arrived at the hill of Uisneach, the very centre of the country, and here they met Éire. She gave them the greatest welcome of all and they said that Eire would be the principal name of the country forever.

The husbands of the three goddesses, Mac Coill, Mac Céacht and Mac Gréine, however, were not quite as accommodating to the newcomers as their wives were, and a great battle between the Tuatha Dé Danann and Clann Mhíle (the Celtic invaders) took place at Tailteann in Co Meath. This is probably Sliabh na Caillí (Loughcrew), the great megalithic cemetery near Kells or modern Teltown. At any rate, the end of the battle was rather indecisive and both parties – the human Celts and the supernatural Tuatha Dé Danann – decided to divide the country between them.

Naturally, one would think that they would have drawn a line from modern Dublin to Galway and assigned one half to the humans and the other half to the divine race. This, however, was not what was done. Each party took the whole of the country, the humans took the surface of the land – where we are – and the Tuatha Dé Danann descended underground into the *síthe* – the hollow hills and megalithic sites throughout the country. In these sacred sites – such as Brú na Bóinne (Newgrange), Sliabh na mBan, Sí Mór, Sí Beag, Cnoc Áine, Lough Gur, Cnoc Sí Úna, Carraig Chlíona – which dot the Irish countryside, the divine race of the Tuatha Dé Danann continue their supernatural life underground. They are normally invisible but can make themselves visible on occasion, as when people claim to hear the *bean sí* (the woman of the *sí* or sacred hollow hill) or have seen her combing her long red hair. In folk tradition it is unlucky to pick up a comb from the wayside as it might be the property of a *bean sí* who dropped it on her way to wail on the death of somebody descended from true Gaelic or Norman aristocracy.

The *sí* is the sacred hill or site and the Tuatha Dé Danann are often called *aos sí,* the inhabitants of the *sí.*

The name *Tuatha Dé Danann* or *Tuatha Dé Anann* (Peoples of the Goddess D/Ana) is derived from Dana or Ana. The 'D' of *Dé* may have come over in front of 'Ana' to make it

'Dana' for ease of pronunciation. In any case, Cormac Mac Cuileannáin, the great tenth century Archbishop of Cashel and King of Munster, described Ana as *'mater deorum hibernensium'* (mother of the Irish gods) in his celebrated dictionary of difficult or obsolete words, *Sanas Cormaic.* (Stokes, 1862, XXXIII, 2)

The special connection of Ana with Munster and with the fertility of the land is pointed out in a manuscript in Trinity College, Dublin, MS H. 3. 18; 565:

> Mumu, i.mo a hana nas ana cach coigid, ar is inti noadrad bandia int shonusa.i.Ana a hainm sain; ocus is uaithi side is berar da chig Anann. (Munster, greater her 'ana' – prosperity/fertility – than any other province, because it is in her – Munster – is adored the goddess of fertility and her name is 'Ana', and it is from her that 'Dhá Chíoch Anann' – the two breasts of Ana – is derived.)

The author is making use of a pun. *Ana* is the word for prosperity/fertility and 'Ana' is the name of the Goddess of fertility. Dhá Chíoch Anann are the two great breastlike hills (The Paps) with a cairn on top of each which dominate the landscape between Rathmore and Killarney. There the Great Mother is outlined in all her glory and what a magnificent and evocative sight that is.

What a mighty religious symbol this must have been – the primordial woman in her nurturing aspect. Even today Dhá Chíoch Anann draws us back past recorded time to the primordial womb, the nurturing breasts, the protecting enfolding arms of the Great Mother. Here is mystery and awe.

It is natural enough to assume that the Tuatha Dé Danann, having been forced underground, would have lost much of their significance. A hilarious passage in the tract, *De Gabáil in tSída,* in the *Book of Leinster,* however, contradicts this assumption.

Hardly had the Tuatha Dé Danann gone underground

than they caused the harvest and milk *(ith agus blicht)* to fail. Then the human population, who had ostensibly won the Battle of Tailteann, had to go hat in hand as it were to the Tuatha Dé Danann asking them to restore the crops. The Daghdha, their king, was most gracious and agreed to restore the fertility of the land:

> Boi rí amra for Tuathaib Dea i nHere. Dagan a ainm. Ba mór di a chumachta. Ced la Maccu Miled iar ngabail in tire. Ar collset Tuatha Dea ith acus blicht im Maccu Miled. co ndingsat chairddes in Dagdai. Doessartsaide iarum ith ocus blicht doib. (245 B)

> (There was a famous king over the Tuatha Dé in Éire. Dagán (the little Daghdha) was his name. Great was his power, however, even over the sons of Míle when they had conquered the country. For the Tuatha Dé destroyed the corn and milk of Clann Mhíle. They made a treaty with the Daghdha. He gave the corn and milk back to them after this.)

The great god of the sea, Manannán Mac Lir who gives his name to the Isle of Man, takes over the leadership of the Tuatha Dé Danann and it is he who divides these supernatural mansions called the *sí* among the princes of the Tuatha Dé Danann and their households.

Among those named are Bodhbh Dearg who takes over the fairy mansion of the Sí mBuidhbh near Loch Deirgdheirc on the Shannon, Midhir is appointed to Sí Truim near Slane and Fionnbharr, goes to Sí Meadha, in Co Galway. In this way, the supernatural race of the Tuatha Dé Danann or *aos sí* are spread throughout the country living in the hollow hills still venerated as sacred places after the lapse of thousands of years. (cf. Map and list of sites in: Logan, P., *The Old Gods,* (Belfast 1981.) These sacred dwellings are modelled on Manannán's own mansion of Eamhain Abhlach or Avalon.

The Tuatha Dé Danann have three great treasures:

The Faeth Fiadha – or supernatural cloak of invisibility by which they are generally invisible to the human population but they can on occasion make themselves visible.

Flea Ghoibhneann – the supernatural drink provided by the blacksmith god Goibniu (Gofannon/Gobán Saor) by which death and old age were avoided by Tuatha Dé Danann.

Muca Mhanannáin – the pigs of Manannán Mac Lir which provided unending food; those killed and cooked today would be alive again tomorrow.

Manannán is accepted as king of Tuatha Dé Danann and is invited to each Sí-Bhrú in turn for a great feast, and a flourishing social life develops among this mystic race.

What we have then, in this country, is two population groups, one human, living on the surface of the land – ourselves; the other divine, immortal, usually invisible, living in the *síthe* or hollow hills and ancient monuments. There is a constant interchange between these two groups. The divine race of Tuatha Dé Danann control the fertility of the land and they expect the human inhabitants on the surface of the land to acknowledge this by making offerings to them. If these offerings are not made, then the Tuatha Dé Danann can cause bad harvests and general misfortune on the land.

In general we can say that these offerings take two forms, formal and informal

Formal:

Offerings made to children or adults going around collecting in masked bands at Samhain.

Killing of a cock and sprinkling of its blood on the threshold and four corners of the house on St Martin's Eve (11 November), Samhain.

Leaving cakes at sacred sites at sacred times, e.g. Samhain, Imbolc, Bealtaine, Lúnasa.

Burying a sheaf of corn on a Lúnasa Hill.

Offerings in a pit, eggs and meat to Donn Fírinne the Irish god of the dead.

The *bainis Rí* in which the king is married to the Tuatha Dé Danann goddess to ensure the fertility of the land.

Informal:

When milking a cow, the first drops are poured on the ground.

Marking the side of cow with sign of cross made by the thumb dipped in milk (two religions mixed).

The first milk of a newly-calved cow is poured out at a *Bile* (sacred tree), *Lios,* or other sacred site.

Three potatoes taken from pot at lunchtime and laid aside for Tuatha Dé Danann.

A slice of bread which drops on floor is laid aside for Tuatha Dé Danann – not an accident but a hint from Tuatha Dé Danann that offering is required.

Similarly in the case of a bucket of milk spilt by a kicking cow. (Tuatha Dé Danann prompt the cow to spill the milk.)

A patch of vegetable garden left unharvested.

Meal left on the table on All Souls' Night (Samhain) for the return of the hungry dead.

Asking house-planning permission from Tuatha Dé Danann. (Four posts with ropes left for some time on the site. If untouched build, if knocked down move somewhere else as the site is on a Tuatha Dé Danann path.)

There are many other observances which formed part of the *creideamh sí* which we can only allude to here – practices such as the use of iron as a protection against harm from Tuatha Dé Danann, the horseshoe over the door, the thongs in the cradle, the *Scian Coise Duibhe* (Black-handled knife); the *leannán sí* or fairy lover; the *bean sí* who cries at the death of a member of the Gaelic aristocracy; the various traditions of skill in music and medicine being given to humans by the

aos sí; stories of supernatural animals coming from the sea; the
four great Celtic Feasts of Samhain, Imbolc, Bealtaine and
Lúnasa celebrating the yearly lifecycle of the goddess.

Literature, folklore and archaeological remains all indicate
that the early founders of Christianity in Ireland, such as
Colm Cille, had to contend with a sophisticated and mystical
religion well integrated with the political and social system.

The underground race, then, has a stranglehold over the
settled population as they control the fertility of the soil.
They have to be placated by little offerings, such as a *bairín
breac* or loaf laid at the foot of the *sí,* respect for their sacred
sites which must not be tampered with. This latter has served
to preserve the sites intact in many cases to the present day
but the decline of the *creideamh sí,* or fairy faith, has led to
much destruction.

Much of the folklore tradition of Ireland concerns the relations between the Tuatha Dé Danann and the human population. Tales of the *bean sí,* of the *leannán sí* or fairy lover
abound. Otherworld figures emerge from the *sí* especially at
Samhain and Bealtaine which are particularly dangerous
times. The various traditions have been, collected and presented in a masterly fashion by Dr Patrick Logan in his book
The Old Gods (Belfast 1981).

The Tuatha Dé Danann or *aos sí* are the ancient goddesses
and gods of the Celts of Ireland. But there may be among
them older divinities from the megalithic period. While
Celtic names such as An Daghdha (the good God), Aonghus
Óg, An Bhóinn, Midhir, Manannán Mac Lir, Eithne, and
others cluster around Brú na Bóinne, Newgrange itself was
constructed thousands of years before the Celts arrived in
Ireland. Did the Celtic gods and goddesses take over the sanctuaries of the megalithic peoples as acts of conquest, or was
there a blending of different cultures – megalithic, bronze age
and Celtic? This would seem to be what happened and per-

haps the different peoples had many religious ideas in common. Then it seems from the folklore traditions of Tech nDoinn (off the coast of Kerry) and Cnoc Fírinne (near Croom, Co Limerick) that the dead were also involved with the Tuatha Dé Danann. (cf. Muller-Lisowski, 1948, 149 ff.)

The Fomhóraigh, or dark gods of the sea whom the Tuatha Dé Danann defeated at the Battle of Maigh Tuireadh, were another group of divinities of immense power.

The fairy faith

The *creideamh sí* or fairy faith was a highly complex religious system. It was above all a fertility cult concerned with food production, health, protection, good harvests, children, large herds of cattle, sheep and pigs. It stood for the ultimately basic things of human life – food and children, the survival of the individual and the survival of the race.

While Christianity has during its history shown a marked tendency to become involved in abstruse theological discussions and dogmatic formulations, the *creideamh sí* was primarily concerned with putting bread and butter on the table, with the secrets of nature and herbs to provide health and well-being, with good law to produce a stable society. In a pre-technological age a succession of bad harvests could decimate a community and so it was all-important to preserve good relations with the goddess and the Tuatha Dé Danann in general, in order to secure the fertility of the land, humans and agricultural stock. We have a fine account of the cult of the goddess Áine Chliach of Lough Gur and Knockainy (Cnoc Áine) in east Limerick, at the end of the nineteenth century, by a local man, David Fitzgerald, whose family were, according to legend, one of the local families actually descended from the goddess.

The ritual in honour of Áine took place out of doors on the sacred hill of Cnoc Áine (near Hospital, *Ospidéal Áine;*

the remains of the Knights' Hospitaller' church is beside the
Catholic church in the village) at a significant astronomical
date, the eve of the summer solstice, 23 June, St John's eve. A
torchlight procession encircled the hill, *deiseal,* and on reaching the top, went around the moat near the large earthworks
there. The *cliars* or torches were then taken and waved among
the cattle and fields to communicate the cleansing, fertilising
fire to the crops and animals.

Behind the ritual was the belief that Áine returned annually
on the holy night to celebrate her own rites. This belief also
formed a major part of the cult of St Brigid and is mentioned
several times in the manuscripts of The Department of Irish
Folklore, University College Dublin:

> People believe that St Brigid comes at night-time and
> blesses the ribbon or handkerchief. (IFC 907: 211);
>
> The door was never locked when they were going to bed
> on that night so that St Brigid might come in and warm
> herself at the fire which is left lighting all night. (IFC 907:
> 231);
>
> In olden times the Cross was put outside the door (on the
> door) on St Brigid's Eve. This was a profession of faith: St
> Brigid was supposed to pass through Ireland on that night
> and she blessed the houses where the cross was displayed.
> (IFC 907: 61-3);
>
> It is believed that St Brigid visits every house on the night
> of the eve of her feast day. She is supposed to kneel in the
> doorway and pray for the people of the house. (IFC 899:
> 167).

Brigid returned then on 31 January, the Eve of Imbolc. The
regular, annual return of a saint from heaven to earth on
his/her feast day does not seem to be part of the ordinary
Catholic tradition. In the case of St Brigid, it would appear
that this was one of the characteristics of the goddess Brigid

which descended to Brigid the saint on analogy with the annual return of Áine.

Another element to be noted in this remarkable account is the allusion to the position of the moon:

Áine is sometimes to be seen, half her body above the waters, on the bosom of Loch Guirr, combing her hair, as the Earl of Desmond beheld her by the bank of the Camóg. The commoner account is that she dwells within the hill which bears her name, and on which she has often been seen. Every Saint John's night the men used to gather on the hill from all quarters. They were formed in ranks by an old man called Quinlan, whose family yet (1876) live on the hill; and cliars, bunches, that is, of straw and hay tied upon poles, and lit, were carried in procession round the hill and the little moat on the summit, Mullach-Crocáin-lámh-le-leab'-an-Triúir (the hillock-top near the grave of the three). Afterwards people ran through the cultivated fields, and among the cattle, waving these cliars, which brought luck to crops and beasts for the following year. There was this about the night of the cliars, that if you came, say, from some neighbouring village to join in the sport it was necessary that on getting on the hill you should look at the moon and mark what her position was in regard to the place to which you had to return: otherwise you would lose your way when the cliars were out, and you had to get back home in the darkness. One Saint John's night it happened that one of the neighbours lay dead, and on this account the usual cliars were not lit. Not lit, I should say, by the hands of living men; for that night such a procession of cliars marched round Cnoc Áine as never was seen before, and Áine herself was seen in the front, directing and ordering every thing. On another Saint John's night a number of girls had stayed late on the hill, watching the cliars and joining in the games.

Suddenly Áine appeared among them, (thanked them for the honour they had done her), but said that now she wished them to go home, as they wanted the hill to themselves. She let them understand whom she meant by (they), for calling some of the girls she made them look through a ring, when behold, the hill appeared crowded with people before invisible. Another time she came one night into the house of some people whose friends are yet living at one end of the hill, and brought them a sheep. So long as the family kept this animal, luck remained with them, and when they parted with it, luck abandoned them.

Áine is spoken of as the best-hearted woman that ever lived; and the oldest families about Knockainy are proud to claim descent from her. These Sliocht Áine (descendants of Áine) include the Ó Briens, Dillanes, Creeds, Laffins, O'Deas. We must add Fitzgeralds, what few remain thereabouts.

The meadow-sweet, or queen of the meadow, is thought to be Áine's plant, and to owe to her its fragrant odour.
(*Revue Celtique* IV (1879-1880) 189-190)

Midsummer fires are known in many parts of Europe and in North Africa. At the summer solstice the sun has reached its zenith to mark the longest day of the year, but from that point onwards it begins to decline so that the nights grow longer and the days shorter. The bonfires and fire-rituals may be a way of strengthening the declining sun and encouraging it to keep going so that the harvest in the more northern parts of Europe might ripen. Áine, the 'fiery driver', is undoubtedly connected with the sun so that the ritual performed by the people could be considered as a joint effort to assist Áine in her cosmic circuit which had repercussions in the livelihood of the local population.

In David Fitzgerald's description of the rite there is no reference to St John. The midsummer fire rituals probably go back to a period long before the Christian era (Frazer, 1923, 622) but were given a Christian slant by attaching the Feast of St John the Baptist to them.

At the other side of Co Limerick (west Limerick) the bonfire was known as *Teine Féil' Eoin,* and prayers were said for the crops and fine weather. In Athea parish, the parish priest, in the early nineteenth century, attended the bonfire and led the prayers. (Danaher, 1972, 134-135) In Knockainy, however, Áine prevailed, with apparently no great fuss on the part of the church. Cnoc Áine, of course, stood within the great Lough Gur complex with its enchanted lake, its profusion of monuments of megalithic and Celtic type, its Norman castles and the massive folklore surrounding Áine and Gearóid Iarla Mac Gearailt who was regarded as the human but enchanted son of Áine herself.

Nevertheless, it is a curious fact that in the Athea area near the Kerry border, a highly developed ritual prevailed for St John's Eve but it seems to have been thoroughly Christianised, and in fact could be said to be a folk-version of the *Rituale Romanum,* whereas at the eastern end of the county, on Cnoc Áine, there seems to have been no attempt at Christianisation and Áine herself was the centre of the observance and invisibly attended the rites celebrated in her honour.

While the people of east Limerick were celebrating Áine and the *aos sí* who accompanied her on the sacred hill in the nineteenth century, centuries before that a cleric was explaining:

For tuaith Herenn bai temel
Tuatha adortais sidi,
ni creitset in fir-deacht
inna Trinoite firi.

(Over the land of Ireland there was darkness, the people
used to worship the *sí,* they used not to believe in the true
divinity of the true Trinity)
(*Liber Hymnorum;* Bernard and Atkinson, 1898, 101)

Undoubtedly there was no lack of faith in the Trinity
among the people of east Limerick. To some extent the ancient *creideamh sí* lived on side by side with the Catholic faith,
or certain assimilation took place, a common enough phenomenon when one religion replaces another and they gradually build up an understanding of each other.

The Gods and the power of nature
To a degree, perhaps, the ancient gods and goddesses, the *aos
sí* or *déithe dúileacha* (elemental divinities), may be explained
as personifications of the forces of nature. One can easily
imagine the Árd Rí or High King standing on the royal hill of
Tara and letting his gaze wander over the vast plain of Ireland.
In this great undulating, fertile, verdant land expanding before him, how easy it was to see the body of the goddess in all
her fruitfulness and variety, a gentle maternal image – she
who made the grass grow, who made the corn ripen, who put
apples on the trees and acorns on the oaks – the mother of her
people. This was Éire.

Or one could look at the Boyne river – *An Bhó Fhinn,* the
white cow – symbol of fertility, and again see in its gentle undulating form the image of the goddess, the giver of salmon.

Standing on a cliff overlooking the raging sea a person
might gaze at the swirling waves topped by great crests of
white foam rolling along on the surface of the ocean to crash
against the strand. He might well see in this vast and threatening panorama the divine figure of the sea – god Manannán
Mac Lir, driving his chariot with break-neck speed as the
manes of his white horses toss to and fro with the speed of
their galloping.

From the end of the nineteenth century we have an example

of this type of personification recorded from the people on the northern slope of Cnoc Fírinne near Croom, Co Limerick. Cnoc Fírinne is the sanctuary of Donn Fírinne, the god of the dead in Irish tradition, no doubt corresponding to Caesar's *Dis Pater* from whom, according to Caesar, the Celts maintained they were descended. But Donn was also associated with storms, weather prediction, fertility of the land, and general luck to those who reverenced him.

Liam Ó Danachair, the folklore collector, took down the following conversation between Pat O'Riordan and Mrs Higgins on a stormy October night:

PAT: Abair go bhfuil Donn ag dul ar cos ináirde sna sgamalla anocht?

MRS H: An airgheann tú anois é ag liúighreach go hard insa ghaoith agus bior nimhneach sa ghlór ghruaimeach? Éist leis sin. Éist leis sin, sin é é, pus a's puicshúil air. Dia idir sinn agus an t-olc. Tá sé ar lasadh le feirg.

(PAT: One may say that Donn is galloping in the clouds tonight.

MRS H: Do you hear him now screaming loudly in the wind, a poison note in his sad voice? Listen to that. Listen to that. That's him with ill-tempered mouth and glowering eye. God between us and harm. He's aflame with anger.) (*Béaloideas* 18 (1948) 159)

While the interpretation of the forces of nature as living and acting personality may be an imaginative and poetic projection of the mind, the actual power of nature is real. The storm is real, the power of the land to produce vegetation and crops is real, the power of humans and animals and birds to reproduce themselves is real, along with thousands of other mysterious activities of the elements. In adopting a sophisticated, superior and rationalistic attitude towards the 'Old Gods' one risks drifting into a cold stony mentality, boring and lifeless.

In the account of St Patrick's meeting with the two daughters of King Laoghaire at the Well of Clebach near Rathcroghan, Co Roscommon, we get a very intimate view of several facets of early Irish Christianity.

The princesses Eithne and Fedhelm come to the well to bathe. Attention is drawn to the east and the rising sun – which with the water indicate the baptismal theme described later.

Then there is the strange episode in which St Patrick and his clerics, dressed in white are actually mistaken for the Aos Sí or Tuatha Dé Danann.

Then there is the dialogue between the representatives of the two religions in which the powers of nature and the elemental gods are discussed and the resolution is arrived at in which the multitude of terrestrial divinities are resolved into the One God.

The princesses are converted and respond to the Creed, which precedes baptism. They are then baptised in the Well of Clebach (now Ogulla, near Tulsk) and then ask to see the Lord. St Patrick assures them that they must receive the Eucharist and die before seeing the face of God. They agree, receive the Eucharist, which for them, as with the Children of Lir in the old legend, is a *viaticum,* or bread for the journey, and straightaway die. The *caoineadh* or lament for the dead is sung for them and they are buried by the well. It becomes a place of pilgrimage for the faithful who visit it on the last Sunday in June. In Tireachán's account we have a moving description of the meeting of the two faiths in a gentle way, devoid of the arrogance which so often characterises these occasions:

The Story of Patrick and the Royal Daughters
But thence went the holy Patrick to the spring which is called Clebach, on the sides of Crochan, toward the rising of the sun, before the rising of the sun, and they sat beside

the spring. And behold, two daughters of Loegaire, Ethne the fair and Fedelm the ruddy, came to the spring in the morning, after the custom of women, to wash, and they found a holy synod of bishops with Patrick by the spring. And they did not know from whence they were, or of what shape, or of what people, or of what region. But they thought that they were men of the *síde,* or of the terrestrial gods, or an apparition. And the daughters said to them: 'Whence are ye, and whence have ye come?'

And Patrick said to them: 'It were better that you would confess our true God than to inquire about our race.'

The first daughter said: 'Who is God? And where is God? And of what is God? And where is his dwelling place? Has your God sons and daughters, gold and silver? Is he ever-living? Is he beautiful? Have many fostered his Son? Are his daughters dear and beautiful to the men of the world? Is he in heaven or on earth? In the sea? In the rivers? In the mountains? In the valleys? Tell us, how is he seen? How is he loved? How is he found? Is he in youth, or in age?'

But holy Patrick, full of the Holy Spirit, answering, said: 'Our God is the God of all men, the God of heaven and earth, of the sea and of the rivers; the God of the sun and of the moon, of all the stars; the God of the lofty mountains and of the lowly valleys; the God over heaven, and in heaven, and under heaven. He has his dwelling toward heaven and earth, and the sea, and all things that are in them. He inspires all things. He gives life to all things. He surpasses all things. He supports all things. He kindles the light of the sun; he strengthens the light of the moon at night for watches; and he made springs in the land, and dry islands in the sea; and the stars he placed to minister to the greater lights. He has a Son co-eternal with himself and like unto himself. The Son, is not younger than the Father, nor is the Father older than the Son. The Father,

Son, and the Holy Spirit are not separated. I truly desire to unite you to the Heavenly King since ye are daughters of an earthly king. Believe (in him).'

And the daughters said, as if with one mouth and heart: 'How can we believe in the Heavenly King? Teach us most diligently, so that we may see him face to face. Point out to us, and we will do whatsoever thou shalt say to us.'

And Patrick said: 'Do you believe that the sin of your father and mother is taken away by baptism?'

They replied: 'We do believe it.'

Patrick. 'Do you believe there is repentance after sin?'

Daughters. 'We do believe it.'

Patrick. 'Do you believe there is a life after death? Do you believe in the resurrection on the day of judgement?'

Daughters. 'We do believe it.'

Patrick. 'Do you believe in the unity of the church?'

Daughters. 'We do believe it.'

And they were baptised, and (Patrick placed) a white garment on their heads.

And they begged to see the face of Christ.

And the saint said to them: 'Unless you shall have tasted death, you cannot see the face of Christ, and unless you shall receive the sacrifice.'

And they replied: 'Give to us the sacrifice, that we may see the Son our Spouse.'

And they received the Eucharist of God, and they slept in death. And they placed them in a bed covered with one mantle, and their friends made a wailing and a great lamentation ... And the days of the wailing for the daughters of the king were ended, and they buried them by the spring Clebach; and they made a round ditch in the likeness of a grave, because so the Scottic men and Gentiles used to do.'

(Sanderson, 1895, 79-282)

Tuatha Dé Danann and the Fallen Angels

From quite an early period, as is seen from *Leabhar Gabhála Éireann,* the Irish embarked on an imaginative effort to situate the Tuatha Dé Danann within the boundaries of Christian theology. Fundamentally, among some, the Tuatha Dé Danann or *aos sí* were identified with the rebellious angels who rebelled against God in heaven. They were led by Lucifer, the dragon, and defeated by the good angels led by St Michael and cast out of heaven as recorded in the Book of the Apocalypse, chapter twelve. This war in heaven seems to have been very important to the Irish from the theological point of view and had a large influence in the conception of Christian life on earth.

The *Leabhar Gabhála* stresses that there were various opinions on the origins of the Tuatha Dé Danann and it is evident that a great deal of creative thinking was going on at this early period:

Atberaid aroile comad deamna grada ecsamla Tuatha Dé Danann, ocus comad iadsiden do deachadar do nim araen risin loinges do deachaid Luitcifear cona deamnaib do nibh; ar faemad chuirp aerda umpu, do milleadh, ocus d'aslach for sil nAdaim. (Macalister, 1940, 3, 154)

(Other people say that the Tuatha Dé Danann were demons of a different grade and that it is they who came from heaven along with the expulsion by which Lucifer and his demons came from heaven, having taken an airy body upon themselves to destroy and to tempt the seed of Adam.)

Here is a clear and cogent connection between the rebellion and war in heaven, the heavenly sphere, and the Christian life on earth, the earthly. Lucifer and the rebellious angels who made war on God in heaven are defeated and, as it were, 'deported' – cast out of heaven down to earth. But in their

new home on earth they do not remain inactive, they begin
the war against God all over again by attacking and tempting
the descendants of Adam, the human race, God's creation. In
this way, the war begun in heaven continues on earth and
Christian life becomes Christian warfare as we take up arms
against Lucifer and his demons on earth, just as the good angels led by St Michael did in the war in heaven. This type of
theological thinking proclaimed a clear line of continuity between the heavenly and the earthly sphere, and Christ could
easily be seen as the *laoch* or hero who descends from the
heavenly sphere to lead his troops against the forces of evil.

The text continues:

Tiagaid thra in lucht sin i sidib. Ocus tiagaid fo muirib,
ocus tiagaid i conrechtaib, ocus tiagaid co hamaide ocus
tiagait co tuaith cingtha. Is as sin is bunudas doib uile, .i.
muintir deamain.

(Those people then, go into the *síthe*. They go under the
seas, they go in wolf-shapes, and they go to fools and they
go to the powerful. This then is the nature of all of them –
demon-people).

Following this tradition, the names *Dream an Uabhair,
Aingil an Uabhair* (People of the Pride; Angels of the Pride,
recalling, no doubt the pride of Lucifer which caused his fall),
were given to the Tuatha Dé Danann by people in parts of Co
Cork. (*Revue Celtique*, 1879-1880, 178)

The same tradition is found in Gaelic Scotland where their
connection with the 'Father of Pride' and deportation from
heaven is admitted by them:

Cha 'n do Shiol Adhamh sinn,
's cha 'n e Abraham ár n-athair;
Ach tha sinn de mhuinntir an Athar Uaibhreach,
Chaidh fhuadach amach a Flaitheas.
(Mackenzie, 1895, 51)

(We are not among the descendants of Adam and Abraham is not our father; but we belong the people of the Proud Father who were cast out of heaven.)

This very definite Christian interpretation of the identity of the Tuatha Dé Danann with the fallen angels was not universal and considerable doubt on the subject prevailed. On the one hand they could be very helpful and magnanimous to the human population, as for instance in the case of Donn Fírinne and the goddess Áine in the folklore of Co Limerick, while on the other hand they could be extremely dangerous. This type of ambiguity is expressed admirably in the folk-prayers:

Gabhaimid le n-a gcoimirce,
agus diúltaimíd d'a n-imirce,
a gcúl linn,
a n-aghaidh uainn,
as ucht báis agus páise
ár Slánaitheoir Íosa Críosta.

(We accept their protection and we refuse their departure, (but) their backs be towards and their faces be away from us, for the sake of the death and passion of our Saviour Jesus Christ.)

This type of ambiguity was catered for within the Irish Christian folklore tradition as it was explained that some of the fallen angels, even though they had been cast out of heaven, weren't really so bad. Some of them had taken part in the rebellion against God in heaven more or less against their wills and their hearts weren't in it. When they were thrown out of heaven, some fell into the sea where they remain, some fell into the *síthe* or hollow hills and some remained in the air. (cf. Logan, 1981, 5)

In practice, then, in accordance with this benign Christian interpretation, they formed a mixed bunch and they could be very generous to the humans. Áine of Lough Gur and Cnoc

Áine was spoken of as 'the best-hearted woman that ever lived', and Bryan Merriman calls Aoibheall na Craige Léithe, *bean sí* of the O'Briens, *Croí gan aon locht* (A heart with no fault). (*Revue Celtique*, 1879-1880, 190)

The Fairies' Question

This situation gave rise to what is known as 'The Fairies' question'. According to the legend, which comes in many versions, the Tuatha Dé Danann were anxious to know if they would be re-admitted to heaven. They approach St Patrick's servant and ask him to ask St Patrick if they had any chance of re-admission. St Patrick, however, comes across as a strict churchman and his reply was quite clear, they would never be admitted into heaven. Patrick warned his servant to be careful when he took this bad news back to the Tuatha Dé Danann as, in their fury, they would try to kill him. Patrick advised him to dig a pit and get into it and then place the shovel and spade he had used to dig the pit over it in the form of a cross.

The servant did all this and the Aos Sí arrived to find out the answer to their question. He gave them the bad news and they flew into a rage and tried to kill him but they couldn't get past the cross formed by the spade and shovel. The custom of putting the spade and shovel in the form of a cross over the grave while the priest recites the prayers for the dead in many parts of the country is said to derive from this tradition. (*Revue Celtique,* 1879-1880, 176)

A somewhat different version of 'The Fairies' Question' tells of them meeting a priest and putting the question to him. He answered, 'You will never enter heaven until this dry dead stick which I have in my hand bears leaves, flowers and fruit.' He threw the stick on the ground and left them lamenting but next day the stick had grown leaves, flowers and fruit. So there is still hope that the *aos sí* will be re-admitted to heaven. (Logan, 1981, 17)

This desire to be admitted to heaven led, it appears, to some surprising developments. The Tuatha Dé Danann had a well-known habit of abducting people, especially at the Feast of Samhain (31 October) when the barriers between this world and the world of the *aos sí* broke down and they could wander into our human world and we could be drawn into theirs. This feast of Samhain was so important among the Celts that it could not be ignored by the Christian church. It is no wonder than that All Saints and All Souls replace it and, as we shall see, appear to be deeply influenced by it.

While healthy children might be abducted by the Tuatha Dé Danann and sickly children left in their place, according to the *Iarlais* or 'changeling' tradition, and women could be abducted as wet-nurses, it does seem that young men were particularly vulnerable to abduction at Samhain and they were well advised to carry the *Scian Choise Duibhe,* or black-handled knife, with them when passing a *sí,* as the *aos sí* feared iron. This may indicate their stone-age connections.

Now, this may be connected with the desire of the *aos sí* to enter heaven. Humans were perfectly eligible for entrance into heaven for humans had red blood. The Tuatha Dé Danann had white blood and so they concluded that to be certain of heaven the thing to do was to acquire red blood. According to the biological thinking of the time, it was thought that the father contributed more to the child than the mother did. If a Tuatha Dé Danann woman, a *bean sí,* married a human man, then their children would have more red blood than if a Tuatha Dé Danann man had married a human woman, hence the demand for young handsome men. By continuous marriage with humans, the number of Tuatha Dé Danann with red blood would gradually increase, in other words they would become human-like and so become eligible for entrance into heaven. (Ó hÓgáin, 1991, 187-190)

Traditionally then, we have a scenario in which supernatural beings proliferate and are intimately involved in the affairs of the human population. As we have seen, they are responsible above all for the fertility of the land which supports the humans. But they also flit to and fro between worlds and may become involved in the personal affairs of individuals. The traditional Irish world is a world of two population groups, one human and the other supernatural, and these two population groups are constantly meeting. In a sense it was something of an enchanted scenario in which two worlds blended and one can easily understand how this must have influenced the lives of the Irish saints, where angels and demons drop in casually for a chat in much the same way as the Tuatha Dé Danann did. This was not the rather clinical rationalistic ethos of much of today's religion, but rather a colourful expression of the relations of the divine with the human, dangerous but very exciting. Even the great Colm Cille had to watch his step. According to tradition a friendly angel visited him regularly. But one day St Colm Cille must have said something out of the way for the angel hit him a slap across the face which left its mark on him for life. This teeming world of supernaturals must have made the doctrine of the Communion of Saints particularly dear and accessible to the Irish. In all this, the divine shows its presence, as it were sociologically, through supernatural persons and this leads us on to consider another type of presence of a more philosophical type – the concept of *Neart*.

CHAPTER SIX

The Concept of *Neart*

In the Introduction we have seen Professor Macquarrie's remarkable insight into the nature of traditional Gaelic spirituality when he stresses the presence of a transcendent reality pervading all things in the world, immanent in human life. We saw also that this idea of a divine presence filling everything seems to correspond to St Paul's phrase in connection with pagan Greek religion: 'In him we live and move and have our being.'

This quotation from Professor Macquarrie highlights the idea of the divine presence, a transcendent reality present and immanent in the world of our own experience. Here it is a question of a supernatural force or power pervading everything rather than that power, as it were, incarnated in the teeming Celtic world of spirits.

As I said, the Celts were *muintir na tuaithe,* people of the land, whose very existence depended on the regular return of the seasons for the provision of food. They were consciously aware of the yearly cycle of decay of vegetation in winter, its resurgence in spring, its maturing in summer, its flowering in autumn. Our greatest mythological text, *Cath Maige Tuired,* expresses it neatly:

> Spring for ploughing and sowing, and the beginning of summer for maturing the strength of the grain, and the beginning of autumn for the full ripeness of the grain, and for reaping it. Winter for consuming it. (Gray, 1982, 157)

Behind this extraordinary cycle of decay and growth, the cyclic movement in nature, the death of one form and the birth of another, the Celts must have seen a strange energy going out from a stable centre filling everything, invigorating everything, constantly changing, leaving aside one form and taking on another.

God in this, his creative energy or *neart,* is seen as going out in six directions in texts such as St Patrick's Breastplate and elsewhere. He surrounds the person on all sides, north, south, east and west, above and below. The points of the compass are set by the phrase *Críst reum* (*Críost romham,* Christ before me). According to ancient custom preserved in the orientation of churches, when praying one turned towards the east, the area of the rising sun and new life. Then one's right hand was to the south, one's back to the west and one's left hand to the north.

The formula of the six directions is expressed neatly in Old Irish in *Lúireach Phádraig* and in Latin in the *Lorica of St Brendan:*

Críst reum (Críost romham); (Christ before me)
Críst dessum (Críost ar mo dheis); (Christ at my right hand)
Críst im degaid (Críost i mo dhiaidh); (Christ behind me)
Críst tuathum (Críost ar mo chlé); (Christ at my left hand)
Críst uasum (Críost os mo chionn); (Christ above me)
Críst issum (Críost fúm); (Christ below me)

Protege me Domine, (Protect me, O Lord)
a dextris et a sinistris, (to the right and to the left)
ante et retro, (in front and behind)
subtus et superius. (below and above). (Ó Duinn, 1990, 93)

The same type of formula is found in the *Chandogya Upanishad:*

The (Infinite) is below,
it is above,

it is to the west,

it is to the east,

it is to the south,

it is to the north.

Truly it is the whole universe. (Ó Duinn, 1990, 170)

The same theme is expressed in the *Atharva Veda,* showing the similarity between Hindu and Celtic thought:

By the Support are held both heaven and earth,

by the Support the broad domain of space,

by the Support the six divergent directions,

by the Support is this whole world pervaded.

(Ó Duinn, 1990, 170)

Curiously enough, this type of layout in six directions is mentioned by St Clement of Alexandria in relation to the creation of the world as described in the Book of Genesis:

There proceed from God, the heart of the world, indefinite extensions upwards and downwards, to right and left, backward and forward. Looking in these six directions, as at a constant number, he completes the creation of the world, of which he is the beginning and the end.

(*Stromata,* VI, 16)

On the seventh or Sabbath Day, God rested after the work of the six days, corresponding to the six rays of creative energy emanating from the centre. In his commentary on the difficult thought of St Clement, Alan Watts draws attention to the fact that this formula of the six directions corresponds to the traditional Chi Rho sign:

What Clement actually describes is the three-dimensional cross, which when represented on a plane surface appears as the six pointed star, and this curiously enough, is the earliest form of the Christian monogram for Christ, made by the superimposition of the initials of the Greek name *Iesous Xristos.* It is for this reason that symbols of the sun –

the astronomical *imago Dei* – may be either four or six-rayed stars, according as to whether the sun is shown in two or three dimensions. Thus the creation of the world in six directions and three dimensions is the primordial crucifixion of the Logos, the slaying of the Lamb at the foundation of the world (Revelation 13:8). Creation is a sacrificial act in the sense that it is God's assumption of finite limitations, whereby the One is – in play but not in reality – dismembered into the Many. (1983, 50-51)

The formula of the six directions was performed as a ritual called the *Comrair chrabuid (Cófra Cráifeachta* – Shrine of Piety) by the ninth century monastic reformers, the *Céilí Dé:*

Pater sair prius ocus Deus in adiutorium usque festine, ocus da dhí láim suas fria nem ocus airrdhe na croise cot laim ndeiss iarum. Similiter in cech aird sic sís ocus suass. Is hi trá comrair chrábuid leosum. (Rule of the Célí Dé, *Hermathena,* xliv, Second suppl. 68)

(The Our Father and 'O God, come to my aid, O Lord make haste to help me' are recited first facing the east with both hands raised to heaven and making the sign of the cross. This is then done for the other three points of the compass; then downwards and finally upwards. This is called the 'Shrine of Piety'.)

This is a very impressive native ritual, easily performed either by an individual or a group. Beginning towards the east one turns *deiseal* or sunwise to the south, then to the west, ending at the north. The downward bowing might be done effectively towards the west where the sun sets and the upward elevation of eyes and body towards the east, the area of the rising sun.

We find this ancient formula of the six directions occurring in a different form in what appears to be an expression of Celtic cosmology in *Táin Bó Chuailnge.* In this case, the sea is regarded as surrounding the world, taking the place of the four points of the compass.

In the story, Cú Chulainn, the great Ulster hero, has to defend Ulster single-handed against the forces of Connacht, who, led by Meadhbh, have invaded Ulster to capture the Brown Bull of Cuailnge. The Ulstermen are unable to fight as they are laid low by the mysterious affliction, the *cess noinden*, imposed on them by the goddess Macha in revenge for having forced her to run a race against the king's horses when she was pregnant. She won the race but died in giving birth to twins.

Cú Chulainn's father, Sualdamh, is furious that his son is getting no help and rides to Eamhain Macha (Navan Fort, near Ard Macha/Armagh) to complain to the king, Conchúr Mac Neasa. He shouts out: 'Fir gontar, mna fuadaitear, ba tiomaintear, a Ulta!' (Men are being wounded, women are being abducted, cows are being taken away, O Ulstermen!)

But it was *geis* (taboo) to speak before the king had spoken and it was *geis* for the king to speak before the druid. Having broken the *geis,* Sualdamh's fate was sealed. His horse reared up and the shield on his arm severed his head from his body. The severed head remained on the shield and again shouted out his protest: 'Fir gontar, mna fuadaitear, ba tiomaintear, a Ulta!' Then the king spoke: 'Tá an nuaill sin beagán ró-mhór, mar tá neamh ós ár gcionn agus an talamh fúinn agus an mhuir umainn uma gcuairt, agus mura dtuite an fhior-maimint lena frasa réaltan ar thonnghnúis na talún, nó mura mbrise an talamh as an dtalamh chumhscu fé n-ár gcosa, nó mura dtaga an fharraige eithreach eocharghorm ar thulmhoing an domhain, dobhearfadsa gach bó agus gach bean díobh ina lios is ina macha féin, tar éis bua catha agus comhlainn agus comhraic.' (Ó Cadhlaigh, 1956, 356)

(This protest is a bit over much. The sky is above us and the earth beneath us and the sea all around us, and unless the firmament with its showers of stars falls on the face of the earth, or the earth itself break up in an earthquake under our feet, or unless the furrowed blue ocean crashes over the hill-clad world, I will bring back every cow that has been taken away and every abducted woman to her farm and land after victory in war and battle.)

The same formula is repeated at a later stage in the *Táin* and here we have in secular literature what is found in some of our earliest religious texts – a sign of how Christianity joined the Celtic stream.

Again in this association between an unjust war, as in *Táin Bó Chuailnge,* and the destruction of world order 'cosmos' by 'chaos', we are led back to the notion of the eternal battle between chaos and cosmos, with God endeavouring to keep the elements in their appointed place – the sky up above, the sea within its boundaries, the earth in a state of stability, and being assisted in this by human intervention. When one element forces its way into the space belonging to another element, it has to be driven back within its proper domain so that harmony may be preserved. When some particular chemical grows to excess in the human body, physicians try to reduce it and produce a state of equilibrium. The created world is not evolving from its beginnings in comfort but with immense struggling and always threatened with the possibility of being dragged back into chaos. War and struggle on a multitude of battlegrounds seem to be part of the pattern of human existence.

Applied to Christian life, prayer, good works, sacrifice, fitting oneself into the creative mind of God who is engaged in keeping the evolutionary process in motion, warring against the forces of disintegration, these are the means we employ as Christian *spreagairí* to urge on and assist God in bringing creation to its final harmonious fulfilment. In this way the Christian programme forms a continuity with the cosmic vision of the Celtic and other ancient cultures.

William Sayers sums up neatly the type of cosmic picture featured in *Táin Bó Chuailnge:*

We have seen in the *Táin* that the threats to order, if they arise, come from just beyond the tripartite sphere of human activity, viz. the lower atmosphere, the coastal area of the sea and the earth's surface, in the form of lightning and storms directed downwards, seas flooding laterally, and quaking and splitting as the underworld thrusts upwards. In all cases, we have the negative consequences of a violation of natural boundaries, a maleficent example of the liminal situations so characteristic of early Celtic literature. (*Ériu*, xxxvii (1986), 105)

St Paul's Letter to the Ephesians, 6:10-17, describes the 'psychomachia' or spiritual warfare in graphic terms as a struggle 'against the sovereignties and the powers who originate the darkness in this world, the spiritual army of evil in the heavens'. He then goes on to describe the armour which the Christian soldier has to put on when going into battle. The opening verse (v. 10) of this section, however, brings in the idea of power/strength: 'Finally, grow strong in the Lord, with the strength of his power' – and this is a word that is highlighted in *Lúireach Phádraig*, St Patrick's Breastplate, which as a protection or 'armour prayer' is related to Ephesians 6:10-17. The Christian needs strength for the spiritual battle.

The idea of power occurs again in Ephesians 1:19-20:

… and how infinitely great is the power that he has exercised for us believers. This you can tell from the strength of his power at work in Christ, when he used it to raise him from the dead and to make him sit at his right hand, in heaven.

In his commentary on this passage, George Hitchcock discusses the four words used for 'power':

There are four words to be distinguished, 'power', 'activity', 'might' and 'strength'. 'Power', the Greek *dunamís*, regards the source, and implies the manifestation of a potency, inherent in God. 'Activity', the Greek *energeia,* or 'energy', looks at the process, the exercise of power, and sees the power in working. 'Might', the Greek *kratos,* used of Divine might in the Greek Testament, except in Heb 11. 14, suggests mastery and victory, and therefore a resistance. 'Strength', the Greek *ischus,* refers simply and absolutely to inherent power. (1913, 111)

Several times in *Lúireach Phádraig* the word *nert* (*neart* in modern Irish) occurs, but while undoubtedly related to *dunamis, energeia,* etc., it may not entirely coincide with them.

This is expressed in Irish texts such as are found in *Lúireach Phádraig* and elsewere: 'Dia/Críost romham; Dia ar mo dheis; Dia i mo dhiaidh; Dia ar mo chlé; Dia os mo chionn; Dia fúm' – in other words, God in his creative power is all around the person, north, south, east and west, above and below.

In St Patrick's Breastplate, the person rises up and binds himself with the *neart* or creative power coming from the Trinity, from the acts of Christ's life, from the angels and saints and from the elements – the forces of nature: sky, sun, moon, earth, sea, rock. In this eighth-century text in Old Irish, this strange power can be utilised for the attainment of eternal life or it can be used for the destruction of soul and body, depending on the intention of the users, so the idea of opposition and of freedom of choice is there all the time.

Now, to examine this basic idea of *neart* a little more closely we will take a simple example.

Some years ago, in Éire, there was a postage stamp depicting a dog, taken from the Book of Kells. The dog was all convoluted, his tail was in his mouth and interlacing lines ran all over him. There was no dog like this to be found in the artist's time and no dog like this could be found today.

So, what was the artist trying to say? I think that he was trying to express a basic Celtic philosophy. In my opinion, he was saying that here we have great lines of creative energy emanating from God to take the form of a dog temporarily. For the dog will die, and perhaps from his grave a flower will grow, and now the *neart* which had formed the dog is taking the form of a flower, and eventually the flower will die and be replaced by grass, shall we say. And now the creative *neart* has taken the form of grass.

This type of archaic religious thought was once common in many parts of the world, like the Indonesian concept of Mana and a similar idea in Hinduism. We find it expressed clearly in a West-Indian text:

> From Wakan Tanka, the Great Spirit, came a great unifying life-force that flowed through all things, the flowers of the plains, blowing winds, trees, birds and animals, and was the same force that had been breathed into the first man. Thus all things were kindred and were all brought together by the one mystery. (Luther Standing Bear, *Laxoto, A Natural Education,* Summerton 1944, 14)

Fundamentally, we have the penetration of matter by spirit and the image of the snake penetrating through rocks and vegetation, casting off his old skin to be renewed, is a valuable symbol of this type of thought. We find it expressed also in the great Welsh Myth of *Ceridwen.* Ceridwen was a Welsh goddess and she had a son call Afag Ddu. Afag Ddu was very ugly and his mother despaired of his ever getting a wife as no woman in her senses would ever look at him. So she decided to compensate him for his ugliness by making him the most brilliant druid and poet in Wales whose fame would last forever.

She went out into the fields and picked herbs to make a magic brew. Her plan was that the brew would be kept boiling for a year and a day and then Afag Ddu would drink some of it and all the wisdom and learning of the ages would enter into him and he would be famous forever as the great sage of Wales.

She got a young boy call Gwion Bach to keep the fire going and the brew stirred, and finally the day came when the magic brew was ready. But at the last moment a drop of the boiling brew shot out of the pot on to the hand of Gwion Bach. He put his hand in his mouth to ease the pain and swallowed a little of the brew. Immediately, all the wisdom and learning meant for Afag Ddu entered into Gwion Bach.

Ceridwen jumped at him to kill him but Gwion Bach turned himself into a hare and ran away from her. She turned herself into a greyhound and pursued him. He reached the sea and jumped in to avoid her and he became a fish. She jumped in after him and became an otter. Just as he was about to be caught he turned himself into bird and soared up into the air. She turned herself into a hawk and soared above him. Then he saw beneath him on the ground a heap of corn, which a farmer had been threshing. He swooped down and became a grain of corn. But Ceridwen swooped down too and became a hen. She gobbled up all the corn and thought that this was the end of Gwion Bach. Then she turned herself into a woman again and found she was pregnant. Nine months later, she had a son and from his infancy he was full of all the wisdom and learning of the ages – this, of course, was Gwion Bach who came back again in human form after all his various transformations and he became known as Taliesin, the great poet of Wales whose fame lives on to this day among Celts. (Rees, 1976, 229-230)

This then, is the *neart,* the creative energy going out from God, ever present, ever changing. One feels this strange power especially in woods where the trees seem to wait in suspense and harbour a hidden power.

As I said, the pagan Celts worshipped in woods and sacred

groves and perhaps a certain nostalgia for the wood can still be seen in our great mediaeval cathedrals where the pillars resemble giant trees, and the groined ceiling looks like arched branches, and the stained glass windows let in a strange light similar to the refracted light of the sun in a wood. We might well ask to what extent these great churches represent the Celtic *Neimheadh* or wood-sanctuary in stone, and to what extent the yew trees in our ancient graveyards represent druidic groves.

At any rate, with this type of philosophical background, it is no wonder that Celtic Christianity emphasised the immanence or nearness of God. God was present everywhere: he was in the trees, he was in the rivers, he was in the woods, he was in animals, he was in people, he was in the sea. When the two princesses, the daughters of King Laoghaire, questioned St Patrick about his God, Patrick answered:

> Our God is the God of all things, the God of sky and earth, the God of sea and stream, the God of sun and moon, the God of the great high mountains and the deep glens, the God above heaven, in heaven and under heaven. And he has a household – heaven and earth and the sea and all that they contain. *(Vita Tripartita)*

Advancement in holiness, according to the Celtic way, involves an effort to develop an awareness of the presence of God in everything and everybody – above us, below us and all around us at the four points of the compass. This awareness of God and its connection with spirituality is well expressed in a story of St Brendan the Navigator.

> One day, he was standing on a cliff looking out to sea and suddenly two whales jumped out of the water and began to fight. A great battle takes place and gradually the smaller whale is getting weaker and St Brendan sees that it is only a matter of time before the bigger whale kills him. But just

as he is about to be killed the smaller whale shouts out with a human voice calling on St Brigit to save him. And with that the big whale stops fighting and goes away leaving the small whale unharmed.

Now, St Brendan was watching all this and he became very upset. He said to himself: 'Why did the whale call on Brigit to save him and not on me? These whales are used to seeing me on the sea; they all know that I am a holy man and that I can get whatever I want from God. Why then, did the whale ignore me and call on Brigit?'

St Brendan could find no answer to this question, so he decided that the only thing to do was to ask Brigit herself for an explanation. So he called his followers and they got into their boat and rowed back to Ireland and proceeded to Kildare to consult Brigit.

When St Brendan met St Brigit he told her what had happened and asked her to explain why the whale had considered her to be a greater saint then himself and had ignored him even though he was actually on the spot when the incident occurred.

'Tell me,' says St Brigit, 'is your mind constantly on God, are you constantly aware of him?'

'Well,' says St Brendan, 'I am generally aware of God, but I live a very busy and a dangerous life. Often the sea is very rough and storms arise and on these occasions I forget all about God as I am so preoccupied trying to keep afloat.'

'That is the explanation,' says Brigit, 'for since the first day I set my mind on God I have never taken it away from him and I never will.'

According to the story, then, the reason why St Brigit was a greater saint then St Brendan was because she never faltered in awareness of the presence of God.

PART TWO

The Easter Mystery

CHAPTER SEVEN

The Caoineadh, the Wake, and the Passion of Christ (Good Friday)

Perhaps the most moving and elaborate descriptions we have of the passion of Christ in the Celtic tradition is to be found in the poems of Blathmac, written towards the end of the eighth century, somewhat earlier than the celebrated Féilire of Oengus Céle Dé *(Félire Oengussa)*. Both men probably belonged to the monastic reform movement the *Céli Dé*. (Carney, 1964, xv)

In this long composition Blathmac asks the Virgin Mary to come to him so that together they may perform the *caoineadh* or lament for her Son:

Tair cucum, a Maire boíd,
do choíniuth frit do rochoím;
dirsan dul fri croich dot mac
ba mind mar, ba masgérat.

(Come to me, loving Mary, that I may keen with you your very dear one. Alas that your son should go to the cross, he who was a great diadem, a beautiful hero.) (Carney, 1964, 2-3)

The tenor of the poem is both devotional and theological as the author traces the life of Christ through its various stages from infancy through his public life to the passion itself:

Your people seized your son, Mary, they flogged him. There struck him the green reed and fists across ruddy cheeks. It was a hideous deed that was done to him; that his very mother-kin should crucify the man who had come to save them.

A crown of thorns was placed about his beautiful head; nails were driven through his feet, others through his hands.

When they thought thus that Jesus could be approached,
Longinus then came to slay him with the spear.
The King of the seven holy heavens, when his heart was
pierced, wine was spilled upon the pathways, the blood of
Christ flowing through his gleaming sides.
The flowing blood from the body of the dear Lord baptised the head of Adam, for the shaft of the cross of Christ
had aimed at his mouth.
By the same blood (it was a fair occasion!) quickly did he
cure the fully blind man who, openly with his two hands,
was plying the lance. (Carney, 1964, 17-21)

Here we see, superbly expressed, the ancient tradition of
the crucifixion taking place on the site of Adam's grave and
Adam being baptised by the blood of Christ. Thus the first
father of mankind and the Redeemer, the second Adam, are
linked together.

Another legend describes the man who pierced the side of
Christ as being blind and being cured by the blood which
spurted on his face. This is what is referred to in the poem,
and the tradition is continued in an Irish folk-prayer:

A Rí na gréacht 'fuair éag i mbarr an chrainn
is croí do chléibh' á réabadh ag láimh an daill
is fuil do ghéag ag téachtadh ar lár 'na linn,
ar scáth do scéithe beir féin go Parthas sinn. (ÁPD 402)
(O King of Wounds who received death on the top of the
tree while the heart in your breast was being torn at the
hands of a blind man. Blood from your limbs flowed to
the ground in torrents; under the shadow of your wings
bring us to Paradise.)

The poem goes on to recall Our Lord's cry on the cross,
'My God, My God, why have you deserted me?' (Mk 15:34)
and then launches out on a graphic description of the effects
of the death of the Redeemer on the elements:

He raises a beautiful protesting voice beseeching his Holy Father: 'Why have you abandoned me, living God, to servitude and distress?'

The sun hid its own light; it mourned its lord; a sudden darkness went over the blue heavens, the wild and furious sea roared.

The whole world was dark; the land lay under gloomy trembling; at the death of noble Jesus great rocks burst asunder.

Jerusalem swiftly released the dead from ancient burial; when Christ suffered slaying the veil of the Temple was rent.

A stream of blood gushed forth (severe excess!) so that the bark of every tree was red; there was blood on the breasts of the world, in the (tree-) tops of every great forest.

It would have been fitting for God's elements, the beautiful sea, the blue heaven, the present earth, that they should change their aspect when keening their hero.

The body of Christ pierced by points warranted severe lamentation; (it would be fitting) that they should keen in a stronger manner the man by whom they were created.

The King was patient at the crucifixion of his only begotten, for had his good elements known, they would have keened sweetly.

That the sky did not fall on them, that great fire did not burn them, that the great ocean did not drown them! Their reproaches (ie. that of the elements) would not have been light.

That the heavy earth did not swallow them, the miserable pack who committed a great crime! That the hasty people led by Annas and Caiphas should not have been turned to ashes! (Carney, 1964, 21-25)

Caoineadh na dTrí Muire
Among the many expressions of Gaelic devotion to the pas-

sion of Christ is the incomparable *Caoineadh na dTrí Muire* (The Lament of the Three Mary's).

A comprehensive study of this has been made by Angela Partridge, *Caoineadh na dTrí Muire: Téama na Páise i bhFilíocht Bhéil na Gaeilge,* (Baile Átha Cliath 1983), in which she has collected the various versions of the *Caoineadh* and related texts from all over the country showing how they were used at wakes, funerals, during Lent and on Good Friday, in a major work of research. If some form of native liturgy were to develop *Caoineadh na dTrí Muire* would doubtless form an important part of the liturgical year centred on the passion of Our Lord.

The 'Three Marys' are the Blessed Virgin Mary, Mary Cleopas and Mary Salome. These are the same as the holy women at the tomb of Christ at the resurrection scene except that there, Mary Magdalene took the place of the Virgin Mary. (Partridge, 1983, 109-111)

The anguish of the Virgin Mary at the foot of the cross is expressed in an introductory text, in which there is a reference to the sword which would pierce Mary's heart according to the prophecy of Simeon at the Presentation in the Temple. (Lk 2:33-35):

Bhí an mháthair ina seasamh ag n-a thaobh,
Is saighde nimhe ag dul fríd a croí;
Níl aon osna dá ndéanadh sé ar an Chroich,
Nar scoilt mar chlaíomh géar a croí. (Partridge , 1983, 57)
(The mother was standing at his side, and poisonous arrows going through her heart; every groan which he made from the gibbet penetrated like a sword through her heart.)

In the Galway version, given here, the cry of lament, *M' ochón agus m' ochón ó,* is repeated after each line. There are several voices involved – that of the Virgin Mary herself who first addresses Peter, then that of Peter who replies to her question, then the voices of the other Marys, and finally the

voice of Christ on the cross promising paradise to those who
lament his death.

A Pheadair, a Aspail, an bhfaca tú mo ghrádh geal?
M'óchón & m'óchón ó *[i ndiaidh gach líne]*
Chonnaic mé ar ball é, i láthair a námhad.
Gabhaidh a leith, a dhá Mhuire, go gcaoinfidh sibh mo
ghrádh geal!
Céard tá le caoineadh againn muna gcaoineamuid a
chnámha?
Cia hé an fear breágh sin ar Chrann na Páise?
An e nach n-aithnigheann tú do mhac, a Mháthair?
Agus an é sin an maicín a d'iomchur mé trí ráithe?
Nó an é sin an maicín do rugadh san stábla?
Nó an é sin an maicín do hoileadh in ucht Mháire?
Agus an é sin an castúr do bhuail thríot na táirngi?
Nó an é *[sic]* sin an tsleagh do chuaidh trí do lár geal?
Nó an í sin an choróin spíonta chuaidh ar do mhullach
áluinn?
Maise, éist, a Mháithrín, agus ná bí cráidhte,
Tá mná mo chaointe le bréith fós, a Mháithrín,
A Bhean atá ag gol, de bharr mo bháis-se,
Beidh na céadta indiu i nGáirdín Pharrthais.
(Partridge, 1983, 158-159)

(O Peter, Apostle, have you seen my bright love?
M'ochón agus m'ochón ó, [after each line]
I saw him a while ago in the presence of his enemies.
Come aside, O two Marys that you may lament for my
bright love.
What is there to lament for except to lament for his bones?
Who is that fine man on the tree of torture?
Is it that you do not recognise your Son, O Mother?
Is that the little Son that I carried for three seasons?

Or is that the little Son who was born in a stable?
Or is that the little Son that was nourished at Mary's breast?
And is that the hammer which drove the nails through you?
Or is that the spear which went trough your bright breast?
Or is that the crown of thorns which was on your beautiful
head?
Listen, O Little Mother, and do not be upset,
The women who will lament for me are yet to be born, O
Little Mother,
O Woman, you are crying on account of my death,
There will be hundreds today in the Garden of Paradise.)

Passion poems were a feature of wakes, funerals, and pre-paration for death and during Lent, especially on Fridays of Lent in some places. Donegal seems to have had a very strong tradition in this respect. Seán Ó hEochaidh describes the recitation of *Gol na dTrí Muire* on Tory Island:

Ba ghnách le seanmhná Thoraigh é a cheol i gcuideachta na n-amhrán diaga eile a bhí acu ar feadh an Charghais. Cha raibh Aoine ar bith ar feadh an Charghais nach ndéan-fadh siad é a cheol trí huaire ar feadh an lae, agus cuid acu níos minicí ná sin dá mbeadh an t-am acu. (Partridge, 1983, 131) (It was usual for the old women of Tory Island to sing it along with the other sacred songs which they had throughout Lent. There was no Friday in Lent when they did not sing it three times during the day and some of them would do it more often if they had the time.)

It was said by some that it was Mary herself who began the custom of the *Caoineadh* when she invited the other two Marys to help her to lament her Son, *Gabhaidh a leith, a dhá Mhuire, go gcaoinfidh sibh mo ghrádh geal,* and that therefore it was right to perform the *Caoineadh* at every funeral. More-over, in some places, it was customary for women on Good

Friday and even at funerals to loosen the hair and let it fall on to their shoulders, and this custom too was attributed to the Blessed Virgin on the first Good Friday. These accounts come from Co Mayo where the tradition of *Caoineadh na dTrí Muire* was very strong. (Partridge, 1983, 99)

The term *Caoineadh* given to this highly Christian text, as well as the fact that it was nearly always performed by women, argues for its connection with the archaic tradition of *Caoineadh na Marbh*, the lament for the dead performed at wakes and funerals, again mostly by women from the most remote period.

In his introduction to Professor O'Curry's *On the Manners and Customs of the Ancient Irish*, (London 1873), Dr W. K. Sullivan gives a marvellous account of the *Caoineadh* as it was traditionally performed, before the Great Famine intervened to disrupt the cultural life of the country. He seems to see in the performance a continuation of the tradition of the *Ceapóg* or *Guba* – the dirge sung by the bards over the dead body of the king or chief at the burial or cremation. Indeed, the six candles traditionally surrounding the coffin in the church may be a remnant of the torches which lighted the funeral pyre. The *Mná Caointe* continue the tradition.

> The usual number was at least four; one stood near the head of the bed or table on which the corpse was laid, one at the feet, who was charged with the care of the candles, and one or more at each side; the family and immediate friends of the deceased sat around near the table. The mourner at the head opened the dirge with the first note or part of the cry; she was followed by the one at the foot with a note or part of equal length, then the long or double part was sung by the two side mourners, after which the members of the family and friends of the deceased joined in the common chorus at the end of each stanza of the funeral ode or dirge, following as closely as they could

the air or tune adopted by the professional mourners. Sometimes one or more, or even all the principal singers, were men. I once heard in West Muskerry, in the county of Cork, a dirge of this kind, excellent in point of both music and words, improvised over the body of a man who had been killed by a fall from a horse, by a young man, the brother of the deceased. He first recounted his genealogy, eulogised the spotless honour of his family, described in the tones of a sweet lullaby his childhood and boyhood, then changing the air suddenly, he spoke of his wrestling and hurling, his skill at ploughing, his horsemanship, his prowess at a fight in a fair, his wooing and marriage, and ended by suddenly bursting into a loud piercing, but exquisitely beautiful wail, which was again and again taken up by the bystanders.

Sometimes the panegyric on the deceased was begun by one and continued by another, and so on, as many as three or four taking part in the improvisation. In the case of Flaths, Rigs, and other distinguished personages, the historian or bard of the family, or some other qualified person selected for the purpose, delivered, in ancient times, the panegyric or funeral oration, recounting the genealogy, deeds, and virtues of the dead, and the loss his friends sustained.

(O'Curry, 1873, CCCXXIV-CCCXXV)

A similar account is given by the Halls in their tour of Ireland in the nineteenth century.

The women of the household range themselves at either side, and the keen at once commences. They rise with one accord and, moving their bodies with a slow motion to and fro, their arms apart, they continue to keep up a heart-rending cry. This cry is interrupted for a while to give the *bean caointe* (the leading keener) an opportunity of com-

mencing. At the close of every stanza of the dirge, the cry is
released, to fill up, as it were, the pause, and then dropped;
the woman then again proceeds with the dirge, and so on
to the close.

The Irish language, bold, forcible, and comprehensive, full
of the most striking epithets and idiomatic beauties, is
peculiarly adapted for either praise or satire – its blessings
are singularly touching and expressive, and its curses won-
derfully strong, bitter and biting. The rapidity and ease
with which both are uttered, and the epigrammatic force
of each concluding stanza of the keen, generally bring tears
to the eyes of the most indifferent spectator, or produce a
state of terrible excitement. The dramatic effect of the scene
is very powerful: the darkness of the death-chamber, illu-
mined only by candles that glare upon the corpse, the
manner of repetition or acknowledgement that runs round
when the keener gives out a sentence, the deep, yet suppressed sobs of the nearer relatives, and the stormy, uncon-
trollable cry of the widow or bereaved husband when allusion is made to the domestic virtues of the deceased – all
heighten the effect of the keen; but in the open air, wind-
ing round some mountain pass, when a priest, or person
greatly beloved and respected, is carried to the grave, and
the keen, swelled by a thousand voices, is borne upon the
mountain echoes – it is then absolutely magnificent.

The highly ritualistic style of the performance of the
Caoineadh is evident from these accounts and naturally the
form varied from place to place according to the circumstances. While the hair of the *Mná Caointe* is said to be un-
loosed in some sources, the painting illustrated on the cover
of Seán Ó Súilleabháin's book shows two youngish women
wearing head scarves as with hands spread wide and raised
above the heads they perform the rite. The other women pre-

sent appear to be wearing a typical form of maids' bonnet. A white sheet covers the corpse and a table with lighted candles is near the head of the bed. Some of the chief mourners wipe their eyes in grief while the general body of people in the house sit around talking and drinking. The cat sitting on a high window looks down contentedly on this picturesque scene in which grief and passion, goodfellowship and entertainment, the living and the dead were all united. As Seán Ó Súilleabháin remarks, 'They [Wakes] were far merrier than weddings.' (1979, 26)

In the description given by Dr W. K. Sullivan of the *Caoineadh* in West Muskerry we saw that the *caointeoir* mentioned certain episodes in the life of the deceased in the course of the lament:

his genealogy,
the honour of this family,
childhood and boyhood,
wrestling and hurling,
ploughing skills,
horsemanship,
fighting skills at a fair,
wooing and marriage,
his death.

What we have here is a short, dramatic, sung form of 'The Heroic Biography' as Tomás Ó Cathasaigh called this type of literary composition in *The Heroic Biography of Cormac Mac Airt,* (Dublin 1977). He discusses the life of the hero in terms of an international pattern in which the birth of the hero is foretold, the birth is often miraculous or unusual, the life of the child is threatened, the *macghníomhartha* or boyhood deeds of the hero, his journey to the otherworld and return, his great exploits and victories, his wooing and marriage, his death – sometimes as unusual as his birth. This pattern is extremely

widespread in ancient literature and even the life of Christ is
to some extent embraced by it as is shown in the Liturgical
Year.

It is obvious that the *Caoineadh* in Muscraí follows this
pattern. In other words, the deceased, in this case a farmer,
had his life cast in the heroic mould. The simple episodes of
his life took on a heroic character, his fight at a fair could be
compared to Cú Chulainn's mighty deeds of valour in *Táin
Bó Chuailnge*. In the *Caoineadh* the dead man became the
ideal Celt – the *laoch* or 'hero'.

The 'Heroic Biography' is best represented in the Kerry
form of *Caoineadh na dTrí Muire,* called *Caoineadh na
Maighdine* (The Virgin's Lament) from the opening words.
This is a long composition and Angela Partridge gives the various manuscript versions so that they can be compared with
each other (1983, 174-193). From these it should be possible to
provide a composite, emended text with regular lines. The
text given here is that of the Gael Linn recording *Caoineadh
na Maighdine* (CEF 084) in which Nóirín Ní Riain gives a sup-
erb rendering of various forms of the *Caoineadh*. This text
corresponds to the first Kerry version given by Angela
Partridge (CI, 174-176):

> *Caoineadh na Maighdine*
>
> *Chronista*
> Caoineadh na Maighdine i ndiaidh a hAon-Mhic.
> Och ochón! agus ochón ó!
> Na trí rithe 's iad a theacht lena chéile:
> Och ochón! agus ochón ó!
>
> *Tres Magi*
> Dá bhfeicimís arís é do gheobhaimís ár leithscéal leis
> Go bhfaighimís maithiúnachas uaidh inar gclaonta
>
> Fé mar fuair Máire Maigdiléana,
> Agus an bhean do chuimil dó an t-éadach.

Nó an bhean thug trí bliana i bhfiabhras aerach
Go bhfuair sí an tsláinte 's na grásta in éineacht

Nó an dall do sháigh an tsleá trína thaobh dheas,
Go bhfaca sé a chuid fola 'n a sruthaibh tréana

Agus dúirt gurbh fhiú na céada gach aon bhraon di
Nó an gadaí dubh do bhí ar a láimh dheas

Virgo Maria
Caithfidh mo Leanbh-sa triall ón gharraí amáireach
Agus Leabhar na Páise a thabhairt ina láimh leis

Christus
Glaoigh chum na hAspail go léifead an Pháis dóibh

Petrus
'A Thiarna,' arsa Peadar 'ní scarfadsa go brách leat.'

Christus
'Is fíor go séanfaidh do bhéal mé trí huaire roimh an lá
amáireach.'

Chronista
Tháinig lúdás dorcha, thug sé póg dó 's chroith sé lámh leis

Christus
A ludáid mhallaithe ní beag duit mé dhíol is gan mé
thabhairt ar láimh dóibh

Chronista
Do cheanglaíodar suas le cordaí crua cnáibe é
Thugadar leo go dtí Pilate a thug spás dó

Pontius Pilatus
'Cad é bhur gcúis ar an bhfear mór breá seo,
Go bhfuil agaibh ina thimpeall a leithéid seo ghárda?'

Synagoga
'Deir sé gurbh é ceann rí na nGiúdach é 's go bhfuilaige na
grásta.'

Pontius Pilatus
Más é sin bhur gcúis air, scagaimse mo lámha as

Chronista
D'ardaíodar leo go dtí Herod gan spás é

Herodes
'Cad é bhur gcúis ar an bhfear mór breá seo,
Go bhfuil aige ina thimpeall a leithéid seo 'gharda?'

Synagoga
'Déir sé gurb é Mac De é 's go bhfuil aige na grásta'

Herodes
'Do réir mar mheasaimse is maith an chúis bháis í
Ceanglaíodh den phola é go dtí an dá uair dhéag
amáireach,
Cuiridh puicín ar a shúilibh agus culaith an amadáin air.'

Ceanglaíodh suas le cordaí crua cnáib é
Caithidh bhur seile air is deinidh fé gáire.
Bíodh buille ó gach duine air – an tAon Mhac Mháire
Téighidh sa gharrdha is bainidh an crann is mó a fás ann.

Cuiridh ar an gCrois é fulang na daor-pháise.
Cuiridh na tairní géara gan truaimhéil dó tréna dhearnaibh.

Chronista
D'árdaíodar suas ar a nguailne go hard é
'S do chaitheadar amach ar chlocha crua na sráide é.

Virgo Maria
Is mithid dom, arsa an Mhaighdean, dul a fiosrú mo ghrá
geal

Chronista
Do bhí a ceann scaoilte is a cosa gan náda,
Is í a bailiú a chuid fola ós cionn an fhásaigh.
Do léim sí isteach is amach thar ghárda.

Virgo Maria
'Dia dhuit a Mhic, nó an aithnid duit do Mháthair?'

Christus
'Bíodh agat an fhoighne agus gheobhaidh tú na grásta.'

Virgo Maria
'A Linbh is mór é t'ualach is lig cuid de ar do Mháthair.'

Christus
'Do gheallas féin dh'iompar ar shon sliocht Áidim.
Iompraíodh gach éinne a chrosa, a Mháithrín.'

Chronista
Nuair a chuala na Giúdaigh na focail sin dá rá acu
Tógadar suas ar a nguailne go hárd í,
'S do chaitheadar amach ar chlocha crua na sráide í.

Synagoga
'Is fíor, más é Mac Dé é, go dtógfaidh sé a Mháthair.'

Chronista
Ansan do thóg sé suas le beartaibh anairde í
Tógadar suas go Crann na Páise é
Agus chaitheadar anuas ina chuailín cnámh é.

Synagoga
'Sin é agaibh anois é agus goilidh bhur sáith air.'

Sancta Brigida
'Ó! is fíor,' arsa Naomh Bríde, 'ná fuil anois ach an scáth ann.
Cá bhfuil na trí Mhuire go gcaoinfidís mo ghrá geal?'

Chronista
Tháinig na trí Aingil is do ghoileadar go cráite air.
Do ghoileadar ar dtúis thar cionn a Athar is a Mháthar
An dara uair thar cionn sliocht Áidim
Agus an triú huair thar cionn an pheacaigh ná filleann go
brách air.

Virgo Maria
'Sin é caoineadh na Maighdine; ach é bheith ró-chráite,
Níl éinne agaibhse go mbeidh aige an dán seo.

Agus éinne a dearfaidh é, is a rá gach lá leis
Ní fheicfidh mo Mhac-sa breith dhamant go brách air.'

The Blessed Virgin's Keening
The Virgin's keening of her only Son,
Och ochón! agus ochón ó!
The three wise Kings were they to come
Och ochón! agus ochón ó!

Could we see him now we would go and ask pardon
For all our sins and our hearts that are hardened.

As Magdalene was forgiven
And Veronica shriven

Or she who for years in a fever had lain
Before God's grace made her whole again,
Or the blind one who pierced his side with a spear
And saw the torrents of blood appear.

Each drop so dear he would fain have stemmed the tide,
Or the black thief on his right side.

My child must go to the Garden tomorrow
And in his hand the Book of Sorrow

'Call my Apostles, the Passion I will read.'
'Lord,' said Peter, 'thy side I shall not leave.'
'Thrice before daybreak you will make me grieve.'

Dark Judas came with a handshake and a kiss,
Accursed one to sell me first and now do this.

With rope of cruel hemp then he was bound
And brought at once to Pilate who looked round:

'What is it this fine man has done, I pray,
That all of you should guard him in this way?'

'He claims to be the King of Jews, the source of every grace,
Then I must wash my hands of him if such be then the case.'

They brought him straight to Herod, making no delay.
'What is it this fine man has done, I pray
That all of you should guard him in this way?'

'He claims to be the source of grace, the Son of the Most
    High
According to my judgement, I deem this man should die.'

Bind him to a pillar and leave him there till noon.
Bandage both his eyes and dress him like a fool.

Get rope of cruel hemp and have him tightly bound,
Spit on him and rail on him with every mocking sound.

Beat him and flog him – Mary's only Son,
Cut down a tree from the garden - the very tallest one:

Let him suffer there his passion high up on the cross,
Drive the sharp nails through his palms without remorse.'
They raised him on their shoulders, his precious arms and feet,
And hurled him despicably on the cold and stony street.

'It is time,' said the Virgin, 'that I my love should seek.'
Her hair was all undone, no shoes were on her feet
And she gathered up the blood that through the grass had
    seeped.

She dashed among the soldiers, in and out in a race,
God be with thee, son – and do you know this face?
Only be patient and you will have grace.

'Child, thy burdens heavy, come and give me my share
For all of Adam's children evermore in my care.'
'No, Mother, each one his own cross must bear.'

When the Jews heard these words, they thought it would
    be meet
To raise her on their shoulders, take her arms and feet
And hurl her despicably on the cold and stony street.

'If he's the Son of God, let him raise her from the street.'
And this Our Saviour did by a miraculous feat

They brought him to his passion hill
His broken body there to kill,
'Behold him now and cry your fill.'

'O truly,' said St. Brigid, 'he's a shadow, nothing more
Where are thee Marys to keen his awesome gore?'
And the three angels came with keening loud and sore.

For their Father and his mother they keened both loud
     and long,
Where then they keened more piteously for all the human
     throng,
And then for the sinner who repents not his wrong.

This is the Virgin's keen in sorrow may you pray
Let him who utters it this way
In reverence, day by day
Know that my Son will never look away!
(Translation by Gabriel Rosenstock)

At the beginning of *Caoineadh na dTrí Muire,* the acts of
Christ's life are subtly conveyed by reference to the visit of the
three kings (Magi). They would ask his forgiveness and obtain from him remission of their sins in the same way as other
characters mentioned in the gospels – Mary Magdalene,
Veronica, the woman sick with a fever, the blind man
(Longinus) who stabbed him, the *gadaí dubh* – the black thief
who was crucified with him. After this account of the acts of
forgiveness performed by Our Lord during the course of his
life, the virgin Mary introduces the narrative of the passion:
'My child will have to go to the garden tomorrow and the
Book of the Passion in his hand.' He will read the passion to
his apostles. Peter's denial is foretold and Judas arrives to be-
tray him. He is bound by ropes and led away to be tried by
Pilate and Herod. He is scourged, spat upon, and led away to
be crucified. They lift him up and throw him down on the
hard stones of the street.

The Virgin Mary arrives looking for her Son. Her hair is let down on her shoulders and she is barefoot. She collects his blood from the path. She jumps past the guards and speaks to her Son, offering to help him bear the heavy weight of the cross. He replies that everybody must carry his own cross and that he himself bears it for the redemption of the family of Adam. When the Jews hear this they lift her up and throw her down on the hard stones of the street but Christ raises her up again. The actual crucifixion is not described in detail, but St Brigid, who according to Irish and Scottish tradition was present at the birth of Christ and as midwife assisted Mary, remarks that only his shadow remains. Other texts say: *Céard tá le caoineadh againn muna gcaoineamuid a chnámha?* (What is there for us to lament except his skeleton?) The three Marys are summoned and they perform the *Caoineadh*. They lamented first for his Father and his mother, secondly for the race of Adam, and thirdly for the sinner who will never return to him.

'This is the Virgin's bitter lament, if somebody has this poem and recites it every day, my Son will never allow him to be lost.'

Caoineadh na dTrí Muire and related songs, such as *Toradh (Tuireadh?) na Páise* and *Caoineadh na Maighdine,* preserve in a Christianised form the archaic custom of the lament for the dead as it was practised throughout Europe and in many other parts of the world.

Mary the Mother of Jesus is presented as an Irish *bean chaointe.* When she hears that her son has been arrested and taken away by the enemy, she rushes off at once, her hair undone, her feet bare, taking a short-cut through the desert, and not noticing the stones on the road cutting her feet. She takes her three jumps:

> Thug sí an léim sin thar an ngarda,
> is an darna léim go Crann na Páise,
> an triú léim chomh fada lena grá geal.

(She took that (first) jump past the guardsman and the second jump to the Tree of the Passion and the third jump to her bright love.) (Partridge, 1993, 94-95)

Some texts make it clear that Mary was going wild with uncontrolled grief: *'Chaill sí a meabhair, a stuaim, 's a tuigse,'* (*Seanmóir na n-Aithreach Naofa,* Partridge, 1983, 204), (She lost her mind, her control, her understanding.) This type of wild passion, even on such an occasion, would not recommend itself to the more restrained, stoical tradition of ecclesiastics but it finds its counterpart in native Irish ethos.

While, for instance, the great *Stabat Mater* (Britt, 1922, 132-136) conceals none of the intense grief of the Virgin Mary as she stands at the foot of the cross while the sword foretold by Simeon pierces her soul, nevertheless, her sorrow is expressed in a controlled measured way:

Stabat Mater dolorosa

Juxta Crucem lacrymosa,

Dum pendebat Filius

Cujus animam gementem,

Contristatam et dolentem,

Pertransivit gladius.

(The sorrowful Mother stood weeping beside the Cross while her Son hung thereon: a sword pierced her sighing, compassionate, and grief-stricken soul.)

Angela Partridge quotes with effect a scene from the life of Peig Sayers (Beatha Pheig Sayers) by M. Ó Gaoithín:

'...B'é an chéad rud a chuala ná scread mhillteach ó Cháit Ní Bheoláin. Do gaibh an scread san siar agus aniar tríom chroí mar a sáfaí biorán cniotála isteach go poll mo chluaise.

'A Dhia láidir', ar sise, 'Seán atá ann is é marbh ag an gcapall.'

Níor fhan sí lena thuilleadh ach imeacht mar imeodh bean gan chiall an bóthar is clocha beaga an bhóthair aici dá chur sa spéir leis an racht neamh-mheabhrach a bhí uirthi, an bhean bhocht.' (1983, 96)

(The first thing I heard was an appalling scream from Cait Ní Bheoláin. That scream went right through my heart like a knitting needle penetrating the depths of my ear. 'O Strong God', said she, 'It is Seán that is there and the horse has killed him'. She waited for no more but off she went like a mad woman throwing up the pebbles of the road to the sky with the unthinking passion that was on her, the poor woman.)

This bears an uncanny similarity to the description of the Virgin Mary's behaviour as she made her way to Calvary. The three jumps are mentioned in the best known Caoineadh of all, *Caoineadh Airt Uí Laoghaire,* in which Eibhlín Dubh Ní Chonail pours out her passionate grief for her husband who has been shot by the English. The horse on which Art had been riding returns to the house riderless and Eibhlín Dubh knows at once what has happened:

Mo chara thú go daingean,
Is níor chreideas riamh dod mharbh
Gur tháinig chugham do chapall
Is a srianta léi go talamh,
Is fuil do chroí ar a leacain
Siar go t'iallait ghreanta
Mar a mbíthea id shuí 's id sheasamh.
Thugas léim go tairsigh,
An dara léim go geata, an tríú léim ar do chapall.

Do bhuaileas go luath mo bhasa
Is do bhaineas as na reathaibh
Chomh maith is bhí sé agam,
Go bhfuaireas romham tú marbh
Cois toirín íseal aitinn
Gan Pápa gan easpag,

Gan cléireach gan sagart
Do léifeadh ort an tsailm,
Ach seanbhean chríonna chaite
Do leath ort binn dá fallaing,
Do chuid fola leat 'na sraithibh;
Is níor fhanas le hí ghlanadh
Ach í ól suas lem bhasaibh. (ÓTuama, 1963, 35)

(You're my firm friend/ and I never believed you were dead/ until your horse came to me and his bridle-reins hanging to the ground/ and your heart's blood on his cheek/ right across to your ornamented saddle/ where you used to be sitting and standing/ I took a jump to the threshold/ the second jump to the gate/ the third jump on your horse/ I clapped my hands quickly/ and made him gallop/ as best I could/ until I found you dead before me/ beside a little low furze bush/ without a pope/ without a bishop/ without a cleric, without a priest/ to recite the psalm over you/ but only an old wasted woman/ who had spread her cloak over you/ your blood streaming from you/ and I did not wait to clean it/ but drank it from the palms of my hands.)

Perhaps the contrast between the reserved dignified Mary of the Roman tradition and the wild Celtic Mary gone mad with grief at the terrible death of her son is presented too extremely. Nevertheless, the question remains: 'Who is the real Mary?', 'Who is the real woman?'

The Irish Wake Tradition

The *Caoineadh* is, of course, closely associated with the tradition of holding wakes for the dead. The wake was essentially a party in honour of the deceased. The purpose was to give him a 'good send-off', to make him feel one of the party while he still remained in some sense among them still.

Why was it considered necessary to give the dead such an

elaborate farewell party? It appears that basic to the whole idea was the survival of the dead in another world. Moreover, the dead had power and could influence affairs in this world of the living from the otherworldly sphere to which they now belonged.

There was the element of pity felt by the mourners for the person who had to leave a comfortable existence in this world, leave behind his family and friends, his land and possessions knowing that somebody else would inherit his property upon which he had devoted so much care during his lifetime.

People could easily see that the deceased might resent all this and return in revenge for what he might consider to be an injustice done to him. The vengeful dead could cause havoc among the community. The main feeling of living people toward the dead in early times all over the world was one of fear. It was fear that sealed the grave, bound or maimed the body, filled the grave with expensive funeral goods.

The purpose of the wake then was to place the deceased, to make him feel a treasured member of his society and so allay any feelings of resentment he may have which would induce him to come back in some form to do them harm. Every effort was made to send him away happy so that he wouldn't consider coming back. Practices such as taking the longest and most complicated way to the graveyard, turning the chairs used to support the coffin upside down, and so forth, must have had the same purpose – to confuse the dead so that they would not return. The primary purpose of the wake was to give a farewell party to the deceased, to give him a great send-off, rather than for the consolation of the bereaved, though of course this was not excluded. It may well be that the *Caoineadh,* wake-games and inhibited expressions of grief, all supported by immemorial custom, may have had a therapeutic effect on the genuine mourners, enabling them to get rid of their grief and sorrow in a socially authenticated way rather than keeping their emotions pent up.

By carrying out the funeral rites, the relatives felt that they had fulfilled the traditions of their ancestors and had earned the respect of the grateful dead. (Ó Súilleabháin, 1979, 170-172)

Seán Ó Súilleabháin draws attention also to a possible connection between the wake-games and the ancient Irish custom of the *Aonach* or meeting of the tribe on the site of megalithic tombs or the graves of the ancestors:

Both pagandom and Christianity were agreed on one thing: the dead were still the concern of the living whether in the otherworld of pagan belief or in purgatory.

Finally, I think that it is possible to make a connection and comparison between wake-games and associated amusements, on the one hand, and what went on at the great fairs (at Teltown, for example) which were held at certain places in ancient Ireland, on the other. Professor D. A. Binchy, in his article about The Fair of Tailtiu and the Feast of Tara, says: 'From several statements in the Laws (e.g. *Críth Gablach* 500f., etc.) it is clear that the king of every tribe was bound to convene an *óenach* at regular intervals. The site of the fair was normally an ancient burial ground: indeed the tradition reflected in many poems and sagas that the *óenach* originated in the funeral games held for kings and heroes may have a kernel of truth. (1979, 173-174)

It would not be rash, to my mind, to see a basic connection between these funeral games in both Ireland and Greece, on the one hand, and the amusements carried on in humble wake-houses in Ireland and elsewhere, on the other. The game at a wake, as well as the keening, are descended from the same ultimate source as the *cluiche caointeach* (game of lamentation) which took place when a great warrior died in ancient Ireland.

The Church's Opposition to Wakes

A promise accompanies *Caoineadh na dTrí Muire* as in the case of some of the Irish folk prayers:

Níl éinne chaoinfeas leat mé, a Mháthair,
Nach geal í a leaba i bhFlaitheas Dé na ngrásta,
Caoinfidh sagairt agus caoinfidh bráithre,
Agus caoinfidhear go fóill mé in Oileán Páraic.
(Partridge, 1983, 150)

(There is nobody who makes the lament for me along with you, O Mother, that will not have a bright bed in the kingdom of the God of Grace; priests and brothers will lament me and I will be lamented in Patrick's Island in time to come.)

This promise and prophecy from the mouth of Christ himself gives authority and justification for the performance of *Caoineadh na dTrí Muire* and similar laments.

This type of justification must indeed have been felt necessary in view of the church's well publicised opposition to the ordinary custom of the lament for the dead sung by women at funerals in many parts of Ireland. The custom lasted well into this century in some areas and is the subject of a remarkable work of research by the folklorist Seán Ó Súilleabháin *Caitheamh Aimsire ar Thórraimh,* (An Clóchomhar Teoranta 1961) and translated by the author into English, *Irish Wake Amusements,* (Cork 1979).

A series of synodal decrees forbade disorderly behaviour at wakes including drinking, dancing, games, erotic plays and so forth and along with all these the custom of the *Caoineadh:*

Synod of Tuam (1631):
Statute 3 ordered that thenceforth exaggerated crying and keening at wakes of the dead should cease.
Synod of Tuam (1660):
The people were advised to discontinue the practice of employing female keeners at wakes and funerals.

Synod of Armagh (1660):

This Synod forbade wailings and crying at funerals, as an unchristian practice.

Synod of Dublin (June 1670):

This was a meeting of the archbishops and bishops of Ireland. Statute 5 ordered each priest in the country to make every effort in his power to bring to an end the wailings and screams of female keeners who accompanied the dead to the graveyards.

(Quoted by Ó Súilleabháin, 1979, 138)

The Synod of Armagh, quoted above as describing the *Caoineadh* 'as an unchristian practice' really got to the root of the problem in recognising that the custom went away back long before the Christian era and was probably an expression of a philosophy quite different from that of Christianity. This is stated in legislation for the Diocese of Leighlin (1748):

Whereas likewise the heathenish custom of loud cries and howlings at wakes and burials are practised amongst us, contrary to the express commandments of St Paul in his Epist. to the Thess. forbidding such cries and immoderate grief for the dead, as if they were not to rise again.

(Ó Súilleabháin, 1979, 139)

Strangely enough, we have an account in the gospels of the meeting of Jesus and the 'keeners' in the story of the young girl whom he raised from the dead. (Mt 9:18-26) Even a poor Jew would have a few hired mourners at the funeral of one of his family. Jesus said: 'Get out of here; the little girl is not dead, she is asleep', for what is 'death' to the ordinary people was only 'sleep' to the power of Christ.

About the year 1800, Archbishop Bray of Cashel issued a pastoral letter

condemning the *Caoineadh* as a 'pagan practice' and advocated that instead of those excesses the mourners show 'in

their whole deportment a most edifying and sober gravity'.
(Ó Súilleabháin, 1979, 140)

The concept of 'control' was important to the church and naturally it came under severe strain in the areas of feasting, faction fighting, and sex. While it may be a cause of some surprise that erotic elements were to be found in some wake games such as 'Building the Ship' (Ó Súilleabháin, 1979, 76-77), nevertheless, it must be remembered that in the subconscious there may have lurked a profound intuition of the complementary functions of death and sex. In a small vulnerable community, say, of one hundred people, if one person dies this constitutes a weakening of the community which is now reduced to ninety-nine. But the birth of a child restores the community to its original strength and confidence.

While bishops and synods proclaimed dire punishment on those who participated in wake-games – which indeed may have been the popular remnants of the *Cluichí Caointe* or funeral games of the Celtic hero – it does appear that some priests had a more benign and tolerant attitude towards the whole situation. When Irish was spoken generally, many people had the gift of poetry as is shown in texts of folk-prayers and in the texts of the *Caoineadh* itself which have come down to us. Seán Ó Súilleabháin gives an example of how hilarious the situation could become on occasion:

Keening over the dead, be it real or artificial, had deep traditional roots, and country people especially were slow to abandon it. In addition to this, the paid keeners themselves were loth to discontinue a custom which was their means of livelihood. A story is told about one of these paid keening women who was being questioned, in a half-jocose way, about her craft; about her it was said that her wailings varied with the amount of whiskey she got. The priest had met her on the road, when she appeared to have had some drink at a wake. 'Where did the raven call today, Mary?'

the priest enquired; the raven was symbolical of the ban-
shee or death. Mary replied in verse:

Do labhair sé thall's abhus,
Do labhair sé thiar is thoir,
Do labhair sé istigh's amuigh,
Do labhair sé i lár an toir;
Agus is duitse is fearr é sin;
Beidh airgead bán id' chrobh,
Is ór ag teacht 'na shruth;
Beidh an coirce dod' láir istigh,
Is féar breá cumhra tirim,
Is ní bhraithfir uait an puins!
(He called here and there,
He called west and east,
He called within and without.
He called in the middle of the bush;
And it was all for your benefit;
You will have silver money in your hands,
And gold coming to you in streams;
There will be oats for your horse,
And fine sweet-smelling hay,
Nor will you be short of punch!)

The priest recognised the intended insult, and said:

A scallaire, do chaoinfeá madra,
Dá bhfaighfeá marbh é!
(You would keen over a dog, you hag,
If you found him dead!)

Mary was still unsubdued; she replied:

Ní gá dhuit, 'Athair, bheith chomh searbh;
Tá a haon ar an mbeo agat, is a dó ar an marbh!
(No need for you to be so bitter, Father;
What you don't get from the living, you get from the dead.)

To this the priest rejoined:

Fear bruíne, bean chaointe ná garbhmhuilleoir,
Ní bhfaighidh sna Flaithis aon leaba go deo.
(Three persons who will get no bed in heaven:
A quarrelsome man, a keening woman and a crude miller.)

Mary had the last word. As she noticed the priest about to spur his horse, she said:

Gaibh an bóthar caol úd soir,
Nó dhéanfainnse do scrios
Ó bhaitheas do chinn go troigh!
(Be off east along the narrow road now,
Or I'll scrape you from the top of your head to your feet!)
(1979, 141-142)

Instruments of the Passion

The hammer, spear and crown of thorns mentioned in the Galway version connect the *Caoineadh* with the mediaeval tradition of the 'instruments of the passion' which form such a marked feature of many tombstones. Perhaps one of the most complete of these to be seen anywhere is the magnificent monument to William Galway in the beautiful mediaeval church of St Multose, Kinsale, Co Cork. A detailed account of the 'Instruments of the Passion' featured on the gravestone is given in the guidebook to the church:

Along the top of one stone is inscribed the motto 'Vita decora mors letac' (sic) – 'A seemly life, a happy death', and around the border (in Latin): 'Here lies William Galway, eldest son of Richard Galway, son of Geoffry Galway and Margaret Yonge, who died 30th day of May, 1628.' This stone is covered with emblems of the passion, all carved in relief. Over the cross, which occupies nearly the whole length and breadth of the stone, are the sun and moon which hid their faces when the Redeemer died, and also the crown of thorns. Lower down, on the left-hand side, are the spear, sponge, ladder, pincers, hammer and nails. Then what are possibly the trees in the Garden of Gethsemane and the scourging pillar entwined with the rope which bound our Blessed Lord, and surmounted by the cock which crowed when Peter denied his Master. Here also are the Apostle's sword and the right ear of Malchus which he cut off, and beneath them the cruel scourges.

On the right side of the cross is the handkerchief of St Veronica which, the story says, was given by her to our Saviour to wipe his face and handed back imprinted with his likeness. Lower down are the pierced hands and feet and the broken heart from which flowed blood and water. There are two staves, one on either side of these emblems, also the thirty pieces of silver, as well as the seamless coat and the dice-box and dice, to remind us how the soldiers cast lots for his vesture. The cup-like object possibly represents the vessel which contained the 'vinegar mingled with gall'. The reed, and the hand which smote the Saviour fill the rest of the panel. At the foot of the cross is Golgotha, the place of a skull, and here are a death's head and cross bones.

The death's head and cross bones are of course those of Adam. Another feature of this remarkable church is the 'Easter Sepulchre', a large arched recess in the north wall near the altar. The cross and sometimes the Blessed Sacrament, or both, was kept here from Good Friday to Easter Sunday according to the custom of the Sarum Rite.

The same type of illustrating the 'instruments of the passion' is evident in the small wooden crucifixes of the eighteenth and early nineteenth century to which the name 'Penal Crucifixes' is given. A. T. Lucas gives a most useful list of the items contained in these:

1. Three dice
2. Pincers
3. Hammer
4. Sun, Moon (and Stars?)
5. Halo
6. Cords
7. Veronica's Veil
8. Jug or Chalice
9. Ladder
10. Spear
11. Skull and crossed bones or Cherub's head
12. Cock
13. Pot
14. Three Nails
15. Scourges. (1958, Fig 15)

These crucifixes, fashioned from a single piece of wood, must have played a singularly important part in the religious life of the people during the Penal Days when the ordinary artistic and devotional items of Catholic life were not available, and indeed, when one considers the terrible condition of the people during that period, what could be more suitable than to have before their eyes the figure of the tortured Christ who, having endured the sufferings of the cross and passion, had entered into glory. The figure nailed to the cross and surrounded by the instruments of torture was the answer to the problem of suffering and evil in the world – an answer not philosophical but archetypal. Instead of presenting a treatise on the meaning and purpose of suffering, the Son of God had himself embraced the agony of the cross and preceeded us on the road on which all of us, to a greater or lesser degree, tread.

Evidently, many of these crucifixes were sold to pilgrims to Lough Derg, Co Donegal. Apparently the crucifix was held in the hand while performing the 'Rounds' or *Iompú Deiseal* –

the sunwise perambulation at the various Stations – and afterwards preserved by the pilgrim with great devotion as a sign
that he or she had performed the pilgrimage, in the same way
as a pilgrim to Compostella would treasure the sea-shell received as a mark of completion of the pilgrimage to the shrine
of St James. The pilgrimage theory would explain the consist-
ency with which the date is marked on the cross. Naturally
the pilgrim would like to remember the year on which he/she
made the pilgrimage to Lough Derg.

One of the items frequently associated with the passion is
the 'Cock and Pot' motif. This is shown both on gravestones
and on the Penal Crucifixes as a cock standing over a pot or
cauldron. The origin seems to be an anecdote from the apocryphal *Gospel of Nicodemus* or *Acts of Pilate* which has passed
into the *Leabhar Breac* and folklore in a variety of forms.

Basically, the story is that Judas, having repented of his be-
trayal of Christ, returned the 30 pieces of silver to the temple
officials and went home. His wife was roasting a cock over the
fire. Judas asked her to get him a rope with which to hang
himself as he was convinced that Christ would rise up again
on the third day. His wife replied scornfully that it was just as
likely that the cock she was cooking would come to life again
as that Jesus would return. At this the cock clapped his wings
and crowed three times. This confirmed Judas' worst fears
and off he went and hanged himself.

In a folk version of the legend, the sound made by the
crowing cock is *Mac na hÓighe Slán* (The Son of the Virgin is
safe), in other words, the cock proclaims the resurrection so
that the bird pictured at the foot of the Penal Crucifix is the
messenger of victory.

In Irish folklore, the Robin Redbreast is a sacred bird, for he
tried to alleviate the sufferings of Christ by using his beak to
pull out the thorns piercing Our Lord's head. Some of the
blood fell on him leaving him with the characteristic red breast.

As the sun darkened and lost its light at the death of Christ so at his Resurrection on Easter Sunday it will be seen to dance. (Danaher, 1972, 74)

In all of this, we see that within the devastating spectacle of the crucifixion there is left a ray of hope, even of confidence, that all is not lost and that behind the terrible catastrophe there remains a promise of resurgence.

CHAPTER EIGHT

Argain Ifrinn – the plundering of hell (Holy Saturday)

In the Apostles' Creed it is said of Christ, *'descendit ad inferos'* (He descended into hell/the underworld). The Apostles' Creed belongs to the fourth century and formed part of the Baptismal Rite of the Western Church. However, it is another ancient text that gives a broad detailed description of this event and explains the reason for Christ's descent into hell in the first place. This is the apocryphal *Gospel of Nicodemus* or *Acts of Pilate,* to which is added in some cases, *The Plundering of Hell.*

Basically, it describes how Christ descended into hell. Adam, Eve, and the saints of the Old Testament – people such as the prophets Isaiah, Jeremiah, John the Baptist, as well as a multitude of other notables, King David, King Solomon among them – are imprisoned in the dark dungeons of hell by Satan and his demons. The prophets continued the work they had been doing among the living on earth and gave the others hope of deliverance.

Eventually, John the Baptist arrived in hell with the same message and he was able to inform the prisoners that it was only a matter of time until the Deliverer arrived to set them free and to lead them into paradise. This eventually occurs. Christ as a conquering hero descends into the underworld, the great fortress of Satan and his demons. He plunders the fortress, chains up Satan and sets the prisoners free. This was known among the Irish as *Argain Ifrinn* – the 'plundering of the underworld'.

The Apostles' Creed gives the order of events, as it were, within the sacred triduum: *'crucifixus, mortuus, et sepultus: descendit ad inferos; tertia die resurrexit a mortuis.'* (*Rituale Romanum*, Tit. II, cap. 4)

This means that the descent to hell occurred in the interval between the death of Christ on Good Friday and his resurrection on Easter Sunday. While the dead body of Jesus was in the tomb the soul of Christ, united with his person was in the underworld.

Jesus himself had declared: 'For as Jonas was in the belly of the sea-monster for three days and three nights, so will the Son of Man be in the heart of the earth for three days and three nights.' (Mt 12:40) According to some ancient authors, it is not the tomb that is meant primarily here but the underworld in which the saints of the Old Testament are imprisoned. (*Dictionaire de Theologie Catholique*, 4, 576)

The popularity of *Argain Ifrinn* is shown by the large number of manuscripts in which it is contained both in Irish and Latin. There is also considerable variety in the versions being ultimately dependent on the *Gospel of Nicodemus*. The picture of the mysterious underworld, and above all the highly militaristic vision of Christ descending to ravage hell, must have appealed immensely to the Celts where the *laoch* or hero constituted such an idealised figure.

A version of *Argain Ifrinn* is to be found in the fifteenth century *Leabhar Breac* (Atkinson, 1887, 392 ff.), in the *Book of Fermoy* (*Ériu* IV (1910), 112ff), and an early dramatised form in the *Book of Cerne* in which much of the dialogue consists of verses from the psalms. (*Journal of Theological Studies* XXII (1972), 374ff) Several other manuscripts add to the diversity of versions of 'The Harrowing of Hell', as it was known in England in the Medieval Mystery Plays.

A particularly interesting version is an abbreviated form of the *Gospel of Nicodemus* composed in Ireland in the fourteenth century and belonging to the Dominicans of Limerick. It has been edited by D. J. Lewis. (*Peritia,* 1986, 262-275) This short text combines neatly the *Gospel of Nicodemus* and *The Descent to Hell.*

In the manuscript, Joseph of Arimathea explains that the leaders of the Jews imprisoned him because he had criticised them severely for putting Jesus to death. However, he wasn't long in prison until he saw Christ coming to him as a ray of sunlight. He took him by the hand and lifted him out of the prison and set him down in his own house in Arimathea. Joseph told his audience then that several people had risen up from their graves along with Our Lord at his resurrection and among them were two sons of Simeon – the old man who had taken the infant Jesus in his arms in the temple. These two are walking around the city of Arimathea in perfect health except that they are unable to speak. Joseph advises the Jewish leaders to meet them. They do this and conjure them to tell them their story. The two sons look up to heaven and make the sign of the cross on their tongues and immediately their speech is restored. They then begin the story of the plundering of hell.

Their story was that they themselves were in hell together with Adam and Eve, King David, Isaiah, Simeon and all the other Holy Fathers of the Old Testament. Suddenly, a marvellous ray of light lit up the intense darkness of the underworld. Adam, the father of the human race spoke:

'This light,' he said, 'is the eternal light. This is the hand of the One who created me.'

Out of the light Christ answered him: 'When I created you it wasn't in this place I put you. Return now to your kingdom.' Then Isaiah spoke: 'This is the light of Jesus Christ, the Son of God, just as I proclaimed while I was still on earth: "The people who lived in darkness have seen a great light".'

Then Simeon spoke to the crowd: 'Let us praise Jesus Christ, the Son of God for his light shines upon us.'

Then John the Baptist spoke: 'This is the Son of God. It was of him I said: this is the Lamb of God who takes away the sins of the world.'

The prisoners have spoken, and now it is time for Satan himself – the Lord of Death – to intervene and also hell itself, which is personalised in the text. It is clear that these two do not get on well with each other.

Satan speaks first and addresses hell: 'Prepare yourself to accept Christ. He boasts that he is the Son of God. But, in reality he is just a human who is afraid of death and he even said: "My soul is sorrowful to the point of death". (Mk 14:34) I afflicted people with blindness and weakness and leprosy and he cured them. Even dead people whom I consigned to your charge, O hell, he took them away from you and they are alive again.'

Hell answers Satan: 'I tell you that if he is powerful in his human nature he will be all powerful in his divine nature. You will be sorry for ever on account of him.'

The dialogue continues in this way with Satan boasting that he succeeded in sentencing Christ to death. But hell maintains that it was through his death that Christ defeated both of them. Christ rose from the grave and neither of them were able to keep a hold on him. Hell asks Satan not to allow Christ in; if he enters he will release the prisoners and lead them off into paradise.

Then a mighty sound as if of thunder was heard and out of it a voice was heard declaiming:

'Tollite portas, principes, vestras, et elevamini portas aeternales et introibit Rex Gloriae.' (Ps 24:7) (Lift up your gates, O Princes, and raise up the eternal doors and let the King of Glory enter.)

When hell hears the voice of Christ in the thunder he gets rid of Satan and prepares for the siege. He starts giving orders to his army of demons: 'Fasten the bronze doors and put bands of iron on them and fight bravely or we will be destroyed.'

Another shout comes from outside: 'Open the gates, O hell.' Hell answers: 'Who is this – this King of Glory?'

King David answers: 'The Lord that is powerful, strong, the Lord that is mighty in war. And now, O hell, open your doors and let the King of Glory enter.'

Satan and Hell cry out together: 'We are in dismay; we are beaten now. Who are you – at once so large and so small, so high and so low, alive and dead, hero and chieftain? At your death all creation trembled. Not only are you not afraid of us but you are going to take our prisoners from us.'

Then Christ takes a hold of Satan and hands him over to hell to keep him in subjection. Then Jesus says: 'Come all you holy people who are in my own image and likeness.'

With this he takes Adam by the hand and draws him out of hell. All the prisoners emerge after him. Christ entrusts them to Michael the Archangel who leads them into paradise.

Basically, the *Plundering of Hell* is an expression of the eternal warfare between good and evil, light and darkness, God and Satan. The war occurs in all three spheres – heaven, earth and the underworld. St Michael figures in all three areas: 'and now war broke out in heaven, when Michael with his angels attacked the dragon. The dragon fought back with his angels, but they were defeated and driven out of heaven. The great dragon, the primeval serpent, known as the devil or Satan, who had deceived all the world, was hurled down to the earth and his angels were hurled down with him.' (Apoc 12:7-9)

In Catholic tradition St Michael fights the dragon in such well-known centres as Monte Gargano and Mont St Michel and he appears here in *Argain Ifrinn* as assisting Christ the dragon-fighter in the underworld.

A continuity of role-playing is apparent. Satan is shown as a jailer who in sickness, poverty and various afflictions as well as in death, makes prisoners of his victims.

On the other hand, Christ is shown as a jail-breaker who

releases Satan's prisoners from their bonds. We have what appears to be a particularly clear example of this in the cure of the crippled woman: 'Is there one of you who does not untie his ox or his donkey from the manger on the Sabbath and take it out for watering? And this woman, a daughter of Abraham whom Satan has held bound these eighteen years – was it not right to untie her bonds on the Sabbath day?' (Lk 13:15-16)

In *Argain Ifrinn,* Christ does not entirely destroy Satan but puts a severe curb on his activities. If he had totally annihilated Satan there would have been no war for us to wage against the forces of darkness and consequently no victory on a personal level.

Behind this theme of the *Harrowing of Hell* is a highly militaristic conception of Christian life which would have to some extent been characteristic of the early church. The forces of evil and death were very real. The Christian was a soldier who by his baptism had undertaken a lifelong battle against these forces. Even today, a little oil is put on the child's breast at baptism. In the early centuries of the church, however, when it was adults who were being baptised, they were plastered all over with oil in the same way as wrestlers entering the arena were plastered all over with oil to make them supple and so that their adversary couldn't get a proper grip on them. This idea was transferred to Christian baptism for the Christian was undertaking a contest with the powers of evil. In the *Harrowing of Hell* Christ met the powers of evil head on, as it were, in their own native territory.

The underworld, which Christ plundered, has many aspects. It stands for any kind of human bondage springing from mankind's alienation from God. The various evils which afflict us, sickness, death, depression, despair, physical and psychological ills, are all aspects of it. And Christ, 'The Plunderer of the Underworld', is the One who has the power to conquer these ills.

Some of the Irish manuscripts seem to reflect the Irish heroic tradition in their description of Christ's onslaught on hell. According to the *Book of Fermoy:*

Do ling an Tigerna isteach,
Énmac Muiri, Dia dúileach,
ní raibhi ann-sin guth ná glór
is-tigh acht uch is ochón.
(The Lord sprang in, Mary's only Son, creative God. Then there was no voice or sound within but ah and alas.)

The *Harrowing of Hell* is portrayed as quite a violent affair and this is indicated particularly in the Irish name for the event, *Argain Ifrinn* – the plunder or destruction of hell. In Gaelic tradition there was a list of stories all under this heading of *Orgna,* and a particularly fine one has been preserved in *Denna Rig* – the story of the plunder of the great fortress of Dind Rig near Leighlinbridge, Co Carlow by the King Labhraí Loingseach:

Dind Rig (is) red – the hill-face (is) a kindled fire.
Thirty chieftains have died in sorrow.
He crushed them, he broke them down, the fierce boar-champion
Labraid, the warrior of Ireland, the grandson of Loegaire Lorc.
Lugaid (was) a bull-calf; fierce, eager for spoils (was) Sétne; famous (was) Cobthach Coel, a chief (was) Muiredach Mál.
He trod down the weapons, the father of the father of Ollom;
The Dumb killed the sons of glorious Augaine.
(*Ériu,* 1977, 2)

A similar heroic bombastic style in an early modern Irish *Argain Ifrinn,* in which several adjectives beginning with the same letter are lumped together to produce an extraordinary effect, gives the impression of a continuity of tradition in Ireland, in which Christ as Plunderer of Hell, is ranked among the great heroes – Cú Chulainn, Conall Cearnach, Fionn Mac Cumhaill and Labhraí Loingseach himself:

The scene describes Christ's arrival in hell and his *Dearg-ruathar* or 'Red onslaught':

Is ann sin do éirigh an léomhan leadurthach laomdha lot,<h> chorcra, & do mhéadaigh a uaill & (a) ar-daigneadh ar faicsin a fhola 'na fhiadhuise; & do ghluais roimhe gu h-uaillmhear aghmhur ionnsaightheach, dána díoghuinn dásachtach, fiochdha feargach faidchémen-dach, cródha cnestollach comharthach, d'argain Ifrinn iargcúlaigh iar sin …

Then the rending, valiant, crimson-wounded Lion arose and his mettle and his high spirit swelled on seeing his blood before him; and he moved forward, proud and lively, victorious, hostile, bold, stout and enraged, fuming, furi-ous and far stepping, hardy, pierced of skin, battle-marked, to harrow furthest hell forthwith, and it is related how he put his feet on the secure, firm heavy-valved strong door of cavernous-hot northern hell, firmly and full fiercely, forcefully and imperiously; and the wearying, noisy-screaming, shadowy-deceptive denizens of upper hell scat-tered with a rush, on seeing the brown-lashed, white-toothed glowing countenance of the Almighty (coming) to extirpate and swiftly scatter them. For he was a ruddy-flaming huge royal candle, and a red-seething mass of molten metal, wide-showering and immense, on the anvil being hammered, and a splendid, flaring warrior's dart, and a white-sided, brilliant, cutting moon having grown and kindled in the truly-dark rain clouds of the firma-ment; and the calm, kingly, shining, wide-eyed, grace-filled countenance of the lovely, noble-great, august High King blazed up throughout the high-showery, bi-partite, concave universe illuminating abundantly with a pure light, from the monster-ridden, dark-caved, remote bottom of cold hell to its harrying, shout-filled, lament-filled topmost part, throughout all that time without darkening or obscurity or gloom. And the saviour extended that long-fingered, noble right hand to the hard iron door, and shattered and violently broke it from its rude, thick, aboriginal hinges, like a sheet of frozen one-night's ice in (its) weakness, so that he (or 'it') released the rich, fair, victoriously-trumpeting, widely-descended, eager, well-born throng up from the stations and mansions of populous hell; for that is the Red Onslaught of the King of the Stars and of the Constellations after his resurrection from death and burial. (*Celtica*, 1980, 40, 47, 50)

We have an extraordinarily early account of the *Harrowing of Hell,* as it was called in Medieval England, and *Argain Ifrinn* in medieval Ireland, in the spirited Easter Homily of Bishop Melito of Sardis in the second century. He puts words into the mouth of the Risen Christ, which are incredibly like the boastful pronouncements of the victorious hero in Celtic literature such as we find them for instance in the early Irish tale, *Scéal Muice Mic Da Thó.* And indeed, the setting is much the same as they are both records of triumphant achievements.

According to Bishop Melito the Risen Christ says: 'Who shall contend with me? Let him stand up to face me. I have freed the condemned, brought the dead to life, raised up the buried. Who will speak against me? I am the Christ,' he says, 'It is I who destroyed death, who triumphed over the enemy, who trampled the underworld underfoot, who bound up the strong one and snatched man away to the heights of heaven; I am the Christ.' (*The Divine Office,* 2, 367-368)

We have a highly original form of *Argain Ifrinn* in a fifteenth century Gaelic manuscript. In this version, Satan and his demons have heard of Christ and the wonderful works he is performing on earth. They realise that he has a lot of power and they become anxious in case he attacks them and deprives them of all the people whom they hold in captivity.

Accordingly, Satan, who realises that Christ derives his power from God and that if Christ were to sin he would lose this power, sends his demons to tempt Christ to sin. They come one by one to tempt him and they are personified as the seven deadly sins. When they get back, Satan questions them individually about how they got on and the seven have to admit sadly that they did not succeed in tempting Christ. Satan sends them away in disgust and tries to fortify hell as best he can against attack. Christ comes along however and liberates the captives and goes away leaving Satan tied to a pillar in the depths of hell. (*Études Celtiques* 1960, 44-78)

The Barking Abbey Rite

The largest and most splendid of Benedictine Nuns' churches in medieval England was Barking Abbey in Essex. Having survived for many centuries it was destroyed at the Reformation and the 100-yard church is now a vague ruin near London. Luckily the Ordinal, describing the various Offices for the Liturgical Year, survives to illustrate the glory of medieval liturgy in England. The *Argain Ifrinn* ritual took place after Matins on Easter Sunday and it is explained that it was the Lady Abbess, Dame Katherina de Suttone (1358-1376) who had arranged it for this rather late time so that a greater number of the faithful would attend the ceremony. Their devotion had cooled and it was easier to get them to church early in the morning than late at night.

The Rite of the Harrowing of Hell in Barking Abbey. The Abbess and Choir of Nuns along with some priests and clerics carrying palm branches and extinguished candles make their way from the choir stalls to the chapel of St Mary Magdalene within the great church. They are a figure of the souls of the Holy Fathers who prior to the coming of Christ descended into the underworld.

The door of the chapel is closed behind them. The presiding priest, wearing alb and cope, makes his way to the chapel. He is accompanied by two deacons – one holding a cross with the banner of the Lord hanging from it while the other deacon swings a thurible. Two boys carry lighted candles. Other priests and clerics accompany the celebrant who represents Christ descending into the underworld to break down the gates of hell, subdue Satan and liberate the captives.

At the door of St Mary Magdalene's chapel the procession halts for the Threshold Dialogue. The celebrant sings three times on a higher note each time:

'Lift up your heads, O gates, and be lifted up, O ancient doors, that the King of Glory may enter.' (Ps 24) Each time, he raps on the closed door with the processional cross.

Probably from inside, he was answered by the verse:

'Who is the King of Glory?' (Ps 24), and then further a verse from outside:

'The Lord, strong man and mighty, the Lord, mighty in battle, the Lord of hosts, he is the King of Glory.' (Ps 24)

Then the doors fall open and the procession of priests and clerics enter the dark chapel. Then from inside is sung the verse: 'From the gates of hell, bring out our souls, O Lord.' At this point the celebrant leads them all out of the chapel, they light their candles and proceed to the Easter Sepulchre to celebrate Christ's rising from the tomb. (Tolhurst, 1927, 1, 107-108)

An ancient prayer relates the *Plundering of Hell* to our own sinful state:

Lord Jesus Christ … you descended into the depths to lead out the bound prisoners from the underworld. Descend now also, we beseech you in the greatness of your mercy, to set us free from the chains of our sins by which we are all bound, O Saviour of the World. (DACL IV, 686)

The Barking Abbey Rite of the Plundering of Hell is both simple and vivid and easily performed. It brought before the minds of the faithful something which was both a doctrine of the faith and an immensely popular emotional experience in which people saw portrayed before them the victory of Christ over sin and death and a decisive defeat of the powers of darkness. The prayer cited above shows how easily *Argain Ifrinn* could be linked to the human condition.

In the Barking Abbey Rite the Harrowing of Hell takes place indoors in a side-chapel. This corresponds to the depiction of hell as a fortress with caves and dungeons whose darkness is lighted up by the arrival of Christ: '… the gates of brass were broken in pieces and the bars of iron were ground to powder, and all the dead that were bound were loosed from their chains and the King of Glory entered in, in fashion as a man, and all the dark places of hell were enlightened', as the *Gospel of Nicodemus* describes the scene. (James, 1924, 134) The broken doors and bolts are often a prominent feature of the descent into hell in ikons of the Byzantine Rite.

But there is an alternative to this 'Hell as Fortress' type of portrayal. This is the 'Hell as Dragon' depiction and, for the Celts, this was a vitally important image with its consequent depiction of Christ as 'dragon-fighter'. This can be recognised most easily in *Argain Ifrinn* of the *Book of Fermoy* and the *Harrowing of Hell* in the English Mystery Plays. The theme developed especially in the apocryphal *Gospel of Nicodemus* and made its way into the areas of liturgical and devotional texts as well as folk drama and art.

CHAPTER NINE

Bealtaine and the Easter Fire
(Easter Sunday)

As regards the idea of the New Fire of the Easter Vigil emanating from the tomb on which the dead body of Christ was deposited on Good Friday, there is above all the present-day rite performed by the Greek Orthodox Patriarch of Jerusalem in which the New Fire emerges from the actual historical tomb of Christ in the Church of the Holy Sepulchre to be spread by means of lighted candles to the waiting crowd. (*Ephemerides Liturgicae*, 1985, 170ff.)

Two early *Ordines* (from the 5th and 7th centuries) describe essentially the same practice. (Capelle, B., *Travaux Liturgiques,* Louvain 1967, T. III, 221-223). The Spanish *Liber Ordinum* gives a marvellous account of the lighting of the New Fire at the Vigil of Easter. It is first explained that the bishop, with only his priests and deacons, enters the sacristy or 'Thesaurus' of the church. Then the doors are closed and the windows veiled so that not even the slightest glimmer of light can be seen coming from outside. From the sacristy the bishop is given a stone or a rock and fuel, and an instrument for striking fire from a stone. And as soon as fire is struck, by the bishop's own hand, flax is lighted; from the flax, a pitch-pine torch is lighted, from that again a lamp; from the lamp a candle is lighted. And, as yet, nobody lights his own candle, but the bishop proceeds to bless the lamp, helped by the deacon who will presently bless it in the choir (of the church). The bishop then blesses the lighted candle held by the deacon who will presently bless it in the church.

This having been done, the bishop lights his own candle from the candle he has just blessed. Then the clergy light their candles from the blessed candle and when all are lighted the bishop stands beside the door. The deacon stands in front of him holding the lighted candle which he will bless at a later stage. Then suddenly, the veil is lifted from the door and the bishop sings: 'Deo gratias' (Thanks be to God). All reply; 'Deo gratias'. This is repeated three times. Then the procession to the choir of the church takes place with the Antiphon: 'Lumen verum inluminans omnem hominem in hunc mundum venientem; Quoniam apud te est, Domine, fons vitae, et in lumine tuo videbimus lumen.' (The true light illuminating every man coming into this world; because with you, O Lord, is the fount of life and in your light we see light.) During the course of the procession, the candles of the faithful are lighted from the blessed candle.

There follows, the solemn blessing of the lamp by the deacon and then the blessing of the candle by another deacon. In this marvellous Spanish ritual the bishop himself acts as fire maker. The method used was probably the sharp striking of flint by a hard iron instrument. When the sparks flew out they ignited a highly combustible material held close at hand. It would appear that this was only a small fire from which the lamp and candle were lighted – not the huge bonfire which was and is to be seen in some churches. This bonfire is probably a feature derived from Celtic sources where bonfires blazed to mark the beginning of the two great periods of the year, the dark period beginning at *Samhain* (November Eve) and the bright period beginning at *Bealtaine* (May Eve).

The great 13th century Bishop Durandus of Mende, in his brilliant exposition of mediaeval liturgy, sees in this the fire of the Holy Spirit which proceeds from Christ to illuminate the church. (*Rationale Divinorum Officiorum*; LIBER VI, CAP LXXX.II) Here, perhaps, Durandus is echoing the words of St

John: 'the Spirit had not yet been given because Jesus had not yet been glorified.' (7:39) The moment of the resurrection of Christ was the moment of the release of the Holy Spirit to the church, symbolised by the spark bursting from the stone which is the tomb of Christ.

It must be remembered that God's archenemy is Lucifer – 'the Light-Bearer', so that we are confronted with a strange situation in which light is in conflict with light and fire fights against fire, as St Patrick's fire at Slane overcame King Laoghaire's fire at Tara.

One might also wonder if the same theme of light over-coming light is not present in the case of Lugh Lámhfhada and Balar. In the great mythological battle, *Cath Maige Tuired,* (Gray, 1982) Lugh, leader of the Tuatha Dé Danann, encounters Balar of the Evil Eye, leader of the supernatural sea-pirates, the Fómhóraigh. Balar has a destructive eye in the centre of his forehead which destroys everything on which it looks. Normally it is kept covered to avoid accidents. In the battle, the eye is uncovered to destroy the army of the Tuatha Dé Danann but Lugh flings a burning slingstone, prepared by the blacksmith god Goibhniu, at Balar which destroys the eye.

In a folk-version, however, Balar's eye is definitely fiery, an image of the sun which scorches perhaps – *súil nimhe tine a bhí inti* (a poisonous eye of fire it was). In this version, Balar lifted off the various coverings one after the other. When the first bandage over his eye was removed, the ferns began to wither with the heat. When the second was removed the grass began to turn brown. At the next uncovering the crows began to squawk and take flight, and for a good reason, as the branches grew hot under their claws. Finally, the entire woods went up in flames. (*Béaloideas,* IV, 88)

These Irish traditions see fire in conflict with fire. The more powerful fire, however, destroys the weaker which is as-

sociated with evil. Perhaps the most dramatic of these 'fire
against fire' conflicts occurs in the great medieval story,
Forbhais Droma Dámhgháire, 'The Siege of Knocklong'. (Ó
Duinn, 1992) This tale tells of how Cormac Mac Airt, King of
Tara, invades Munster to collect taxes. Cormac sets up camp
on the hill of Knocklong on the borders of Cork and
Limerick. His druids dry up the wells and water supply and
the Munster army is in dire straits. In their terrible predicament they call on the brilliant Munster druid Mogh Roith
(who, by the way, in Irish tradition, was the man who beheaded
John the Baptist). Mogh Roith lights a magical fire well to the
south of Knock Long with the intention of driving it northwards towards the enemy camp. He chants a spell which, with
its strange rhythm and sustained alliteration, may indicate the
type of ritual incantation in use among the druids:

Tairgim tine threathnach thréan,
réiteoidh fiodh, feofaidh féar,
lasair lonn, leor a luas,
sroichfidh snas sruith neamh suas,
cnaífidh fioch, fiocha foinn,
cloífidh cath ar chlann Choinn.
(I kindle a fire, powerful strong, it will level the trees, it will
scorch grass, an angry flame, great its speed, it will rush up
to the heavens above; it will destroy forests, the forests of
the earth, it will subdue in battle the people of Conn.)

At the same time Cith Rua, Cormac's druid, lights his own
magical fire with the intention of driving it southwards towards the camp of the Munstermen.

The two fires begin to rage and make for each other, leaving the central plain of Munster level to this day. They wind
around Tory Hill in Co Limerick, turn in the direction of the
Shannon and back again. They rise up to the sky:

Tá siad imithe suas go dtí an fhirmimint agus go dtí néalta

neimhe, agus tá siad cosúil le laochra lonna lúfara nó le
dhá leon alpacha ag leanúint a chéile. (102) (They have
gone up into the firmament and to the clouds of heaven,
and they are like two ferociously agile warriors, or like two
devouring lions attacking each other.)

Mogh Roith then dons his druidic attire of bull-hide from
a hornless brown bull, and his speckled bird mask with bil-
lowing wings. He soars up into the sky and keeps beating the
fire northwards until Cormac and his army have to flee for
their lives back to Tara.

In accounts of St Patrick's conflict with the druids, similar
stories are told in which, of course, St Patrick is victorious.

St Patrick's companion, in a typical story, is clothed in a
druid's clothes and placed inside a wooden hut. The hut is set
on fire, Patrick's companion emerges unharmed but the
druid's dress is burned to cinders. Then a druid, clothed in
Patrick's clothes is put inside a hut. The hut is set on fire and
the druid is burned to ashes while St Patrick's dress is unharmed.

In the story of St Patrick and the two snakes who escaped
his purge, one went to Loch Dearg where he swallowed
Patrick, who, however, hacked his way out of the monster's
belly, in consequence of which the lake turned red with the
dragon's blood and became a place of Christian pilgrimage, as
the site of Patrick's great victory over the forces of evil.

The other snake made his way to Co Mayo and set up his
headquarters in a rock near Ballina called Carraig Seircín,
from the snake's name. He caused terrible devastation to the
people of the locality. His practice was, at nightfall, to stand
erect in the mouth of his cave holding a lighted candle in his
mouth. All who saw the light of the candle dropped dead.

St Patrick arrives on the scene to confront the serpent. A
local woman gives him lodging for the night and she is careful
to close her door before sunset to exclude the serpent's fire. St

Patrick takes some lard from Fiontan (Fionn-tan? – white fire?) his servant's belly and with the aid of rushes supplied by the woman a candle is made. Then Patrick goes to the door holding aloft his lighted candle as in the distance the serpent holds up his. But Patrick's light is greater than the serpent's light and the serpent drops dead. The people thank St Patrick and he baptises them, explaining to them the mighty power of God. (Hyde, 1915, 287-288) Fire and baptism are closely linked here as in the Easter Vigil. Reminiscent of patrician legend of St Patrick lighting his fire on the hill of Slane to challenge the ritual fire of Tara to the south, and the fire of Mogh Roith challenging the fire of Cormac Mac Airt on Knocklong, Co Limerick, in the epic *Forbhais Droma Dámhgháire* (Ó Duinn, 1992), this episode of the fire-bearing snake brings together the two elements, fire and serpents, which in Patrick Ford's study are the great characteristics of the pre-Christian religion of Ireland. St Patrick, in his efforts to replace the old religion by the new, is much preoccupied by these two things. (1983, 29-49)

The serpent and the fire brings us to the *Arundina Serpentina*. This was an instrument well-known in medieval liturgical rites of which the fire candle-bearing serpent of Ballina is an obvious memory. The *Arundina Serpentina* was a long staff at the top of which was serpent holding a candle in his mouth. The *Regularis Concordia* of the tenth century describes its ceremonial use during Holy Week:

> On Maundy Thursday after none, a procession went down to the church door, bearing with it a staff which ended at the top in the shape of a serpent. There, fire, struck from a flint, was first hallowed, and then used for lighting a candle which came out of the serpent's mouth. From this all other candles were lighted; and the same ceremonial was repeated on Good Friday and Easter Eve. (King, 1957, 281)

One wonders how an ancient liturgical instrument used in the great liturgical centres of Europe in the middle ages could have found its way into a folktale centred on St Patrick and his adventures in the west of Ireland.

The Bealtaine Fire

By combining several accounts of local Bealtaine rituals in Scotland and Ireland in the eighteenth century, as given by Sir James Frazer, we arrive at a very clear picture indeed of the elaborate celebration of Bealtaine. Several distinct elements can be distinguished: (cf. Frazer, 1923, 617ff.)

1. The Rite of Bealtaine takes place on the eve of the feast, that is on the evening of 30 April. According to Gaelic custom the feast begins on the evening before.

2. The household fires of the area are extinguished.

3. The rites are performed out of doors on a hill or eminence.

4. Frazer quotes John Ramsay, Lord of Ochtertyre: 'They (the Druids) thought it degrading to him whose temple is the universe to suppose that he would dwell in any house made with hands.' A square or circular trench was cut and the turves placed about it to serve as a seat for the company.

5. The wood and fuel for the fire was set up in the centre. This seems like the plan of a Celtic/Romano temple with the shrine of the deity in the centre and an ambulatory all around for the *iompú deiseal* or clockwise procession of the worshipers, as can be seen at Holy Wells.

6. The fire is kindled in the *tine-éigin* fashion: two pieces of wood are rubbed together until the friction produces sparks. A species of agaric, which grows on old birch trees and is highly inflammable, is held close to the sparks until a fire is kindled. In some places, 9 or 27 men (multiples of the sacred number 3) are employed to make the fire.

7. Dance three times *deiseal* (clockwise) around fire.

8. A special meal is taken, in some places a caudle of eggs, butter, oatmeal and milk, as well as large quantities of beer and whiskey.

9. Singing, dancing, entertainment, take place around the fire.

10. A special cake, called *An Bonnach Bealtaine,* is baked. This large cake was broken into small pieces, one for each person present, and one piece was blackened with soot. The pieces were put into a bag and each person drew out a piece. Whoever drew out the blackened piece became the *Cailleach Bealtaine* or 'May Hag'.

11. The company took hold of him and made a show of putting him into the fire, but were restrained by others. In some places they laid him flat on the ground, making as if to quarter him. While the feast remained fresh in people's memory they spoke of him as if he were dead. 'Whoever draws the black bit is the devoted person who is to be sacrificed to Baal, whose favour they mean to implore in rendering the year productive of the sustenance of man and beast.' The drawing of the pieces of the Bealtaine cake from a bag or cap is clearly a selection rite to discover the sacrificial victim.

12. The household fires were relighted from the great Bealtaine bonfire.

13. The belief that by leaping three times over the bonfire, or running between two fires thrice, would produce a good harvest is worthy of note and the use of the ashes or cinders as charms.

14. On May Eve, Walpurgis Night, witches were believed to be abroad and to be particularly active in casting spells, depriving people of their dairy produce, and so forth. In some places the Crois Cuirn *(Cros Chaorthainn),* a cross made of the sacred tree, Rowan, was put up on the wall of the byres to protect the cows. In other places, young people danced

around the fire shouting, 'Fire, fire, burn the witches.' (1923, 617-622)

Many of these customs belong also to the midsummer bonfires on St John's Eve (23 June), the Summer Solstice, which, as regards the ritual, seems to be a duplicate of Bealtaine.

A particularly interesting fire from the Celtic point of view is that of Auvergne, discussed by Frazer in his comprehensive treatment of the Fire-festivals of Europe. (1923, 639-658)

Perhaps the most elaborate of the Christian fires was that of 'The Burning of the Easter Man' at certain villages in South Bavaria.

The ceremony was very closely associated with the Easter Vigil which, of course, until the recent reform of Holy Week had for centuries been pushed back to the morning of Easter Saturday. This extraordinary occurrence of anticipation resulted in such strange anomalies as the deacon proclaiming solemnly 'O vere beata nox ...' (O truly blessed night ...) while the sunlight streamed in through the windows. Unfortunately the tendency in many churches today is to have the vigil at an early hour on Holy Saturday evening so that everything is over at 9.00 or 10.00 pm.

At any rate, the 'Burning of the Easter Man', as described by Sir James Frazer (1923, 616-617), took place on Holy Saturday night between nine and ten o'clock. On a hill near the village, known in some places as 'The Easter Mountain', the young men set up a tall wooden cross wrapped in straw so that it looked like a man with his arms extended. One man stood beside the 'Easter Man' with a lighted candle. This had been brought from the church and had probably been lighted from the paschal candle which had been blessed that morning. The rest of the men stood at regular intervals in a great circle around the cross. A signal was given and the men raced around the circle three times. They then stopped, each in his place, and another signal was given. At this they ran to the cross and the man holding the candle beside it. Whoever reached the cross first was given the candle and it was his privilege to set fire to the Easter Man. Great shouts of jubilation rose as the Easter Man blazed.

On Easter Monday, the villagers came back to gather the ashes. They strewed it on their fields to improve the fertility of the land. In some areas in Germany the charred sticks from the Easter bonfire were kept until Bealtaine and thrown into the fields as a preservative – Bealtaine being a particularly dangerous time in which the crops were at risk.

In this system a link was forged between the Christian Feast of Easter based on the spring equinox and the Celtic Feast of Bealtaine coming half way between the spring equinox (21 March) and the summer solstice (21 June).

The old palm branches from Palm Sunday of the previous year, which had been hung up in peoples' houses, were taken down and burned with the Easter Man or 'Judas Figure', as he was known in some places. In this way the two types of ashes are mixed and the old year and new year united. This ashes is preserved and mixed with the seed corn being sown in the spring of the following year, so that the sacrifice of vegetation in the old year gives rise to the growing corn of the new year, like the *cailleach,* or last sheaf of the harvest being buried in the soil in which the corn for the following year is being sown. Out of death life springs.

Similarly, the palms carried in the Palm Sunday procession are burned and the ashes preserved to be used in next Ash Wednesday's ritual of spreading ashes on the foreheads of the faithful. In this way, the liturgy of the church has retained archaic practices in which one year leads into another and death will produce new life. How marvellous it is that the church has preserved these old rituals in a new way and joined an ancient stream of tradition linking itself to the experience of mankind throughout untold ages. In integrating these ancient rites into her liturgy, the Catholic Church has shown herself to be worthy of the word 'catholic', that is 'universal', for she has honoured the diverse practices of the various peoples which form the age-old experience of the human race. A long tradition lies behind the succinct rubric in the *Roman Missal* for Ash Wednesdays: 'The ashes used today come from the branches blessed the preceding year for Passion Sunday.'

We have seen that in many areas in Europe the bonfires blazed on a hill near the church at the Easter Vigil.

A straw effigy was burned on this occasion and the whole operation was known as 'Burning the Judas' or 'Burning the Easter Man'. (Frazer, 1923, 616) These two appellations can be seen to be complementary as describing the two aspects of sacrifice, the burning or destruction – leaving aside – of the old (sinful) form (the Judas figure), and the exaltation – the taking up to a more glorious higher form of existence, in the Easter Man figure.

Our Lord's sacrifice on the cross, culminating in his ascension to the shining glory of heaven, has the same double polarity. By the 'Judas figure' sinful mankind is symbolised and Christ on the cross took on himself the weight of all our sins: 'He was bearing our faults in his own body on the cross, so that we might die to our faults and live for holiness; through his wounds you have been healed.' (1 Pet 2:24) In this connection, St Paul makes an even more dramatic statements: 'For our sake God made the sinless one into sin, so that in him we might become the goodness of God.' (2 Cor 5:21) In both quotations the double polarity is maintained, the wounding and the healing, the destruction and the exaltation, so that the 'Judas figure' and the 'Easter Man figure' are fundamentally one. They are two aspects of the Redeeming Christ who 'became as men are; and being as all men are, he was humbler yet, even to accepting death, death on a cross. But God raised him high and gave him the name which is above all other names.' (Phil 2:7-9)

The Easter Man ceremonial carries with it an atmosphere of archaic ritual and ancient thought patterns, and yet it can contain in its ideology something of the most profound Christian mysteries.

The triple circumambulation of the sacred site, then the approach to the centre, the burning of the effigy and the return later to spread the ashes on the soil, leads the mind back to distant ages of mankind's mythic past. The spreading of the ashes of the burnt Easter Man on the soil can be seen as the fields' communion in the sacrifice. The Easter Man has been transformed and admitted to the otherworld and from this arena of power he returns to fertilise the earth. We have seen already that there is an echo of this ancient system in the spreading of the ashes on the forehead on Ash Wednesday. In this case, it is a change of heart that is envisaged: 'Turn away from sin and be faithful to the gospel.' *(Roman Missal)*

CHAPTER TEN

Dragon-Fighting at Bealtaine (Eastertide)

In a penetrating article in which he shows the importance of serpents and fire as major symbols of the old Irish pagan religion, Patrick K. Ford (1983, 29-49) brilliantly illustrates the use of these same two items in the life and legends of St Patrick.

What concerns us at the moment is St Patrick's contention with the powers of darkness whether in the form of black birds, or dragons *(ollphéisteanna)* or snakes. In whatever form it takes, this is essentially the 'dragon-fight' in which St Patrick endeavours to participate in the great dragon-fight of Christ against Satan, the primordial dragon, and put Christ's victory into operation on the local level. Many other Irish saints were dragon-fighters, with the same intention of extending Christ's victory over the powers of darkness into their own territories. Hence the importance of the local Celtic saint operating within a small well-defined area. Essentially, then, when we read of St Patrick's exploits against a dragon or *ollphéist,* what we are seeing is the Easter victory of Christ – his victory over death when he rose from the grave and ascended in a triumphal procession into heaven like a Celtic hero returning from a successful battle carrying his spoils. St Patrick or some other saint delivers the local community from the slavery and depredations of a local potentate in human or animal form, just as Christ descended into hell, the great potentate's fortress, to subdue the dictator and set the prisoners free. It is essentially an Easter spirituality, spreading the Easter

Fire of Victory. The *Dinnseanchas* tradition in Ireland – that is the lore of place names – makes this very real. Sometimes the spot can he pointed out where the dragon-fight took place as, for instance, at *Baile na nDeamhan* in Glencolumkille, Co Donegal, now marked by a cross-pillar standing on a cairn. It was here that the demons turned on St Colm Cille.

According to the legend in the *Vita Tripartita,* St Patrick stayed on Croagh Patrick for the forty days of Lent. Since Croagh Patrick is a *Lughnasa* (August) pilgrimage site, it is possibly the *Samhcharghas Maoise* of the Irish Celts that is meant. This was the summer lent and may possibly have come to an end at the Feast of the Transfiguration on 6 August thus coinciding with the great Celtic feast of *Lughnasa,* in honour of the god Lugh who defeated the stingy oppressive god Balar at the battle of Magh Tuireadh and liberated the Tuatha Dé Danann from his domination. The three lents of Irish monastic tradition are mentioned in *Félire Oengusso Céilí Dé: Carghas Éilí sa Gheimhreadh,* the winter lent of Eilias corresponding probably to our Advent; the ordinary lent, *Carghas Íosa san Earrach,* and the summer lent of Moses. (Stokes, 1905/1984, 42) The winter lent may have been 'St Martin's Lent', beginning after the feast of St Martin, 11 November.

Notice that the three Lents are named after the three who appeared transfigured at the Transfiguration. (Mk 9:2-10)

If there were three Lents then there must have been three 'Easters', Lent being a preparation of Easter, so that Christmas would have been considered as the 'Winter Easter' and the Transfiguration *(Tarmchruthud),* celebrated on 26 July, according to *Félire Oengusso,* would be the 'Summer Easter'. Perhaps it was celebrated on the following Sunday to coincide with *Domhnach Crom Dubh,* for the last Sunday in July or the first Sunday in August was so-called to recall St Patrick's defeat of the pagan god Crom Dubh or Crom Cruaich. At any rate, the particularly mystical character of the Feast of the Transfiguration, in which the glory of the Risen Christ is prefigured, aligns it with the Feast of Easter.

If the theory of the three Easters is correct then their dates would correspond to significant astronomical occurrences: the winter solstice at Christmas, when a ray of the rising sun enters Newgrange; the spring equinox modified by the time of the full moon at Easter, and the Transfiguration at Lughnasa, half way between the summer solstice and the autumn equinox.

According to the story, St Patrick, while spending Lent on Croach Patrick *(Cruachan Aigli),* was menaced by a great flock of demon birds who blacked out the sky above him and encircled the mountain on all sides. He rang his bell against them and finally dispersed them by throwing it at them in somewhat the same way as Lugh had vanquished Balar of the Evil Eye by throwing a stone from his sling, sending it right through his forehead and putting the venomous eye through the back of his head where it burned up a part of Balar's own army, as recorded in the Battle of Maigh Tuireadh. (Gray, 1982, 61) Having got rid of the demon birds, an angel came to comfort him.

Obviously, this story has associations with Our Lord's conflict with Satan in the desert and on a high mountain (Mt 4:1-11), the traditional gospel pericope for the First Sunday in Lent.

This is the dragon-fight in which the dragon takes on the form of monstrous birds. The victim in this case is the people of Ireland who are being attacked by the forces of darkness and St Patrick, the hero, intervenes to rescue them.

Another legend of St Patrick concerns his conflict with the snakes. Like the birds, these are demon entities. A folk story recorded by Douglas Hyde recalls St Patrick's exploits.

Many of the serpents had gone up to the top of Croagh Patrick (the Reek) to escape from the saint. He, on his part,

dug a large pit at the foot of the mountain and then went up
and proceeded to hunt the serpents down. They fell into the
pit and were killed. Two, however, escaped. The first escapee
charged across the country making for Lough Derg *(Loch
Dearg)* in Co Donegal, with St Patrick chasing him. The
snake made it to the island. He was known as Bolán Mór for
he was as big as a round tower. When St Patrick arrived at the
lake he had no boat. He threw off his clothes but, keeping his
crozier, he swam across the lake. The huge serpent saw him
coming and advanced to meet him. A terrible fight ensued
but in the end the dragon made a mighty swoop and swallowed St Patrick. St Patrick, however, had taken the precau-
tion of taking his crozier in with him and succeeded in hack-
ing his way out. He killed the dragon in the process and the
lake turned red with blood. Up to then it had been known as
Fionnloch (White Lake) but ever since it has been known as
Loch Dearg (Red Lake). This scene of St Patrick's Easter victory
became the site of the great pilgrimage, St Patrick's Purgatory.
There was great rejoicing among the local people as Bolán
Mór had caused terrible destruction in the area. (1915, 287 ff.)

This account approximates to the Jonas model as the hero
is actually swallowed by the monster.

A similar dramatic dragon-fight of the same Jonas model is
found in secular literature in *Duanaire Finn*.

A great dragon from Greece called Ard na Catha arrives in
Loch Cuan and challenges Fionn Mac Cumhaill and the
Fianna to battle. The beast proved impervious to swords and
spears. He killed a large number of the Fianna and swallowed
others. Fionn attacked him but, to the consternation of the
Fianna, he swallowed Fionn also. But Fionn had taken his
sword inside with him and this proved to be decisive:

> 'Dorus ar gach taobh dá chorp, do rinne Fionn nar bh'olc
> réim, gur leig amach gan fhuirech, gach nech dar sluigedh
> don Fhéin.' (Mac Neill, 1908, I, 79)

(A door on each side of its body, Fionn of no ill-fame made, and he let out without delay every one of the Fianna that had been swallowed.)

The poem (No. 24) gives a long list of the dragons and various monsters killed by Fionn.

The great thirteenth-century bishop and liturgist Durandus gives a warm and spirited account of the dragon-fight as it was performed in some places with all the colour and buoyancy of the Middle Ages. It is associated above all with the 'Major Litanies' on the Feast of St Mark (25 April – the Bealtaine period) and the 'Minor Litanies' or 'Rogation days' on the Monday, Tuesday and Wednesday before Ascension Thursday, in the Bealtaine period also.

The Rogation Processions seem to have been very popular especially in France. The custom was begun by St Mamertus, Bishop of Vienne, in the fifth century to counteract the public calamities which affected his diocese, such as flooding, earthquakes and the appearance of wolves in the streets of the city. Penitential processions were begun to avert God's anger and drive off evil forces. In areas where the Ambrosian Rite of Milan was in use, however, the Rogation Processions around the town and into the surrounding farmland were held on the Sunday after the Ascension on the grounds that 'the friends of the Bridegroom cannot fast while the Bridegroom is still with them'. (Mk 2:19)

Bishop Durandus describes the *Processio Septiformis,* consisting of clerics, monks, nuns, boys, old people, widows, married people. The Litany of the Saints is sung seven times each day as the procession winds it way through the streets and surrounding countryside, led by the cross and relics of the saints, so that the banner of the cross and the prayers of the saints may repel the demons. The priests wore black vestments in token of penance.

It was also the custom to have a huge artificial dragon

going in front of the cross and banner on the first two days of
the Rogations. On the third and last day, however, the dragon
is at the very end. For this dragon is a symbol of the devil who
through three Ages – before the Law, under the Law and in
the Age of Grace – symbolised by the three Rogation Days –
deceived the human race and desires to keep on doing so. For
the first two Ages he reigned proudly, and Christ himself referred to Satan as 'Prince of this World'. On the third day, the
Age of Grace, Christ has defeated the dragon and so he walks
(carried by men hidden in the framework) at the end of the
procession, his pride curbed. He does not dare any more to
reign powerfully but seduces people slyly by suggestions –
those whom he sees to be sluggish in good works and remiss
in following the Christian way of life. The dragon keeps looking behind him as a thief does, looking out for those who
wander and fall away from the rectitude of faith. (MDCV, 393)

The mood of our present liturgy is far removed from this
long, naïve, boisterous, dramatic, popular type of ritual. But
we can only wonder at the marvellously effective means
which earlier generations had to get across the idea of the
'Psychomachia' or spiritual warfare in which the forces of evil
are conquered by prayer and fasting. Our Lord, in the processional cross, the saints in their relics, the people in their various categories – the Communion of Saints – are seen to make
a concerted attack on the Powers of Darkness.

In the lives of many of the Irish saints, stories occur of
their exploits with *péisteanna* or dragons.

St Finbarr overcomes a dragon at Gougane Barra, Co
Cork. The saint approaches the dragon in the lake, prays and
sprinkles him with holy water. The dragon emits a mighty
roar, makes his way through the river Lee to Cork harbour
and disappears into the sea. (*Béaloideas,* 1983, 99-100) In a
spectacular episode, St Mac Creiche is shown confronting a
fire-spitting dragon called 'Broicseach'. He strikes his bell fur-

iously and recites a very fine example of the Celtic *Lúireach* or spiritual battle song, *Do neimh ar ccul go ccuire Crist:*

May Christ repel your venom …

O savage 'Broicseach', press not upwards,
O dumb 'Broicseach', though rough the encounter,
I am to subdue you, trusting in holy Christ.

The seven archangels from the fair city (heaven),
God has ordained them to repel you from me;
The four noble evangelists shall lower your strength,
Matthew and Mark in their mighty host, Luke and John.

I entreat the saints, I entreat the virgins,
I entreat them all, that they may be a strong band,
to help me, all the saints of the lasting world,
That all of them, north and south will assist my prayer.
(Plummer, 1925, 40, 80)

As is the case in other *Lúireacha*, not only is Our Lord's help invoked but that of the various categories of saints in the heavenly city. In this case, the dragon is overcome only with the greatest difficulty. As he traverses a river he spits out balls of fire. Mac Creiche prays to God as a bull-fighter prays before entering the ring. He beats his bell and at the third stroke a ball of fire shoots out from the bell and sets the monster's maw ablaze. The dragon plunges into the river with horrible screams and Mac Creiche, with his *bachall* in his hand, pursues him along the river, men, women and children following behind him in a procession comparable to that of the Rogation Procession described by Bishop Durandus. The dragon arrives at Loch na Rátha and plunges in and a great shout arises from the crowd. The victory is short-lived, however, for soon the monster puts his head above the lake, causing it to overflow its banks. Mac Creiche prays again, clutches his hat and flings it at the monster. The hat enlarges miraculously and takes on the form of a great metal cover as it descends on the head of the dragon forcing him down into the depths of the lake, *Poll na Broicsí*, where he remains to this day. Loch na Rátha itself, near Corofin, Co Clare, is known as Loch Broic Sí, from this episode, the lake of the fairy badger. (cf. Plummer, 1925, 80-82)

Here the engagement with the demon is laid out on the Clare landscape and it is ultimately connected with Christ's temptation in the desert and the prayer for Ash Wednesday:

Concede nobis, Domine, praesidia militiae christianae sanctis inchoare jejuniis: ut contra spiritales nequitias pugnaturi, continentiae muniamur auxiliis.

(Grant us, O Lord, to begin our Christian warfare with holy fasts; that as we are about to do battle with the spirits of evil we may be defended by the aid of self-denial.) (Trans. *The Saint Andrew Daily Missal*, 1945, 272)

This wonderful prayer, found in both the old and the new rite, is faithfully translated as above in the *St Andrew Missal* as it is in the Irish version:

Deonaigh dúinn, a Dhia, go gcuirimid tús leis an gcath Críostaí seo le troscadh naofa. Go mba sciath chosanta againn ár smacht ar ár gcolainn agus sinn ag dul chun troda le cumhachtaí na n-ainspiorad. (*An Leabhar Aifrinn*, 1978, 67)

In the English language version of the *Missale Romanum* (Dublin, 1974, 74) the translation is as follows:

Lord, protect us in our struggle against evil. As we begin the discipline of Lent, make this season holy by our self-denial.

This text appears to be a somewhat inadequate rendering of the original.

PART THREE

Celtic Piety

CHAPTER ELEVEN

Traditional Gaelic Prayers

In the Gaelic tradition of Ireland and Scotland there exists a remarkable collection of folk-prayers which have their own quite distinctive style. In recent years, a large selection of the Irish prayers has been gathered together in one volume by Diarmuid Ó Laoghaire SJ. (*Ár bPaidreacha Dúchais,* F.Á.S., Dublin, 1975). A similar collection was made in Scotland by Alexander Carmichael (*Ortha nan Gaidheal,* Edinburgh, 1972, VOLS 1-3).

The Irish prayers are generally short and in verse form and this naturally made for easy memorisation without the use of books.

The vast majority of these prayers are in a simple colloquial style which indicates that they were composed for the most part by non-professional poets during the past few centuries. Nevertheless, some of these relatively modern compositions embody ideas which go back to remote antiquity.

It is probable that the collection originated in the following way: After the battle of Kinsale at the beginning of the seventeenth century, the Celtic order of society finally collapsed. The chieftains immigrated or were dispossessed leaving the *filí* or court-poets without patronage. They were forced to take up whatever occupation was to be found and, especially in Munster, made a desperate attempt to keep the ancient culture alive by the establishment of the *Cúirt filíochta* at various centres such as Blarney, Baile Bhuirne, Teampall Geal, Carraig na bhFear, Cois Mhaighe. In this they partially succeeded and so the Celtic culture has passed down to our own day.

But, the aristocratic poets now found themselves among the ordinary people and had to accommodate themselves to the new situation. The highly sophisticated metrical compositions of bardic poetry were gradually abandoned for simpler and more popular forms of versification. It would appear that this contact with the disinherited professional poets had the effect of inspiring even ordinary people to attempt to compose their own verses and, naturally, some of these were of a religious nature.

This would explain to some extent the proliferation of the folk-prayers during this period. Almost all of these are in the Irish language and in Father Ó Laoghaire's collection practically none have come from Leinster, as the language began to disappear in that province much earlier than elsewhere. These texts are so unequivocally Gaelic and embody so much of the Celtic mentality that no translation can do them justice. When, finally, the language disappeared from common use in most parts of the country, the folk-prayer tradition disappeared also, leaving a lacuna in the spiritual life of the nation which has never been filled. Ireland became the dumping ground for a host of individualistic and sentimental pious practices introduced from England and the Continent in an endeavour to fill the gap. These, unfortunately, were often of a highly individualistic and sentimental character little suited to the native temperament.

While the great religious poem, *Gile mo Chroí,* attributed to Tadhg Gaelach Ó Súilleabháin, could hardly be classed as a folk-prayer because of its incredible sophistication and artistry, nevertheless, I would like to include part of it here as an example of religious poetry which could be ranked among the greatest composed in any language:

Duan Chroí Íosa

Gile mo chroí do chroí-se, a Shlánaitheoir,
is ciste mo chroí do chroí-se a dháil im chomhair;
ós follas gur líon do chroí dem ghrá-sa, a stóir,
i gcochall mo chroí do chroíse fág i gcomhad.

Ar fhuilingis trínne, a Rí ghil ard na gcomhacht,
ní thigeann im smaointe a shuíomh ná a thrácht i gcóir,
's gur le gora-ghoin nimhe do chroí 's do chneá-sa, a stóir,
do bhrostaigh na mílte saoi go sámh i gcoróinn.

An uair chasfadsa arís led ghuí-se, a bhláth na n-ord,
fá thearmainn Chríost is díon a ghrás 'om chomhad,
beidh garbhchnoic fraoigh na líog do chráigh mé romham
'na machairí míne síoda 's 'na mbánta sróill.

(The light in my heart, O Saviour, is Thy heart,
the wealth of my heart, Thy heart poured out for me.
Seeing that Thy heart, Love, filled with love for me
leave Thy heart in keeping, hooded in mine.

The pains we have caused thee, bright high King of the
Powers,
their nature and number, truly my mind cannot hold.
The noxious hot hurt in thy heart and thy wound, O
Love,
sweetly hurried the just in thousands to their Crown.

And when I return and have prayed to thee, Flower of the
Orders,
in the refuge of Christ, with the guard of his grace about me,
the harsh stony heathery hills that troubled me once
will alter to silk smooth plains and pastures of satin.
(Ó Tuama, agus Kinsella, 1981, 190-193)

We have here undoubtedly a Gaelicisation of the newly-introduced devotion to the Sacred Heart. But with the internal rhyme and the controlled emotion it has undergone a metamorphosis. The beautiful imagery of the last lines suggests the Celtic supernatural where the poet, worn out by tramping through the rough heather-covered mountains, sees them transfigured into gentle folds of silk and plains of satin in a world made new.

A highly distinctive feature of Celtic Christianity is the way in which the native culture and the teaching of the gospel were intermingled. This trait can be found in many folk-prayers and can be illustrated in *Ortha na Féile* or 'Hospitality Prayer' from Scotland:

Chonaic mé coigríoch inné,
Chuir mé bia in áit idhidh dó,
Deoch in áit óil,
Ceol in áit éisteachta,
is in ainm naofa na tríonóide
do bheannaigh sé mé fhéin
is mo theach,
mo ní is mo dhuine;
is dúirt an fhuiseog
is í ag seinm
gur minic, minic, minic,
a thagann Críost i ríocht an choigrígh.
(Scottish Council for Research in Education, 1964, 96)
(I saw a stranger yesterday, I put food for him in the eating place; drink for him in the drinking place; music in the listening place. And in the sacred name of the Trinity he blessed myself and my house, my possessions and my people; and the lark said as she was singing: that it is often, often, often Christ comes in the form of a stranger)

Here, the man of the house sees a stranger coming; he prepares food in the eating place, drink in the drinking place, music in the listening place. The stranger blesses him and his household in the name of the Trinity. Meanwhile, the lark sings and provides the interpretation of the occurrence. 'Often, often, often,' she says, 'Christ comes disguised as a stranger.'

Obviously, this is based on the scriptural text: 'I was hungry and you gave me to eat ...' But, notice how the idea of music, not found in the biblical text, is introduced. The speaker is thinking of a harper at a Celtic feast. As we know from the old stories, hospitality was a virtue among the Celts before the introduction of Christianity and a stranger was often entertained royally for several days before being asked what his business was. *(Is túisce deoch ná scéal.)* But, perhaps the most remarkable part of the text is the commentary supplied by the lark. The 'minic, minic, minic' imitates the notes of the lark and she supplies the Christian interpretation of the occurrence. Here we have an illustration of the Celtic pre-occupation with nature. The Celtic culture, unlike the cultures of Greece and Rome, was a rural culture in which the life of the people was intimately bound up with the land and with the sea. The Celtic Christian God is often referred to as *Rí na nDúl* – the King of the Elements – earth, air, fire, water and perhaps a fifth element, spirit, joining the other four. There may be here also a dim recollection of an archaic philosophy of integration in which one thing influenced another. In any event, it is unlikely that in other cultures the interpretation of a supernatural event would be left to a lark's singing.

This short text also involves a journey into the realm of pagan mythology. According to the legend, the mother of Oisín (Son of Fionn Mac Cumhail) had been changed into a deer by a druid. Oisín used to visit her on the mountain where she lived and,

Chuir sí bia in áit ithidh dó,

Deoch in áit óil,

Ceol in áit éisteachta.

The *Ortha na Féile,* then, provides a key to the understanding of Gaelic folk-prayers as it shows the essentially integralist character of Celtic Christianity in which demarcations between old and new break down and a unique type of Christianity emerges which is a composite of the many facets of the Celtic culture and the teaching of the gospels.

The *Altú roimh Bhia* or Prayer before Meals illustrates the use of archetypes in folk-piety:

Bail na gcúig arán agus an dá iasc
a roinn Dia ar an gcúig mhíle fear.
Rath ón Rí a rinne an roinn
go dtaga sé ar ár gcuid
agus ar ár gcomhroinn. (ÁPD 36)

(The blessing of the five loaves and two fishes that God divided among the five thousand men – the blessing from the King, who made the division, may it come on our portion and on our sharing.)

There is obvious reference here to the miracle of the loaves and fishes and the speaker requests that the sacredness of this action descends on the action of eating now being performed. The use of the archetype represents a return to archaic thought-patterns to be found in many ancient cultures, particularly in New Year Festivals. The narrative of the creation is recited or sung or danced at the beginning of the year. This primordial event took place in 'the age of the gods', 'in illo tempore', 'in arche', 'in the time outside time', 'fadó, fadó'.

But in the ritual it is brought into relationship with the present time and the sacredness of the primordial event descends into the present. We have an example of this in the Christian Easter Vigil in the lighting of the new fire and the recitation of the creation narrative. While the miracle of the loaves and fishes is a historical event, it is treated here as the work of a divine Person taking place in the 'time outside time' and its power descends into the present time. (Eliade, 1954, 21-27)

A very beautiful prayer after meals is as follows:

Míle buíochas duit, a Thiarna Dia;
an té 'thug an bheatha seo dúinn
go dtuga sé an bheatha dar n-anamacha.
Más fearr atáimid inniu,
Go mba seacht bhfearr
a bhéas muid blian ó inniu,
ár gcuid agus ár ndaoine
slán i ngrá Dé
agus i ngrá na gcomharsan,
i dtrócaire agus i ngrásta,
i saol agus i sláinte. (ÁPD 46)

(A thousand thanks to you Lord God. The One who gave
us this food/life may he give food/life to our souls. If we be
well off today, may we be seven times better off a year from
today, our possessions and our people safe in the love of
God and our neighbours, in mercy and in grace, in life and
in health.)

Here the idea of earthly life, sustained by food, is elevated
to the idea of heavenly life sustained by the Eucharist. The
next part contains the idea of thanksgiving for present prosperity and the hope that this would continue and increase. I
suspect that the phrase 'bliain ó inniu' refers to the common
idea of 'a year and a day' *(bliain agus lá),* since at the evening
meal a day would already have gone by. It is thought the 'bliain
agus lá' of Irish and Welsh legend refers to a Celtic lunar calendar of 13 moons of 28 days each. This would make up 364
days. An extra day was needed to reconcile it with the solar
year.

The calendrical motif is found again in a bedtime prayer
which also attempts to describe the Trinity in terms of contradiction to illustrate its mystery:

An Triúr is sine, an Triúr is óige,
an Triúr is treise i gcathair na glóire,
an tAthair, an Mac is an Spiorad Naomh
do m'shábháil, do m'ghárdáil
ó anocht go dtí bliain ó anocht
agus anocht féin. (ÁPD 265)
(The Three that are the oldest, the Three that are
youngest, the Three that are strongest in the city of glory –
the Father, Son and Holy Spirit – may they be protecting
me, saving me, from tonight until a year from tonight and
tonight itself.)

The Theme of Protection
The 'protection theme' is also found here and this theme is of
great importance in Gaelic spirituality.

It was customary to bless the bed with a short formula and
the Sign of the Cross made over it from bottom to top and
across the centre, before going to sleep at night. Sometimes
this was done three times and sometimes the Sign of the Cross
was made with the thumb – a very ancient usage conserved at
the announcement of the gospel and at baptism in the Roman
Rite. The idea of protection is a feature of this ritual. The Sign
of the Cross stands between the person and all harm:

Cros Chríost idir mé agus namhaid m'anama is mo choirp.
(Ag déanamh fíor na croise trí huaire ar éadach na leapa.)
(ÁPD 279). (The Cross of Christ between me and the
enemy of my soul and body. – *Making the Sign of the Cross
three times over the bedclothes.*)

The identity of the *namhaid* (enemy) is made clear in an
alternative blessing; it is the Adversary/Devil/Satan:

Fíor na croise naofa céasta cumhachtach idir mé agus an
tÁibhirseoir. (APD 277) (The sign of the holy powerful
cross of crucifixion be between me and the Adversary.)

Another simple night prayer is similarly concerned with protection:

Go raibh ar leaba chodlata
na leaba shocair shuain,
is go n-éirímid ar maidin
i ndídean Dé go buan. (ÁPD 285)
(May our bed of sleep be a bed safe for repose and may we arise in the morning in the permanent protection of God.)

There is found also a prayer for making the bed which invokes the Trinity. This probably recalls the Sign of the Cross made over the bed at night to which the invocation of the Trinity was added in some places. (ÁPD 278) The mention of the Trinity leads to the idea of heaven in which the saints and apostles mentioned in the prayer surround the throne of God. The idea of conception associated with the darkness of the night leads to the notion of the birth into the new life of the Trinity in baptism in the light of day. In this prayer, said in association with the simple operation of making the bed, ideas related to the sacrament of baptism can be discerned. There are echoes here of Our Lord's teaching on baptism: 'Unless a man is born through water and the Spirit, he cannot enter the kingdom of God: what is born of the flesh is flesh; what is born of the Spirit is spirit.' (Jn 3:5-6) Baptism is performed in the name of the Father, Son and Holy Spirit and in Jesus' own baptism (Mt 3:16-17) the Trinity is present – the Holy Spirit descends in the form of a dove and the voice of the Father is heard announcing: 'This is my Son, the Beloved.'

A certain chain of ideas leads from a prosaic natural operation to a consciousness of the divine – bed, night, conception, darkness, supernatural birth, the Trinity, the court of heaven, light:

Cóirím an leaba seo anocht (inniu)
in ainm an Athar, an Mhic agus an Spioraid Naoimh,
in ainm na hoíche a gineadh sinn,

in ainm an lae a baisteadh sinn,
in ainm gach naoimh is gach aspail
dá bhfuil sna Flaithis. (ÁPD 160)
(I make this bed tonight (today) in the name of the Father,
the Son and the Holy Spirit, in the name of the night in
which we were conceived, in the name of the day on which
we were baptised, in the name of every saint and every
apostle in heaven.)

Another night prayer is concerned with disturbed sleep
and puts the cross of Christ and the three holy women as a
protection against nightmare. These same three women are
invoked for a safe childbirth and this may have been the original situation for these three had unusual births. Mary was a
virgin and Anne and Elizabeth were barren. The connection
with sound and healthy sleep may be a transfer from the original case, (Ó Duinn, 1990, 61):
Anna, máthair Mhuire,
Muire, Máthair Chríost,
Éilís, máthair Eoin Baiste,
cuirim an triúr sin idir mé agus
éagruas na leapa,
agus an crann ar céasadh Mac Dé air
idir mé agus an tromluí go lá. (ÁPD 312)
(Anne, mother of Mary, Mary, mother of Christ, Elizabeth,
mother of John the Baptist, I put these three between me
and sleep-weakness, and the tree on which Christ was tortured between me and nightmare until day dawns.)

From this we move to a very short but widely known
morning prayer to be said when getting up:
Éirím suas le Dia,
go n-éirí Dia liom.
Lámh Dé i mo thimpeall,
ag suí is ag luí
is ag éirí dom. (ÁPD 8)

(I rise up with God, may God rise up with me. The arm of
God around me, when going about and in bed and at rising.)

This would mean then, that God is with me while I am
performing all three activities – getting up, going about my
business during the day and going to bed at night – and in all
of these his protecting arm encircles me. Now, as well as God
and myself performing these three actions, is there anything
else which acts likewise? And of course, there is – the sun. The
sun rises in the east in the morning, it goes about its business
travelling around the earth during the day, and goes to bed in
the west when night comes. Here then, we have a cosmic vision
in which God, myself and the sun are united in the mystery of
movement and repose.

The Cosmic Vision
In the Hebrides, it was customary for men to uncover the
head on seeing the sun – the 'Eye of the Great God' – in the
morning:

Súil Dhé mhóir
Súil Dhé na glóir'
Súil Dhé na slogh,
ag doirteadh orainn
go fóill agus go fial. (Slightly adapted: *CG* 3, 316)
(The eye of the great God, the eye of the God of glory, still
beaming down on us generously.)

A note in *Carmina Gadelica* describes the ritual of greeting
the rising and setting sun:

The reciter said: There was a man in Arasaig, and he was
extremely old, and he would make adoration to the sun
and to the moon and to the stars. When the sun would rise
on the tops of the peaks he would put off his head-covering and he would bow down his head, giving glory to the
great God of life for the glory of the sun and for the good-

ness of its light to the children of men and to the animals of the world. When the sun set in the western ocean the old man would again take off his head-covering, and he would bow his head to the ground and say:

Thá mise an dóchas na thráth
Nach cuir Dia mór nan ágh
As domhsa solas nan grás
Mar thá thusa dha m'fhágail a nochd.

(I am in hope, in its proper time,
That the great and gracious God
Will not put out for me the light of grace
Even as thou dost leave me this night.)

The old man said that he had learned this from his father and from the old men of the village when he was a small child.

Having seen the traditional veneration of the sun in Gaelic Scotland, we now look at the particular importance of the moon in the case of the people of the Hebrides off the western coast.

Fishing on a moonless night amidst tortuous reefs and rocks was not only hazardous but could be a matter of life and death. Among several 'Moon-Prayers' we have a very short one remarkable for its poetic beauty and its emphasis on the sound 'ú':

Glór duit féin, a Dhé na nDúl,
ar son lóchrann iúil an chuain,
do lámha féin ar fheilm mo stiúir,
is do rún ar chúl nan stuagh. (Slightly adapted: *CG* 3, 305)

(Glory be to you, O God of the Elements. for the shining lantern of the ocean; may your own hands be guiding my rudder and your mysterious love behind the waves.)

The people of the Island of Barra saluted sun, moon and stars as is told so graphically by Mór Mac Néill:

Nach mór is córa dhomhsa mo cholann a chlaonadh dh'an
ghréin agus dh'an ghealaich agus dha na reultaibh a
chruthaich Dia mór nan dúl dha mo mhath seach do
mhac nó do nighean talmbaidh mar mi féin?" (*CG* 3, 303)
(Is it not much more proper for me to bow my body to the
sun, moon, and stars that the great God of the Elements
created for my benefit, than to a son or a daughter of the
earth like myself?)

The simple ritual of saluting the new moon is given in the
Rann:

Tá mé ag lubadh duit mo ghlún,
tá mé ag tabhairt duit mo lámh,
tá mé ag tógail duit mo shúl,
a ghealach úr na dtráth. (Slightly adapted, *CG* 3, 306) (I am
bending my knees to you; I am extending my hands to you;
I am lifting my eyes to you, O New Moon of the periods.)

Caesar, in *De Bello Gallico* (VI), describes the druids as having many discussions about the stars and their movements,
the size of the universe and of the earth, the order of nature,
the strength and powers of the immortal gods and says that
they pass on this lore to their young students. It may be that
Christian tradition, in native folk-prayers, has preserved certain remnants of ancient pedagogy.

In the Islands, it was thought that meat, from a pig or a
sheep killed during the *earradhubh* or waning of the moon
would be tasteless, and that likewise, the sap of hazels and wil-
lows used to make baskets and pine wood for boats, descended
into the root during the waning period of the moon rendering the wood quite unsuitable. All these operations should be
performed *ri líonadh nó ri airde na gealaiche* – with the waxing
of the moon or the full moon. In other words, it was understood that the phases of the moon affected certain materials
used in daily life. (*CG* 3, 304) In all this we have an illustration

of a civilisation in which the person was conscious of living within an ordered reality which had its own rules. He had an awareness and a knowledge of this ordered machinery of the universe and, by respecting it and integrating himself into it, he could survive in an environment in which nature was not particularly bountiful. As we have seen, in the texts, God was seen as *Dia na nDúl,* the God of the Elements, so that all the immense variety of nature with its complex laws and operations was referred back to its central source in the Deity, the Lord of the Universe.

Among our collection of Irish folk-prayers we have one from Co Mayo which in a very comprehensive way invokes blessings on a living person in a manner somewhat reminiscent of *Lúireach Phádraig.* It is a very useful type of intercession to be made on behalf of somebody for whom one should pray and tends to be repetitive in the sense that, having said it once, one remembers others for whom one should also pray.

Go mbeannaí Muire
is go mbeannaí Dia thú.
Go mbeannaí na haspail (haingil?)
is go mbeannaí na naoimh thú.
Go mbeannaí an ghealach gheal
is go mbeannaí an ghrian thú.
Go mbeannaí an fear thoir
is go mbeannaí an fear thiar thú
is go mbeannaí mé féin
i ndeireadh thiar thú. (ÁPD 382)
(May Mary bless you and may God bless you. May the apostles (angels?) and the saints bless you. May the bright moon and the sun bless you. May the eastern man and the western man bless you. And last of all may I myself bless you.)

One could expand this text by inserting *muir agus tír, thuaidh agus theas* (sea and land, north and south) to provide something close to some sections of St Patrick's Breastplate.

The prayer begins with an invocation of God and Mary, Mary being placed before God on account of the rhyme.

Possibly *aingil* is a better reading than *aspail* and this provides us with the idea of the heavenly court made up of angels and saints. Here a kind of hierarchy is established in the otherworld. God and the Virgin Mary are kept close together and traditionally Mary is queen of angels and queen of saints.

The next stage downwards from the supernatural sphere of heaven is to the sun and moon as representing the major cosmic elements which give light and life and heat to our world and control the ordered movement of the seasons. In our prayer, then, we not only invoke God, the Virgin Mary, the angels and the saints, but also the forces of nature, the elements themselves, to shower a blessing on the person for whom we are praying. We see the four elements expressly mentioned in the long and curious religious poem, *Ateoch friut an dechmad.* (Plummer, 1925, 102-107):

Aiteoch muintir nime,
Co Michel ngland nglesda;
Atteoch friut in treidhe,
Gaith, is grein is escca.

Atteoch friut an usci,
Ocus inn aer nangbaid;
Atteoch friut in tenid
Atteoch friut in talmain.

Modern Irish:
Achainím ar Mhuintir Neimhe
le Micheál glanghléasta;
achainim ort tríd an tréidhe
– gaoth is grian is éasca.

Achainím ort tríd an uisce
agus tríd an aer glan anfach;
achainím ort tríd an tine,
achainím ort tríd an talamh.

(I entreat the company of heaven with bright-armed Michael; I entreat you by the trinity – wind and sun and moon. I entreat you by water and the cruel air; I entreat you by fire. I entreat you by earth.)

Here the elements are used as intermediaries between the person making the prayer and God, in much the same way as we say: 'We make our prayer (to you, O God) through Christ our Lord', *per Christum Dominum nostrum.*

In Irish God is called *Dia na nDúl,* the God of the Elements, earth air, fire and water, and the invocation of the elements is a feature which occurs fairly frequently in ancient and more recent texts. This makes the Celtic texts rather distinctive and unusual – and seems to point to the immanence of God. The two stanzas of *Ateoch friut an dechmad* are part of a long poem which Plummer names 'Litany of Creation' and in his introduction he makes an interesting commentary on the unusual nature of this text:

> But the peculiarity of the piece consists in this: that although a few of the petitions are based on the ordinary objects of Christian devotion, in the great majority of them the appeal is made by means of purely natural objects: I adjure Thee by wind and sun and moon; by water, air, fire and earth; by the torrid zone, the temperate and frigid zones; the stars, the animals, and the inanimate creation. Is it a faint echo of ancient nature worship? Or is it the work of a physicist proud of his knowledge of nature? (1925, xxiv)

Again, Plummer remarks on the curious syncretic piece describing the securities for the observance of the law, *Cáin Adamnáin:* 'grian ocus esca, dúle Dé arcenaeg Petar, Pól, Andreas.' (1910, cxxxv) (sun and moon and other elements of God, Peter, Paul, Andrew.)

In matters of legal sureties, the matter arises again in the case of King Laoghaire whose periodic incursions into Leinster to collect taxes was a constant source of annoyance. Finally, Laoghaire was beaten in battle and he swore on oath to the Leinstermen that he would never try to collect booty from them again as long as he lived. The Leinstermen released him on this condition. He took as his sureties: 'grian ocus ésca, usci ocus aer, lá ocus adaig, muir ocus tír' (sun and moon, water and air, day and night, sea and land). But Laoghaire broke his oath. Soon he was back again but this time the elements killed him:

Atbath Loegaire mac Neill
for táeb Chassi glas a tír,
duli Dé adroegaid raith
tucsat dal báis forsin rig. (Best and Bergin, 1970, 294-295)
(Laoghaire Mac Neill died beside Caisse – green its land, his sureties – God's Elements – it was they who killed the king.)

The elements, earth, air, fire, water, sun, moon, etc., appear to have been used to swear by as people in Christian countries swear by the Bible. This placed a very serious compulsion on the person to abide by his oath or promise. While a modern perjurer may not feel that the Bible is going to rise up and strike him dead, it does appear that in ancient Ireland swearing by the elements was considered to be a very serious matter and that the elements had the power in themselves of avenging their misuse. However difficult to explain on a philosophical basis, it is clear that a divine power impregnated the elements.

In the celebrated conversation between St Patrick and the daughters of Laoghaire at the well of Clebech, as described in the *Vita Tripartita*, St Patrick explains that God is behind the elements and more fundamental than they, even though he resides in them, *Inspirat omnia, vivificat omnia, superat omnia, suffultat (suffulcit) omnia. Solis lumen illuminat et lumen lune.* (Stokes, 1887, 100-102) (He breathes into everything, he enlivens/gives life to, everything, he surpasses everything, he supports beneath/underprops everything. He lights up the light of the sun and he lights up the light of the moon.)

The universe is filled with God's active power as the Burning Bush was filled with his divinity. (Exod 3:2-6) But even though the bush was a theophany, a manifestation of God, it still was not consumed, it retained its own shape and form even while radiating the fire of God. It seems that to the Celts every bush was a burning bush – a manifestation of the divinity behind it and that theophany, the showing forth of God in nature, was a vital element in the Gaelic way to the world of the divine.

One of my earliest recollections as a child in the countryside is of taking a horse to the forge for a new set of shoes. As we jogged along, the marvellous sound of the anvil being pounded could be heard in the quiet air, more mysterious because more irregular than church bells. The forge always appeared to be dark and cavernous and filled with the shadows thrown by the fire, ever changing, as the assistant blacksmith operated an enormous bellows making the fire glow with an intensity of heat. The blacksmith himself, stripped to the waist, with mighty chest and muscles, pounded the glowing metal on the anvil to mould it into the form of a horseshoe. When ready, he plunged it into a tank of water and a sizzling spurt of steam shot up into the air. No wonder that for the Celts the blacksmith, the *gabha,* was a revered figure, a man of magic who understood the mystery of transformation to the extent that he could convert this heavy colourless iron into a glowing fiery mass and then mould it into the forms necessary for agriculture. The forge was a place of mystery. Here was life, men, women, horses, fire and water, rhythmic sound, the strange mutual relationship between the man and the horse and their relationship to metal through fire and water. Obviously the blacksmith (Old Irish *gobae*) has his archetype in Goibniu, the smith-god of the Tuatha Dé Danann.

Highly prominent in *Cath Maighe Tuireadh,* where he forges the weapons for the Tuatha Dé Danann in their war against the Fomhóraigh, the dark gods of the sea, he is also the host at the underworld feast, *Fled Goibnenn.* He provides the guests with enormous quantities of intoxicating drink, but instead of getting drunk they receive protection against old age and decay. (MacKillop, 1998, 227-228)

But the great mystery is in the flaming molten metal. The dark heavy material has been penetrated by fire and taken on its colour and form. The transformation is little less than incredible. How could such a metamorphosis take place? After a little while, when taken from the fire, released from the penetrating source, the iron will again return to its original form, but while penetrated its nature is so changed that we are confronted by a flaming mass of fire. Something like this must have occurred at the transfiguration of Christ: 'his face shone like the sun and his clothes became as white as the light.' (Mt 17:2) Here the divinity of Christ manifested itself in the flesh for a brief moment only to be replaced again by the familiar figure. But, of course, the divinity was always there, hidden behind the mask of Christ's body. The transfiguration is the great scene in which we see the form of the Risen Christ in heaven and the form which our own risen bodies will have: 'For when they rise from the dead, men and women do not marry; no, they are like the angels in heaven.' (Mk 12:25) This great feast of the fiery transformation of Christ into his risen form on 6 August deserves far greater recognition than it gets. It illustrates Christ's and our own final state and is well placed to coincide with the Festival of Lughnasa in the Celtic tradition, the beginning of harvest and the pilgrimage season. In Irish monastic circles, it may have been the third Easter, Christmas being the first.

St Patrick's Breastplate and the Concept of Neart
We may see fire as the overall symbol of divinity penetrating matter, transforming it, sustaining it. This idea of a strange power or life-force permeating everything, can perhaps be best seen in St Patrick's Breastplate, the well-known protection prayer of the eighth century. On several occasions the word *nert/niurt* occurs corresponding to the modern Irish *neart* – 'strength', 'force', 'power'. The omission of the preposition but the retention of the dative case makes the interpretation difficult.

This archaic poem is divided into sections and the first five of these begin with the phrase *Atomriug indiu* – 'I arise/raise myself up/put around me'. It is a morning poem containing the idea of getting up and putting on one's clothes. In this case it is layers of spiritual armour one puts on to protect oneself from the attacks of malignant enemies who seek to destroy both soul and body. The poem is reminiscent of the scene in *Táin Bó Chuailnge* where Cú Chulainn puts on several layers of armour as he sets out to fight the terrible battle of Muirtheimhne.

Atomriug indiu
niurt trén togairm trindóit
cretim treodatad
fóistin oendatad
in dúleman dail.
(I arise today
through a mighty strength, the invocation of the Trinity
through belief in the threeness
through confession of the oneness
of the beloved Creator.)

The *neart* filling the person comes from the invocation of the Trinity, the confession of the one nature and three divine Persons. It is noticeable also that the Creator is mentioned in association with the Trinity. In other words, we are led to the idea of the power of the Trinity going outside itself to form the universe.

This first Trinitarian section may be compared to the opening of the Litany of the Saints, which similarly invokes the Trinity:

Pater de caelis, Deus, miserere nobis.

Fili Redemptor mundi, Deus, miserere nobis.

Spiritus Sancte, Deus, Miserere nobis.

Sancta Trinitas, unus Deus, miserere nobis.

(God the Father of heaven; God the Son, Redeemer of the world; God the Holy Spirit; Holy Trinity, one God, have mercy on us.)

The second section concerns the *neart* emanating from the acts or deeds of Christ's life:

Atomriug indiu

niurt gene Crist cona bathius

nuirt a chrochtho cona adnacul

niurt a essérgi cona fresgabáil

niurt a thóiniuda fri brithemnas mbrátho.

(I arise today

With/through the strength of the birth of Christ with his baptism,

through the strength of his crucifixion with his burial,

through the strength of his resurrection with his ascension,

through the strength of his descent for the Judgement of Doom.)

Again, a corresponding section is found in the ancient Litany of the Saints: *Per Adventum tuum, per Nativitatem tuam, etc., libera nos, Domine.* (Through your coming, through your birth, etc. set us free, O Lord.) While the preposition *per* (through) is given in the litany, the preposition is omitted in St Patrick's Breastplate but in English translations is often given as 'through' as in the Latin. We have seen already that this carries the idea of communication, of opening a gap so that the human and divine may come into contact with each other.

This section is an 'anamnesis' – a recalling of the works of Christ performed for our salvation – as we have it in the Eucharistic Prayer: 'Father, calling to mind the death your Son endured for our salvation, his glorious resurrection and ascension into heaven, and ready to greet him when he comes again, we offer you in thanksgiving this holy and living sacrifice.' (No 3)

We have here in embryonic form the feasts of the year, the Nativity, the Baptism of Christ (Epiphany/Sunday after Epiphany), good Friday, Easter Sunday, Ascension, Parousia or Final Coming in Judgement – last Sundays of the liturgical year.

Like the trinitarian formula with which the *Lúireach* began, this second section also forms a 'prayer unit' which goes back to a very early period of the church. The impression is given that certain 'prayer units' were available from a very remote period which could be used in different situations such as general intercessions, protection prayers and Eucharistic celebrations.

The thought here, however, seems to be that these acts of Christ's life contain *neart* – a kind of dynamic power which gives protection to the person against evil whenever he invokes these acts, that is, when he says with confidence:

Éirím inniu
trí neart breithe Chríost lena bhaisteadh,
trí neart a chrochta lena adhlacadh,
trí neart a aiséirí lena dheascabháil,
trí neart a thuirlingthe do bhreithiúnas brátha.

In saying the formula, he is gathering, binding about himself, the armour power of Christ's acts. Here we are in the presence of powerful, archaic thought forms. It is as if we plunged the iron in the fire and watched it become suffused with the mysterious flaming element.

Section Three:
Atomriug indiu
niurt gráid Hiruphin
i nerlattaid aingel
i frestal na narchaingel
hi frescisin esséirgi archenn fochraicce
i nernaigthib huasalathrach
i tairchetlaib fáthe
hi praiceptaib apstal
i nhiresaib fóismedach
i nenccai nóebingen
i ngnímaib fer fírien.
(I arise today
through the strength of the order of cherubim,
in obedience of angels,
in the service of the archangels,
in hope of resurrection to meet with reward,
in prayers of patriarchs,
in predictions of prophets,
in preachings of apostles,
in faith of confessors,
in innocence of holy virgins,
in deeds of righteous men.

This section concerns the heavenly world, and the communion of saints. The person rises up and binds about himself, equips himself, with the power of the Angelic Order of Seraphim. In the vision of Isaiah 6:1-7, the Seraphim surround the throne of God and cry out 'Holy, Holy, Holy'. The name means 'the fiery ones'. (*Dictionary Concordance* 1970, 615) Then the angels and archangels are invoked. These are the celestial spirits. This part corresponds to the Litany of the Saints: *Omnes sancti angeli et archangeli.* (all ye holy orders of blessed Spirits, pray for us.)

   The second part of this section turns to the orders of saints and each order is identified with the activity which characterises it – prayers of patriarchs, predictions of prophets, and so forth. This is the teeming world of the communion of saints. This supernatural throng had its counterpart in the antique world of the Tuatha Dé Danann and its multitude of spirits.

Section Four:
Atomriug indiu
niurt nime
soilse gréne
etrochtae ésci
áne thened
déne lóchet

lúathe gáithe
fudomnae maro
tairisminge t[h]alman
cobsaide ailech

(I arise today
through the strength of heaven
light of sun.
brilliance of moon,
splendour of fire,
speed of lightning,

swiftness of wind,
depth of sea,
stability of earth
firmness of rock.) (Stokes and Strachan, 1903, 354-356)

This passage has no parallel in the Litany of the Saints and echoes an archaic philosophy of the unity of Being. The elements themselves will build a protective circle around the person to defend him as they, on a contrary mission, brought destruction on King Laoghaire who had insulted them.

The *neart neimhe* is undoubtedly the 'firmament with its

showers of stars' mentioned by Conchúr Mac Neasa in *Táin Bó Chuailnge*. The list of elements are those which are most spectacular and effective in nature, causing both growth and destruction. The person praying feels himself to be an integral part of the universe made up of these elements. This type of cosmic consciousness in which the *file/*god identifies himself with the actual forces of nature, reaches its fullest extreme in the poem of Amergin:

Am gaeth i muir,
Am tonn treathain,
Am fuaim mara,
Am dam secht ndirend,
Am seg for ail,
Am der ngreine … etc.
(*Lebor Gabála Érenn,* Macalister, 1956, v, 110)
(I am wind on sea, I am an ocean wave, I am sound of sea, I am an ox of seven fights, I am a hawk on a cliff, I am a tear of the sun.)

In the so-called *Lorica of Leyde* (ZCP, 2, 1898, 66-72) the elements are invoked directly in the same way as the angels and saints are called upon, nor are birds, beasts and reptiles excluded: the piece is obviously related to the canticle of the Three Young men in the Fiery Furnace (Daniel 3:57-88, 56), in which the three young men who have been thrown into the fire suffer no harm and call on all creation to bless the Lord: 'All ye works of the Lord, bless the Lord; O sun and moon, bless the Lord; O nights and days, bless the Lord', etc. Here the various elements, as well as the angels and saints, are called upon directly to bless the Lord as if they had understanding and could respond to the invitation.

The same phenomenon occurs in Leyde, but here the motive is different. The reciter, probably a love-sick man spurned by the woman he loves, calls on the angels and saints and forces of nature/elements to empty the woman's heart of all other affections or distractions it may have, so that it may be fully open to receive his own love:

Adiuro uos throni, dominationis, chiruphin et seraphin, ut euacuatis cor N. pro amore meo.

Adiuro uos martires ut euacuatis cor N. pro amore meo.

Adiuro uos caelum et terram et solem, et lunam, et omnes stellas fulgora et nubes et uentos et pluuias et ignis et calorem ut euacuatis cor N. pro amore meo.

Adiuro uos noctes et dies, tenebre et luna, ut euacuatis cor N. pro amore meo.

Adiuro uos ligna omnia et lapides et onore et momenta ut euacuatis cor N. pro amore meo.

Adiuro uos uolucres caeli et omnes bestiae agri et iumenta et reptilia ut uacuatis cor N. pro amore meo.

Adiuro uos mateus, marcus, lucas et iohannes, ut euacuatis cor N. pro amore meo.

(I implore you, O Thrones, Dominations, Cherubim and Seraphim, you empty out the heart of (Name) for my love. Martyrs, sky and earth, sun, moon and all stars, lightening, clouds, winds, rain, fire and heat, night and day, darkness and moon, all trees and stones, hours and moments, birds of the air, all beasts of the field, herds and snakes, Matthew, Mark, Luke and John.)

The likeness between Leyde and *Canticum Trium Puerorum* is quite clear. In one case those addressed, whether rational or non-rational, are told to 'Bless the Lord' *(Benedicite Domino)* and in the other case an appeal is made to them *(Adiuro vos)* to do something. Texts such as 'Leyde' are sometimes spoken of rather lightly as pantheistic. It is unlikely, however, that those pious priests, who recited the *Canticum Trium Puerorum* as found in the *Missale Romanum* as a part of their thanksgiving after Mass, could be accused of pantheism. However, one can appreciate the difficulty in the matter of addressing non-rational and non-living objects.

In the Canticle, a person can say, *Benedicite omnia opera Domini Domino* (O, all you works of the Lord, bless the Lord) and so forth, with a vague feeling that this is a poetic way of praying and that as spokesman for creation one is glorifying God in all his works, in the various areas of creation. The issue is clearer and more difficult to explain in the case of Leyde and St Patrick's Breastplate.

In the case of Leyde, for example, we can see this man passionately in love with this woman. But she won't look at him. Her mind is on other things. He is left desolate. He begins to pray. He prays to God, the angels and saints and this presents no difficulty since all these are living and can understand what he is saying. In Ireland, it is a well known practice for a woman in search of a husband to go to the church, light a candle and pray devoutly:

Holy St Brigid and Blessed St Anne

get me a man as fast as you can.

In the Leyde example, there is no problem while the man addresses the angels and saints. The difficulty begins when the man goes out and implores sun and moon, clouds and winds, trees and rocks, birds and cows to help him. People will begin to mutter that no woman is worth this trouble.

We have in *Leabhar na hUidhre* the dramatic account of Cú Chulainn calling on the river Cronn *(Glas Cruind)* to rise up against the army of Meadhbh and Ailill:

Adeochosa inna husci do chongnam frim. Ateoch nem ocus talmuin ocus Cruinn in tsainrethaig.

Gaibid Crón cóidech fríu

nis leicfe Muirthim(n)iu

co rroirc (rroisc) monar Féne

isin tSléib túath Ochaíne.

La sodain cotnoccaib in t-usci suas co mboí i n-indaib crand. (*LU* 5512-5520)

(I beseech the waters to help me; I beseech heaven and

earth and especially Cronn. Cron takes to fighting against them. Muirtheimne will not release them until warriors' work/destruction reaches them on the northern mountain Ochaine. With that the waters rose to height of trees). Thirty horsemen were drowned.

In a very similar martial situation, Joshua commanded the sun and moon to stand still but in this case it seems that Joshua first consulted God and was not exercising independent power over the elements:

Then spoke Joshua to the Lord in the day when the Lord gave the Amorites over to the men of Israel; and he said in the sight of Israel: 'Sun, stand thou still at Gibeon, and thou Moon in the valley of Aijalon.'

And the sun stood still, and the moon stayed until the nation took vengeance on their enemies. (Josh 10:12-13)

What is very clear in the biblical tradition is that the Creator is outside of his creation. There is a sharp distinction between God and the universe. In other traditions the distinction is less sharp and creatures appear to be suffused by divinity though in a limited and transitory way as illustrated in the Welsh myth of Ceridwen.

With a philosophical background of this type, where a life-force penetrates everything to give a unity in diversity, the rigid distinctions between objects may on occasion become vague. Cú Chulainn and the river Crón are both made up of essentially the same elements and may interact with each other. The bull Donn Chuailnge, though an animal, has the intelligence of a human. The Badhbh, or War Goddess, in the form of a crow, can warn him of danger and advise him to get out of the area. Animals speak to the hero in folktales and the boundaries between species are sometimes fluid. In this type of archaic thought the *neart* or 'mana' suffusing everything creates an essential unity.

While the older more archaic philosophy may not be entirely absent from the Bible, and phrases such as 'In him we live and move and have our being' (Acts 17:28) as well as passages on divine Wisdom, hint at a reconciliation between two worldviews, the famous mythologist, Joseph Campbell, elucidates the distinction between them very clearly:

> Christian writers, even of the most liberal sort, have never been able to appreciate the piety of the pagan Romans: for instance, that veneration of the emperor which the patron of Virgil, Augustus, caused to be instituted as a policy of state.
>
> For, after all, where every fish and fly carries divinity within why should not the master of the state be revered as *primus inter pares?* No comparison is to be made of such an attitude of respect with the Christian deification of Augustus's contemporary, Jesus. For in the Christian view the world and its creatures are not suffused divinity. The deification of Jesus marks a radical designation far beyond anything possible where all things are in essence *numina.* And from the Roman point of view the Christian refusal to concede a pinch of incense to an image of the emperor was an act not only of rebellion but also of atheism, vis-à-vis that divinity of the universe which every myth and philosophic view in the known history of mankind (save only that of the up to then completely unknown Bible) had taught as the ultimate truth of truths. (1976, 330-331)

The Purusa Myth

It is unlikely that any informative, factual and positive statement can be made about ultimate reality and the exact relations between creator and creation. Certain fragmentary clues may be gathered here and there and, perhaps, somewhere near the heart of the matter is the Indo-European creation myth of *Purusa,* found in the Sanscrit *Rig Veda,* x, xc. (Zaehner, R. C., *Hindu Scriptures,* London 1978, 9-10)

According to the myth, Purusa was the primordial man. He was slain in sacrifice and dismembered. From the various parts of his body the various parts of the universe were created; from his mind the moon was created, from his eye the sun, his breath became the wind, his feet the earth, his head the sky, and so forth. In this way, the universe was built up from the dismembered body of primordial man.

Now, in the case of Purusa, all this happened in the beginning, *in illo tempore, fadó fadó, en arche,* in mythological time. But the sacrifice to Purusa had to be continually renewed in historic time to keep the world in existence and in order. Every sacrifice was a re-enactment of the Purusa sacrifice for the constant renewal of vegetation, food, and world order.

This explains why the continental Celts, who appear to have preserved ancient Indo-European traditions long after they had been abandoned by the Romans, are described, as we have seen, as practising human sacrifice on a fairly large scale, particularly in the case of prisoners of war and criminals.

According to the *Seanchas Mór* – the Code of Brehon Law – the druids of Ireland said that it was they who made heaven and earth, the sun and moon, and so forth. (1;22) What is meant obviously is that the sacrifices performed by the druids kept the world in being and motion. 'It was not their (Celts) custom to make a sacrifice without a philosopher (druid)', remarks Diodorus Siculus. (Tierney, 1960, 251)

The classical author Strabo remarks that the druids believed that 'when there are many murder cases there will be a fruitful yield from their fields'. (Tierney, 1960, 269)

This seems quite an enigmatic statement, as there is no obvious connection between murder cases and good crops. It becomes perfectly clear, however, in the light of the Indo-European *Purusa* myth, under which the Celts were operating. The committing of murder gave the Celts an excuse for sacrificing the murderers and this promoted the fertility of the land.

A Christian form had been given to the *Purusa* myth at an
early period in what is known as the *Homo Octopartitus.*

Fundamentally, the human body is made up of the four elements – earth, air, fire and water – the sun, the sea and so
forth. As the Anaphora of the Apostolic Constitutions puts it:
'You made him with an immortal soul and a mortal body, the
soul was created out of nothing, but the body was made from
the 4 elements.' (*Enchiridion Euchologicum,* Roma 1979, 388)

The key to this doctrine is found, I believe, in the clearest
fashion in that marvellous Irish MS, *An Teanga Bhithnua.* This
long and extremely curious document describes the Apostle
Philip as having his tongue cut out nine times, but it was always replaced and so the name, 'The Evernew Tongue'. In
this MS, among the elaborate discussions on the relationship
between the body and the elements, we have two statements
which, taken together, give the philosophical justification for
the theory and explains the glorious profusion of sculptured
vegetation which adorn the great medieval cathedrals.

The first statement from *An Teanga Bhithnua* is:

Mar, tugadh le chéile gach ábhar agus gach dúil agus nadúr
atá le feiceáil sa domhan sa cholainn inar aiséirigh Críost.

(For, every material, and every element and nature that is
to be seen in the world was brought together in the body
in which Christ arose from the dead.)

In other words, the whole world is contained in the
human body in which Christ rose from the dead.

The second vital statement from *An Teanga Bhithnua* is:

D'éirigh an domhan uile leis, óir, bhí nádur na ndúil uile
sa cholainn a ghlac Íosa chuige féin. (Stokes, W., The
Evernew Tongue, *Ériu* 2, 1905, 102-104) (All the world rose
up with him, for the nature of all the elements were contained in the body which Jesus possessed.)

In other words, Our Lord's Body contained the elements

of the whole of creation, so that when this body was glorified the whole of creation was glorified with it.

It would appear to me, then, that there is an echo here of St Paul's teaching about all creation waiting in expectation for the revelation of the Sons of God, when creation itself will be set free from its bondage to decay. (Rom 8:18-30)

We have a wonderful example of how widespread the *Purusa* myth was from the elaborate form it took in Ireland in the myth of *Miach*.

In the Battle of Maigh Tuireadh Conga, Nuada the King of the Tuatha Dé Danann had lost his right arm fighting against the Fir Bolg. He had to resign immediately as no one with a defect of this kind was allowed to be king. However, Dian Cécht, the great physician of the Tuatha Dé Danann, made a silver arm for Nuada and hence, he was known as Nuada Lámh Airgid. This was good and it wasn't bad.

Dian Cécht had a son called Miach who was a much better doctor than his father. He considered his father's work on Nuada to be a botched job and he proceeded to make a better arm for Nuada which, as events turned out, was almost as good as the natural one. When Dian Cécht saw that his son had surpassed him, he was furious and, in a fit of temper, murdered him.

They buried Miach and from his grave 365 herbs sprang up. Then Miach's sister, Airmedh, came along to the grave; she took off her cloak and laid it out on the edge of the grave and proceeded to pluck the herbs very carefully and lay them out *'in ord is in eagar'* on the cloak. The point being, of course, that the herb that sprang from Miach's head would cure headache, the herb that sprang from his heart would cure heart disease, and so on. However, before she had time to memorise the exact position of each herb on Miach's body, Dian Cécht arrived. He snatched up the cloak and scattered the herbs, and from that day to this, no one knows which herb will cure which disease. And this is why our medical system is in a state of confusion. (cf. *Cath Maige Tuired,* 33-35)

In the myth of Miach we get an indication of the complete cycle of interaction between man and the universe. The dismembered body of Miach – the microcosmos – produces herbs to build up the universe or macrocosmos. But these parts of the universe or macrocosmos can be referred back to the body of a man – the microcosmos – to repair any damage done to him and to sustain him in being.

> The picture presented is that of a cycle, in which cosmogony and anthropogony ceaselessly alternate: the body being created out of the world and the world out of the body, with the creation of the one always implying and resulting from the (temporary and partial) de-creation of the other. (Lincoln, B., *Death, War, And Sacrifice,* Chicago 1991, 170)

Much research remains to be done in relation to all this and the doctrine of the *Logos,* the 'Word'. The Prologue to St John's gospel deals firstly with the nature of the *Logos* and his relation to God: 'In the beginning was the Word: the Word was with God and the Word was God. He was with God in the beginning.' (Jn 1:1-2)

Then comes the Word's relation to creation, to the universe and to the human race. 'Through him all things came to be, not one thing had its being but through him. All that came to be had life in him and that life was the light of men, a light that shines in the dark, a light that darkness could not overpower.' (Jn 1:3-5)

It does seem that some of these ancient texts retain fragment's of an archaic and widespread philosophy of communion with the universe which is of supreme value to us today. For we live in a world in which we feel alienated and divorced from our environment and in which exploitation of natural resources sometimes goes unnoticed. Thomas Berry describes eloquently the neolithic vision of 5000 years ago – the period in which Brú na Bóinne, the great monuments of the bend of the Boyne were constructed:

During the first period the human order was intimately associated with the physical and biological earth processes. Mankind lived in an ocean of energy in which the physical and psychic forces of energy were intimately related. Men found the meaning of their own existence in response to the energies about them. These men perceived as divine forces supporting him with an abundance of their products. During this period the physical energies of the earth and its resources were little affected. As specifically human energies were awakened and utilised in harmony with the earth process, there was little disturbance of the integral earth process. There was even a certain benefit in its new capacity to bring forth grain and other fruits under human cultivation. This is a period when there was a dominance of the unconscious depths of the human psyche, when the great visions took place. The feeling of identity with the earth was it its height. The response of man to the earth process was immediate. Earth was experienced as the Great Mother, heaven as a comprehensive providence. The ultimate mystery of things was venerated with special forms of worship.

The sequence of the seasons was celebrated with a variety of festivals that contributed much of the charm and fascination of life and evoked much of the cultural creativity associated with this age. Man had a feeling for the cosmic dimensions of his own being. Even beyond the Cosmic there was communion with the world of the sacred, that benign presence guiding and supporting all things in heaven and on earth. It was the period of the great symbolisms. Mythical narratives were created that provided man with a revelation of the deepest realities of the universe. (1976, 163-164)

CHAPTER TWELVE

Celtic Monasticism and the Célí Dé

A cursory glance at the Map of Monastic Ireland prepared by the Ordinance Survey Office will indicate the large number of monastic foundations in Ireland from roughly the sixth century, a period of 1000 years. The scattered remains of these can still be seen throughout the country and certain of these, such as Clonmacnoise and Glendalough, have extensive archaeological material and are as well centres of pilgrimage. By the time of the Reformation and the subsequent suppression of the monasteries, many of the existing houses seem to have been at a low ebb and probably would have died anyway even if they had never been suppressed.

The first period, from the sixth to the twelfth century, is the Celtic Period or period of native monasticism.

The second period, from the coming of the Normans in the twelfth century to the suppression in the sixteenth century, is the period of the European or continental monasticism – the Orders we are familiar with today, Benedictines, Cistercians, Augustinians, Dominicans, Franciscans, etc. It happened that, on occasion, Celtic monasteries which survived until the introduction of the continental Orders took on the observance of the new Orders. It seems, for instance, that some of the native foundations became Augustinian. For this reason, in many sites the ruins of the Celtic foundation and those of the later continental foundation are found together.

Here, we are concerned with the first period of monasticism, the Celtic period, and indeed only with a portion of this period, from 750-900, which was especially noted as a time of great spiritual and monastic reform. The reformers were known as the *Célí Dé* (Servants/Clients of God).

Before speaking of reform we must know what there was to reform and so a short introduction to the whole area of ancient Celtic monasticism may be in order.

Following the traditional dates, Christianity was introduced into Ireland in the fifth century. The impression has often been given that the whole island was evangelised during St Patrick's lifetime. This is extremely unlikely and it is far more probable that it took centuries for the faith to spread into every hill and valley in the country. Moreover, Ireland had never been conquered by the Roman Empire and Celtic Ireland was above all a rural civilisation having no towns or cities.

The normal evangelising methods followed in the East and throughout the Roman Empire – sending out missionaries to the chief cities and towns of the Empire, setting up bishoprics, organising dioceses and provinces on the lines of the civil administration of the Empire – were hardly practical in Ireland. There were very few roads and such settlements of people as there were, were undoubtedly separated by dense forests. In short, the machinery of the Roman Empire, used by the church so effectively in practically every other country, was inoperable in Ireland, as this type of political machinery did not exist.

Nevertheless, the church founded by St Patrick seems to have been primarily episcopal and clerical, not monastic. According to a seventh century biographer of St Patrick, Tíreachán, St Patrick consecrated 450 bishops. This must be wildly exaggerated. (cf. Ryan, 1931, 85-86) Nevertheless, considering the large number of petty kingdoms and tribal territories, a very large number of bishops may have been needed.

From the beginning of the sixth century, monasticism began to develop to such a degree that the episcopal organisation of the church, if ever such a phenomenon really existed to any degree in Celtic Ireland, fell into the shade, and from this on to the coming of the Normans and the introduction of the continental diocesan system, the history of the church in Ireland is dominated by monasticism.

Among the great founders of monasteries in the sixth century are St Enda who founded a monastery in the Aran Island (*Árainn Mhór*), the ruins of which or still be seen, and St Finnian of Clonard (Co Meath).

These two great founding figures had contacts with monasticism in England and Wales (Ryan, 1931, 114-116), which in turn got its monasticism from Gaul and especially Lerins, which in turn came under the influence of the Fathers of the Egyptian Desert. The route by which monasticism came to Ireland seems clear – from Egypt to Gaul, from Gaul to Britain and from Britain to Ireland.

Clonard especially became famous for its school and had an enormous number of students by the standard of those times. According to later writers, Finnian had 12 disciples called the 12 Apostles of Ireland. These were the founders of other great monasteries branching off from Clonard, among them Ciarán of Clonmacnoise, Colm Cille of Iona, Breandan of Clonfert (Brendan the Navigator), Colmán of Tír dá Glas, Molaisse of Daimhinis, Ruadán of Lothra, Cainneach of Achadh Bó and various others. From this early period we have the spread of monasticism and the rise of monastic schools devoted to both religious and secular learning, and from this period also, we have the two great illuminated copies of the gospels, the *Book of Durrow* and the *Book of Kells,* as well as the liturgical work, the *Antiphonary of Bangor.*

The typical Celtic monastery was quite different in appearance from the continental type with its huge stone buildings. A typical Celtic monastery would consist of a circular earthen or stone wall and inside this ring were the buildings of wood with straw, thatch or shingles. Around the late ninth and tenth centuries, stone came to be used. The monks lived in these small huts and even some of the churches are tiny. If the community increased in numbers, the indications are that instead of enlarging one big church, as we would do today, they simply built another small one. Also inside the enclosure there would be a large stone cross, perhaps, a graveyard, a kitchen, possibly workshops, a schoolhouse, etc. The population must have been very small and so we are speaking of small communities. Perhaps an abbot and 12 monks, after the manner of Christ and the apostles, were considered an ideal size for a monastic community. There is a tenth-century poem in archaic Irish in which the monk Manchán describes his ideal monastery:

Dúthracar, a Mhaic Dé bí,
a Rí suthain sen,
bothán deirrit díthraba
commad sí mo threb.

(I wish, O Son of the living God, eternal ancient King,
for a hidden little hut in the wilderness that it might be my dwelling.

All-grey shallow water beside it, a clear pool to wash away sins through the grace of the Holy Spirit.

A beautiful wood close by, surrounding it on every side,
for the nurture of many-voiced birds, for shelter to hide them.

A few young men of sense, we shall tell their number,
humble and obedient to pray the King.

Four threes, three fours (to suit every need), two sixes in the church, both north and south.

Six couples in addition to myself ever praying to the King who makes the sun shine.

This is the farming I would undertake and openly choose:
genuine fragrant leek, hens, speckled salmon, bees –
Raiment and food enough for me from the king whose
fame is fair, to be seated for a time, and to pray to god in
some place.)

Mo lórtu bruit ocus bíd
ónd Ríg as cháin clú,
mo bithise im shuidiu fri ré,
guide Dé in nach dú. (Murphy, 1956, no. 12)

This little poem is typical of early monastic poetry, of
which there is a considerable amount. It shows how simple
the monastic setting was – the little hut, the well, a small vegetable garden, the proximity of the forest, an ideal rural setting – what we would call a 'Back to Nature' movement
today.

By the 'two sixes in the church, north and south' is meant,
of course, the liturgical layout for the Divine Office, with the
altar in the east and one choir of six people at the north side
singing the psalms against the second choir of six at the south
side.

Then he mentions the light farming – leeks or onions,
looking after the hens, bee keeping and a little fishing.

Finally, there is the phrase, 'To be seated for a time', and
this I imagine refers to the tradition of study and writing carried on in the monasteries.

In this little poem we have the three principal activities of
the Celtic monks – the recitation of the Divine Office, some
manual work and study. In fact they correspond to the three
activities of the day in the Rule of St Benedict – the *Opus Dei*
or Divine Office, Work, *Lectio Divina,* sacred reading or
study. What is different from Benedictinism is the simplicity
of the buildings and the intimate link with nature.

This poem may represent an ideal, and perhaps it is really

part of the Célí Dé reform, for many monasteries must have become large and complicated, with many students, many guests, many tenants, large lands and interference from lay lords. This primitive simplicity was no doubt part of the reformers' dream.

This brings us then to the reform movement connected with the group of monks called the *Célí Dé,* a spiritual movement of great vitality covering the period 750-900.

The *Annals of Ulster* for the year 780 state that a Synod was held in Tara to draw up a penitential with the aid of the anchorites and scribes. Before this, in 737 *(AU)* another royal meeting was held in Terryglass, Co Tipperary, which proclaimed the Law of Patrick throughout the country. This *Cáin Pátraic* was often renewed throughout the eighth century and forbade the killing of clerics. These entries in the *Annals* proclaim officially that the spirit of reform was in the air.

As regards the Penitential, perfection consisted in distributing all one's goods to the poor and going on a pilgrimage or else living in destitution or living in a monastery until death. The Abbess of Clonbroney (Longford), who is associated with the Célí Dé reform, is described as 'poor in spirit and in goods'. She also refused to possess fields: 'never had she more than six cows at a time'. (cf. O' Dwyer, 1981, 9)

This may have been a reaction to the tendency to amass wealth and property in other monasteries and to achieve that simplicity of life described in the poem we have seen. Moreover, it is not always necessary to see the Célí Dé as a highly distinct group. In many monasteries some monks may have followed the older observance now gone lax while others followed the stricter reformed observance, in much the same way as different types of observance are to be seen in monasteries of the Orthodox Church. Nevertheless, the monasteries of Tallaght and Finglas, both near Dublin, are regarded as the great centres of the Célí Dé, and from Tallaght a great deal of literature emanated, including the teaching of Mael Ruain and the *Rule* of the Célí Dé.

From this centre the influence of the reform spread out to a number of other monasteries such as Terryglas, Lorha, Lismore, Dairinis and Doire na bhFlann where the Doire na bhFlann chalice and Paten were found some years ago.

We are speaking now about the eighth century and this was an era which was characterised by certain widespread abuses, not only in Ireland but in Europe.

One of these was the interference of lay people in the monasteries and, of course, this was a particular difficulty in Ireland, the *Comharba* or successor of the saint being sometimes a descendent of one of his relatives. This meant in practice that a particular family was associated very closely with a particular monastery and the *airchinneach* or lay administrator passed on the abbacy to his son. For instance, we have some examples from the *Annals of the Four Masters (Annála Ríochta Éireann):*

Gormán, comarba of Mochta in Louth FM 753

His son Torbach, scribe and Abbot of Armagh FM 807

His son Aedhagán, Abbot of Louth 834

Aedhagán's son Eoghan, an anchorite in Clonmacnoise 845 and so it goes on for several generations – a tradition of monastic learning and piety passing from father to son.

While celibacy was the monastic ideal, its absence did not prevent somebody from attaining learning, piety, and esteem within the Celtic monastic system. However, with the Célí Dé the emphasis was on celibacy and, in the same ascetical and even puritanical spirit as the Penitentials which were being produced, heavy penalties were imposed on clerics who became involved with women.

What must also be kept in mind is that a large Celtic monastery had not only the community of monks and clerics as we know them today but also students receiving religious and secular education. As well as these there were the *Manaig*. *Manaig* is the ordinary word for monks in Irish but originally it had a wider use than today – the *Manaig* were the tenants on monastic land and naturally most of these were married. These tenants were regarded as part of the monastic set-up or plant. They generally worked for the monks, paid taxes to the community in exchange for land and they had certain rights – religious instruction, and pastoral care, burial in the monastic graveyard, the eldest son was educated in the monastic school. The Penitentials tried to extend the ideal of chastity to these people – no sex on Wednesdays and Fridays or during Lent and so forth. We may wonder how realistic this type of legislation was in a country where Brehon Law was easy going about matters of marriage and divorce.

These same problems of church discipline were also prevalent on the continent at this time, problems such as lay-interference in church affairs, celibacy, the low standard of learning among the clergy, lack of pastoral care of the faithful and related matters. The Venerable Bede (8th century) complained about the state of affairs in England. Boniface was endeavouring to reform the Frankish clergy. St Chrodegang, Bishop of Metz, drew up a *Rule* and formed a group of canons to recite the Divine Office in his cathedral. Then there was the great monastic reform undertaken by St Benedict of Aniane. All this was taking place in the eighth century and some have seen the Célí Dé movement as being influenced by the continental situation. It is more likely, however, that the reform movement of the Célí Dé was an independent phenomenon, the two movements being reactions to similar abuses. (O'Dwyer, 1981, 1-4)

The words *Célí Dé* mean Client of God, possibly with some of the legal connotation of the *célí* as client of a wealthy landowner in civil law with the mutual obligation which bound client and lord together. In other words there may well

be the suggestion that not only had the person obligations towards God but that God had obligations towards his faithful
servant – that God was expected to have a gentlemanly respect for Brehon Law.

We have two fairly extensive manuscripts from the
monastery of Tallaght, near Dublin, which between them and
along with some other monastic *Rules* of the eighth and ninth
centuries, provide us with considerable information on the
life and spirit of the Célí Dé.

The first manuscript is *Teagasc Maoil Ruain* (Teaching of
Maol Ruain, Abbot of Tallaght), and the second is *Riagail na
Céle nDé*, (The Rule of the Célí Dé). (Gwynn, E., (Ed), 'The
Rule of Tallaght', *Hermathena* XLIV (1927) second Supple-
mental Volume)

We can summarise the material under a number of head-
ings:

Ascetic Practice
Prayer, Liturgical Regulations
Pastoral Care of the Faithful.

Asceticism
Despite the considerable amount of space devoted to diet in
the Tallaght documents, it is very difficult to say exactly how
much food was allowed. Common sense would seem to be
the hallmark of the rules concerning food but certainly it can
be said that it was meagre and simple by present day standards. (cf. O'Dwyer, 1981, 70ff) Bread, milk, cheese, butter,
cabbage, leeks, fish, dry eggs and apples were allowed in
Tallaght. The documents do not give a clear picture of regulation on eating meat. It seems to have varied among the different monasteries. And of course this is true of other points in
the observance also – a great deal depended on the abbot, and
this is especially obvious in the document *Teagasc Mhael
Ruain*. It was what some outstanding figure taught and prac-

tised that counted and not a rigid written code covering every detail and embracing a number of houses.

As regards beer, it was permitted on certain occasions at least in some monasteries but not by Mael Ruain of Tallaght. Dublittir, Abbot of Finglas, approached Mael Ruain and asked him to allow the Tallaght community to drink beer on the three great feasts (Christmas, Easter, and Pentecost). But Mael Ruain refused: 'As long as I shall give the rules, and as long as my injunctions are observed in this place, the liquor that causes forgetfulness of God shall not be drunk here,' said Mael Ruain. 'Well,' said Dublitter, 'my monks shall drink it and they shall be in heaven along with yours.' 'Anyone of my monks that shall hearken to me,' said Mael Ruain, 'and keep my Rule, shall not need to be cleansed by the fire of Doomsday, nor to come to judgement, because they shall be clean already. Not so with your monks, however, they will have something to be cleansed of in the fire of Purgatory.' (*Teag. M.* no. 40)

So from this we see how subjective dietary laws were and how much they depended on the individual abbot. Mael Ruain seems to have been particularly strict, and all those who had him as their *anamchara* or spiritual director had to fast on bread and water for three periods of forty days – probably the three Lents of the Celtic liturgical year. Also, Wednesdays and Fridays were Fast days and from these we have the modern Gaelic words for Wednesday and Friday: Dé Chéadaoin (day of first fast), Dé hAoine, day of fast.

There was the peculiar custom of fasting against a person by whom one had been wronged until one obtained redress. The plaintiff took up his position outside the person's house and fasted there in the sight of everybody and no doubt caused the household acute embarrassment. Mael Ruain of Tallaght fasted in this way against the local king, Artrig Mac Fael Mhuire, on three occasions. On the first occasion the king broke his leg; on the second occasion fire fell on him and he was burned from head to food; on the third occasion the king died. (*PRIA* xxix, 157)

Prayer and Liturgical Regulations
The Rule of the Célí Dé states: 'Three profitable things in the day: prayer, work and study; or it may be teaching or writing or sewing clothes, or any other profitable work that he can do so that none be found idle, as the Lord has said: "Thou shalt not appear in my sight empty".' (no. 55)

Naturally a large section of the documents is devoted to prayer as one of the principal means of uniting oneself with God and pride of place is given to the Canonical Hours or Divine Office, of which the Psalter of 150 Psalms was the principal part. 'Continue in prayer, in pondering on what you have read, and in teaching' – this was the advice of Mael Ruain. (*Teag. M.,* 12)

The Divine Office was said in choir in the church, and among the Célí Dé there were 8 Hours or divisions: Lauds, Prime, Terce, Sext, None, Vespers, Compline and Matins. Moreover, during the night two of the community in turn re-cited the psalms in the church while the others were in bed. (*Riag.* 30)

We don't know precisely how the psalms were distributed among the various Hours but the whole psalter of 150 psalms had to be recited each day. Mael Ruain's method of reciting the psalms was to divide the psalter into four divisions and he genuflected and said the Our Father and *Deus in adjutorium meum intende* before and after each division. (*Teag. M.,* 99) He said each division of about 38 psalms standing and sitting alternately. (*Teag. M.,* 100) (*Riag.* 22)

As well as the psalms there was the regular recitation of the canticles *Benedictus* and *Magnificat.*

The long Psalm 118 called the *Beati,* which is divided into sections following the letters of the Hebrew alphabet, was a favourite one and Muircheartach mac Olcobhair, Airchinnench of Clonfert, used to say it 12 times instead of the psalter. (*Riag.* 23)

Then, as a kind of devotional ritual, there was the *Comhrair Chrábuid* or *Lúireach Léire.* The person stood facing the east and, with raised arms, said the Our Father and then the verse, 'O God come to my aid; O Lord make haste to help me', and the sign of the cross. This was repeated facing south, west and north and then towards the earth and finally towards the sky. (*Riag.* 14)

This appears to have a cosmological significance among the Celts who considered the sea to surround the land (hence the four quarters), the sky above and the earth beneath.

The Mass was said on Sundays and on Thursdays as well as on Holy Days, and we have a ninth-century Missal, the *Stowe Missal,* from this period which preserves, in a highly Romanised form, the early Celtic liturgy. Underneath the later Romanisation one can discern a form of Gallican liturgy. 'They were unwilling to kill any insect whatever between the chancel-rail and the altar, for by custom, only the body of Christ and his blood might be sacrificed in that space.' (*Teag. M.,* 16) This very realistic notion of sacrifice is also clear from another portion of Mael Ruain's teaching (*Teag. M.,* 70): 'As to those who shed blood, if they do so intentionally, he is unwilling that they should ever be priests from that time forth, that they should be ordained; for he holds it unfitting that one who sheds blood should afterwards make an offering of Christ's body.'

The Pastoral Care of the Faithful

The final section of the rule of the Célí Dé deals with the pastoral care of the faithful. The faithful were the tenants of the monastery and the students and then, perhaps, outlying small churches serving local populations.

The ordinary church services of baptism, Sunday Mass, confessions, intercession for the living and the dead, celebration of the Canonical Hours must be provided by a fully competent priest and any bishop who ordains somebody not capable of performing the priestly duties competently is culpable before God and man.

The people pay tithes for these services and the tithes are collected in this way: the animals that a man owns, cows, sheep, goats, are put into a field and driven out through a gap one by one; every tenth animal is given to the church.

The end of the Célí Dé reform movement is generally given as the year 900. All that this can mean is that we don't hear much about the Célí Dé after this date. Around this period the Viking attacks began to take place, devastating monasteries and church buildings. But the influence of the movement must have lasted on long after this and there is even some indication that some monasteries in the south of Ireland retained Célí Dé elements until the dissolution of the monasteries in the sixteenth century. Some Celtic monasteries adopted the continental Rules when the European Orders were introduced in the twelfth century.

CHAPTER THIRTEEN

Intercession for the dead

The cult of the dead seems to have been an important part of early Celtic spirituality. *The Rule of the Céilí Dé* is quite forthright in this respect:

> There is nothing that a man does on behalf of the soul of one who dies that does not help it, whether vigil or abstinence, or requiem *(gabháil n-écnairce)* or frequent benediction. Sons ought to do penance for their dead parents. Maedóc of Ferns and all his community spent a full year on bread and water in order to gain the release of the soul of Brandub mac Echach from hell. (Gwynn, 1927, 76-77)

This Brandub was King of Leinster and died at the Battle of Slaibre in the year 601/604. Maedóc fought with the demons who were trying to get possession of the king's soul. (Gwynn and Purton, 1911, 167) Obviously, it was a long drawn out conflict in which Maedóc and his community in Ferns were finally successful.

Similarly, in early secular literature, we have the story *Siabur-Charbat Con Culain* from the 11th century *Leabhar na hUidhre,* in which St Patrick succeeds in getting the great pagan hero Cú Chulainn out of hell for the purpose of persuading King Laoghaire to become a Christian. He succeeds in this and Patrick rewards Cú Chulainn by transferring him from hell to heaven. (*JRSAI,* 1871, 371ff)

A particular connection appears between the cult of the dead and the recitation of the 'Beati' (Psalm 118), called 'Biáit' in Irish. This long psalm, with its 22 divisions and 176 verses, seems to have had enormous importance in the lives of clerics and nuns of the early period and had a special efficacy in saving a soul from hell. (O'Dwyer, 1981, 100-101) Eláir of Loch Cré used to divide the daily recitation of the psalter into three fifties and recite the *Biáit* and the *Magnificat* after each fifty psalms. (Gwynn and Purton, 1911, 129)

From the opening words, *Beati immaculati in via,* the psalm (118/119) was associated with a journey and hence the journey to the otherworld in death. 'The Biáit brings a soul from hell within a year' (*do beir in biát anmain a hiffurn hi cind bliadna*), it was said, (DIL, 73), and 'the Biáit every day for my soul' (*in biáit cech dia ar m'anmainse*). (DIL, 73)

Both the Milan Glosses and the so-called Psalter of St Caimín of Inis Cealtra on the Shannon (*PRIA,* 1973, 246-249) connect this psalm with the Babylonian captivity. The captives finally make their way out of captivity back to Jerusalem. The journey takes one year, 365 days. They travel 176 paces each day and there are 176 verses in the psalm. Interpreted mystically, Babylon corresponds to hell and Jerusalem corresponds to heaven. If the psalm with its 176 verses is recited, then, every day for 365 days on behalf of a dead person it will bring his soul from hell into heaven. (*Ériu,* 1932, 103-106)

A story from the *Book of Lismore* illustrates the power of the *Biáit:*

Maol Póil Ó Cinnaetha, abbot of the monastery of Cill Becain, had been discussing astrology with another monk. After that, in his sleep, he saw this Gospel Nun who had died six days previously coming towards him complaining bitterly that it didn't matter to him that she was dead. 'How are things with you there, O Woman?' said he. 'Little you care, indeed,' said she, 'discussing astrology without making intercession for me *(ocus gan m'écnairc-si do ghabháil).* Miserable your performance,' said she. 'What form of intercession do you require from me, O Woman?'

said he. 'The *Biáit,* of course,' said she, 'the *Biáit* after the
Biáit, the *Biáit* above the *Biáit,* the *Biáit* below the *Biáit,*'
said she, all in one breath, ordering that the *Biáit* should
be said often for her, for nothing except the Mass for the
Dead alone is held in greater esteem by God than the *Biáit.*
(Fraser, Grosjean, O'Keefe, 1931, 1, 44)

In the *Rule* attributed to St Colm Cille the hermit is exhorted to 'Perform the prayers for the dead with fervour as if
every one of the faithful who died were a special friend yours.'
(*Hallel,* Spring 1987, 63) It does seem that intercession for the
dead was a very important and time-consuming element in
Celtic monasticism and it may be that the numerous small oratories of the early monasteries were used for this Office of
the Dead in somewhat the same fashion as chantries and side-
chapels came to be used for Requiem Masses.

Perhaps too, some association with the cult of the dead
may be found in one of the most extraordinary monastic sites
in the world, Skellig Michael. This is a small rocky island off
the coast of Kerry on whose incredibly precipitous and dangerous heights a monastery was founded sometime between
the sixth and eighth century. As well as the recently discovered ruins of a hermitage on the South Peak, clinging precariously to a rock formation 700 feet above the sea, six beehive
huts and two oratories remain on the more eastern ledge. The
sheer isolation, the exposure to nature in its most elemental
forms of rock, wind and sea, the cry of sea-birds, the continual
danger in which one false step could plunge a person hundreds of feet into the ocean, create an atmosphere that is at
once dramatic and awesome. The stone beehive huts and oratories may have housed an abbot and twelve monks. (Horn,
White Marshall, Rourke, 1990, 7) A small garden forms part
of the layout and the absence of frost on the island may have
allowed vegetables to grow in a way hardly to be expected in
such an inhospitable setting. Fishing must have been the chief

source of food, however, and alternation with the mainland, possible only in good weather, may have been the only means of survival. The deterioration in climate in the thirteenth century may have led to a more complete withdrawal to the mainland monastery of Ballinskelligs, but the island continued to be maintained as a place of pilgrimage. (Horn, White Marshall, Rourke, 1990, 10)

The *Annals of the Four Masters* announce for the year 950, *Bláthmac Sgeillice decc* (Bláthmac of Skeillice dies), but for 1044 it records the death of Aodh of Sccelicc Mhichíl. (O' Donovan, 1856, 2, 666, 844). The dedication to St Michael may have taken place between these two dates. Given the predilection for giving rocky heights overlooking the sea to Michael, as at Monte Gargano, Mont St Michel, St Michael's Mount, etc., this was only natural but we may well wonder if the death cult we mentioned had a particular significance for this site. To the south of Sceilig Mhichíl is a tiny rocky island called Tech nDuind (the House of Donn). Donn was the god of the dead among the pagan Irish and it was here that the dead assembled: *Co Tech nDuind frisndailit mairb* (tenth century poem) (to Donn's house where the dead assemble). According to *Lebor Gabála* (Book of Invasions) Donn left as his last bequest: *Cucum dom thig tissaid uili iar bar n-ésaib* (To me, to my house, you shall all come after your death). (*Béaloideas,* 18, 1948, 148, 152)

In Christian tradition, St Michael is the 'psychopomp', the person who guides the souls of the dead into heaven. We might wonder, then, if the dedication of Skellig to Michael were a direct challenge to Donn, the pagan psychopomp who was engaged in the same kind of operation a few miles to the south. The monastic community would then be involved as associates of Michael in war against the demons for possession of souls, in the very area where the fight was at its fiercest, at Donn's doorstep.

In the eleventh century the cleric and poet, Maol Íosa Ó Brolcháin of Armagh, addressed St Michael thus:

Dom anmain
tuc cobair, tuc comdídnad
i n-uair techta don talmain.

Co daingen
ar chenn m'anama ernaides
tair co n-ilmílib aingel.
(Ní Bhrolcháin, 1986, 42)

(To my soul, give help, give protection at the hour of its departure from the world. Come firmly for my waiting soul, come with many thousands of angels.)

In the Offertory for the Mass for the Dead, Michael the standard-bearer is the one who is to lead the souls of the faithful into the holy light (*sed signifer sanctus Michael repraesentet eas in lucem sanctam*).

A folklore tradition among the fishermen of that area of Kerry connects Sceilig Mhichíl with Tech nDuind:

On moonlight nights old fishermen were said to have seen over Skellig Rocks the souls of the dead on their journey to Tír na nÓg – the otherworld. (*Béaloideas* 18, 1948, 149)

One of the ancient traditions connected with Sceilig is as a place of pilgrimage, and the question has been asked if the beehive huts were for pilgrims or for a resident community of monks. (Harbison, 1991, 89) At any rate, the pilgrimage involved the most terrifying exercise of squeezing through an opening in the rock called 'The Needle's Eye'. After this, the 'Stone of Pain' and the 'Eagle's Nest' had to be negotiated. A stumble meant a fall on to the projecting rock or into the sea. A long narrow fragment of rock jutting out from the summit over the raging ocean had to be traversed inch by inch. This was known as the 'Spit' or 'Spindle' and led to a stone perched precariously at the end, which the pilgrim kissed. This is prob-

ably the stone referred to as the 'Stone of Don', a possible cor-
ruption of Donn. This brings us back again to the alleged
connection between Sceilig and Tech nDuind. (Horn, White
Marshfall, Rourke, 1990, 15-16)

This appalling ordeal reaches its climax about 700 feet
above the sea and, by making this pilgrimage, the devotee believed that he was expediting the journey of his soul to the
otherworld after death. (Rees, 1976, 98, 371) On his way he
had to overcome the demons of fear and panic. There is little
doubt but that this pilgrimage was a rehearsal for the soul's
journey to eternity and belonged to the same tradition of the
Celtic culture as the *eachtra* (adventure) and the *iomramh* (adventure by sea). Only by performing heroic deeds and over-
coming seemingly superhuman odds could the hero arrive at
the otherworld and share its spoils, for the gods do not easily
part with what belongs to them. The 'Stations' of Sceilig have
their analogy in the 'Plain of Ill-Luck', the 'Valley of Monsters',
the 'Wild Mountain' and the 'Perilous Bridge' which the hero
Cú Chulainn had to traverse before arriving at the otherworld
residence of the female warrior Scáthach, who was to train
him in all the feats of battle. (Gregory, 1970, 44-45) Similarly,
the hero Fionn Mac Cumhaill attacks a *sí*, a dwelling-place of
the supernatural race of the Tuatha Dé Danann. His thumb is
caught in the door and when he returns to earth he finds that
when he sucks his thumb he is filled with supernatural knowledge, for he has arrived at the very threshold of the otherworld where all knowledge resides. (Rees, 1976, 66) Perhaps a
similar idea of divine illumination and rehearsal for the otherworld journey defined the pilgrimage to the monastic sanctuary of Sceilig Michíl. In other words, the pilgrimage may have
served as a kind of preparation for death – to give the pilgrim
a pre-view and rehearsal for the long and dangerous journey
which he must undertake before his arrival in the otherworld.

In the heroic deeds, extraordinary asceticism and individualism of some of the great Celtic monastic figures, a line of continuity may perhaps be discerned with the druidic past of which Pelagius, with his teaching of absolute confidence in the individual to will and work towards his own salvation, was the heir of the past and the link with the future. The individual had received the *neart* (power) and he could use it, as indeed could be inferred from the Parable of the Ten Talents. (Markale, 1983, 109) Life was a quest for the Holy Grail.

CHAPTER FOURTEEN

Christian Spirituality in Gaelic Scotland

We derive a great deal of our knowledge of Gaelic spirituality from the highlands and islands of Gaelic Scotland.

At the beginning of the twentieth century a magnificent work was published containing prayers, hymns, rites, ancient traditions of all kinds, which summarised the life-work of the great collector of folklore Alexander Carmichael. The work covers six volumes and gives an English translation along with the original texts in Gaidhlig. The whole is known as *Carmina Gadelica* or *Ortha nan Gaidheal*. The first three volumes are the most important from our point of view as they contain the more specifically religious material. Alexander Carmichael spent forty-four years collecting the material, from 1855 to 1899. (*Carmina Gadelica*, I, XIX)

The greater portion of the collection came from Eileana Bride, the Outer Hebrides, embracing the long line of islands stretching for 120 miles on the north-western coast of Scotland and comprising the islands of Barra, South Uist, Benbecula, North Uist, Harris and Lewis. (*CG* I, XIX) Four times a day, the Atlantic tide sweeps through the gaps in this wild treeless terrain in which a livelihood is wrested from the sea and land with great difficulty. This group of islands, known collectively as *Inis Fada* or Long Island, had 44,000 inhabitants at the lend of the last century. Under British rule, about 44 families occupied two thirds of the land, leaving the vast majority of small farmers and cottiers crowded into the rest in relative poverty. (*CG* I, XXI)

There are no intermediate farms, no gradation holdings, to which the industrious crofter might aspire, and become a benefit to himself, an example to his neighbour, and a lever to his country. (*CG* I, XXI)

While the economic life of the ordinary people was quite poor and precarious, the cultural life was extraordinarily well developed. This seems to have been due to the institution known as the *Céilí.* In Ireland, at present, this is largely a musical and dancing session but storytelling also forms part of it, at least on occasion. The Céilí was highly developed in the Hebrides, as far as we know, and may have been more or less a nightly event throughout the year. In Ireland the equivalent institution was the *Cuartaíocht,* in which the people of the neighbourhood gathered in a particular house each night and sat around the fire telling stories, singing and generally entertaining themselves.

The immense collections of folklore in Ireland and Scotland show the basic unity of the Gaelic culture in both countries and the extraordinary extent of its content and vibrancy.

Neither in Ireland or Scotland was there any shortage of *seanchaithe* or storytellers, historians, musicians or reciters. The subjects which formed the repertoire for these fireside sessions was quite varied: Stories of the Fianna *(An Fhiannaíocht),* adventure stories, ghost stories, romance, and all the folk versions of the great classical literary tales. In Scotland, historical tales were told which held fairly rigidly to known facts, while other storytellers took the same episodes but elaborated on them. Riddles, conundrums, rhymes and poetry were other features of the programme.

Luckily, some of the most ritualistic elements of the Céilí have been recorded on tape in Scotland. Among these are the *Dánta Fiannaíochta* or Ossianic Ballads recounting the heroic deeds of Fionn Mac Cumhaill, Oisín, Diarmaid Ó Duibne,

Caoilte, and Fianna Éireann in general. These were chanted to a kind of monotone, a tradition which is also found in some area of Eastern Europe. Women seemed to specialise in ancient songs sung to weird airs and some of these were ballad versions of the Legends of King Arthur and the Knights of the Round Table. (*CG*, I, XXII)

The recordings which we have of the great *seanchaithe* show them to be true artists. The ability to hold an audience enthralled throughout a long story demanded a developed sense of drama and rhetoric as well as an incredible feat of memory. Some of these stories were too long to be told in one night and were divided into sections. For instance, the tale *Sgeul Coise Céin* was divided into twenty-four parts and took twenty-four nights to tell. (*CG*, I, XXIII)

In the *Book of Leinster* it is laid down that the *file* or Court Poet was expected to know 350 stories. (Rees, 1961, 208) This is in fact a story for every night of the year except for fifteen days holidays. A list of subject matter of the stories is given: destructions, cattle-raids, courtships, battles, feasts, adventures, elopements, slaughters, visions, loves, expeditions, invasions, caves, voyages, violent deaths, sieges, conceptions and births, frenzies. (Ibid 208) While these lists represent the repertoire for the aristocratic audience of the king's *dún*, all the indications are that this ancient tradition had passed to the small farmer's fireside.

Caesar, in discussing the Celts of Gaul, remarks that the druids in their schools insisted that their students commit enormous amounts of poetry to memory. They believed that in writing things down the memory grew weaker, a sentiment with which Caesar agreed. At any rate the huge collections of stories, songs, ballads, etc. which we have today in both Ireland and Scotland are a product of oral tradition and have been written down only in this and the last century.

The Céilí or Cuartaíocht can be seen as a school of native

learning which the ordinary person attended nightly all his or her life.

One account says: 'I remember myself, though I was little at the time, when the Christian folk crowded into one another's houses, telling tales and histories, invocations and prayers, runes and lays, sweet, beautiful and soft.' (Tha cuimhne agam fhin ge bu bheag mi san am, dar a bhitheadh daoine Criosdail na duthcha cruinneachadh ann an taighean cach a cheile, ag innseadh sgialachd agus eachdraidh, achan agus urnaigh, a 'seinn laoidh agus luinneag, a 'gabhail dhuan agus oran binn boidheach reidh.) (*CG* 3, 21/20)

'The old people conversed about the state of the world and about changes in the weather, about the moon and the sun, about the stars of the sky, about the ebbing and flowing of the sea, about the life in the depths of the ocean, and about the hot and cold lands of the earth.' (*CG* 3, 21)

It is remarkable how closely this resembles the type of cosmological knowledge required of learned clerics by the *Seanchas Mór* (Brehon Law) and indeed of the druids of Gaul. Perhaps it can be said with some degree of truth that the *aos dána,* the aristocratic druids, *filí* and *baird* of the classical Celts of Europe, lived on in the *seanchaithe* and *mná feasa* (women with knowledge of herbal cures, etc.), the *mná caointe* and the *mná glúine* (midwives) of recent centuries.

The immensity of the folk tradition which has survived should come as no surprise in view of these considerations and the people of this heritage, though poor economically, were a people of high sophistication in terms of native culture. But at the end of the last century the ancient culture in the islands of Scotland began to disappear just as it was disappearing in Ireland at the same period.

The Highland Clearances, like the Potato Famine in Ireland, proved disastrous for the old culture and way of life. Large numbers of people were evicted as the landlords found that sheep rearing on a ranch scale was more profitable than keeping small farmers on the land. The descendants of these evicted people are still in parts of Canada (Nova Scotia).

More subtle causes also contributed to the decline – the gradual change from Gaelic to English. In accordance with Celtic tradition, a huge proportion of the texts were in poetry. This of course could not be adequately translated into another language.

Gaelic oral literature has been disappearing during the last three centuries. It is now becoming meagre in quantity, inferior in quality, and greatly isolated. Several causes have contributed towards this decadence – principally the Reformation, the Risings, the evictions, the disruption, the schools, and the spirit of the age. Converts in religion, in politics or in ought else, are apt to be intemperate in speech and rash in action. The Reformation action condemned the beliefs and cults tolerated and assimilated by the Celtic church and the Latin church. Nor did sculpture and architecture escape their intemperate zeal. The Risings harried and harassed the people, while the evictions impoverished, dispirited, and scattered them over the world. Ignorant school-teaching and clerical narrowness have been painfully detrimental to the expressive language, wholesome literature, manly sports, and interesting amusements of the Highland people. Innumerable examples occur.

A young lady said, 'When we came to Islay I was sent to the parish school to obtain a proper grounding in arithmetic. I was charmed with the schoolgirls and their Gaelic songs. But the schoolmaster – an alien like myself – denounced Gaelic speech and. Gaelic songs. On getting out of school one evening the girls resumed a song they had been singing the previous evening. I joined willingly, if timidly, my knowledge of Gaelic being small. The schoolmaster heard us, however, and called us back. He punished us till the blood trickled from our fingers, although we were big girls, with the dawn of womanhood upon us. The thought of that scene thrills me with indignation.' (*CG* I, xxv-xxvi)

The strict form of Protestantism introduced into Scotland did not prove favourable to the blending of pagan with Christian elements which the Catholic Church had accepted with equanimity. In the traditional system, 'Religion, pagan or Christian, or both combined, permeated everything – blending and shading into one another like the iridescent colours of the rainbow. The people were sympathetic and synthetic, unable to see and careless to know where the secular began and the religious ended.' (*CG* I, xxxiii)

When Alexander Carmichael visited the Island of Lewis he found that much of the mentality of the people had changed through the evangelising efforts of the Protestant clergy, aided and abetted by the elders. He found it difficult to collect native material. As he says himself:

It was with extreme difficulty that I could obtain any information on the subject of my inquiry, because it related to the foolish past rather than to the sedate present, to the secular affairs rather than to the religious life of the people. When I asked about old customs and old modes of working, I was answered, 'Good man, old things are passed away, all things are become new'; for the people of Lewis, like the people of the Highlands and Islands generally, carry the Scriptures in their minds and apply them in their speech as no other people do. It was extremely disconcerting to be met in this manner. (*CG* I, xxvii)

With self-righteous satisfaction, a woman of Lewis explained the changes that had come about:

There were many sad things done then, for those were the days of foolish doings and of foolish people. Perhaps, on

the day of the Lord, when they came out of church, if indeed they went into church, the young men would go to
throw the stone or to toss the cabar, or to play shinty, or to
run races, or to race horses on the strand, the young maid-
ens looking on the while, say, and the old men and women.
'And have you no music, no singing, no dancing now at
your marriages?' 'May the Possessor keep you! I see that
you are a stranger in Lewis, or you would not ask such a
question,' the woman exclaimed with grief and surprise in
her tone. 'It is long since we abandoned those foolish ways
in Ness and, indeed, throughout Lewis. In my young days
there was hardly a house in Ness in which there was not
one or two or three who could play the pipe, or the fiddle,
or the trump. And I have heard it said that there were men,
and women too, who could play things they called harps,
and lyres, and bellow-pipes, but I do not know what those
things were'. 'And why were those discontinued?' 'A
blessed change came over the place and the people,' the
woman replied in earnestness, 'and the good men and the
good ministers who arose did away with the songs and the
stories, the music and the dancing, the sports and the
games, that were perverting the minds and ruining the
souls of the people, leading them to folly and stumbling.'
'But how did the people themselves come to discard their
sports and pastimes?' 'Oh, the good ministers and the
good elders preached against them and went among the
people, and besought them to forsake their follies and to
return to wisdom. They made the people break and burn
their pipes and fiddles. If there was a foolish man here and
there who demurred, the good ministers and the good elders themselves broke and burnt their instruments, saying:
'Is fearr an teine beag a gharas la beag na síthe,
Na 'n teine mor a loisgeas la mor na feirge.'

(Better is the small fire that warms on the little day of peace,
Than the big fire that burns on the great day of wrath.)
The people have forsaken their follies and their Sabbath-breaking, and there is no pipe, no fiddle here now,' said the woman in evident satisfaction. 'And what have you now instead of the racing, the stone-throwing, and the cabar-tossing, the song, the pipe, and the dance?' 'Oh, we have now the blessed Bible preached and explained to us faithfully and earnestly, if we sinful people would only walk in the right path and use our opportunities. (*CG* I, XXIX–XXX)

A famous violin-player died in the island of Eigg a few years ago. He was known for his old style playing and his old-world airs which died with him. A preacher denounced him, saying: Tha thu shios an sin cul na comhla, a dhuine thruaigh le do chiabhan liath, a cluich do sheann fhiodhla le laimh fhuair a mach agus le teine an diabhoil a steach' (Thou art down there behind the door, thou miserable man with thy grey hair, playing thine old fiddle with the cold hand without, and the devil's fire within.) His family pressed the man to burn his fiddle and never to play again. A peddler came round and offered ten shillings for the violin. The instrument had been made by a pupil of Stradivarius, and was famed for its tone. 'Cha b'e idir an rud a fhuaradh na dail a ghoirtich mo chridhe cho cruaidh ach an dealachadh rithe! an dealachadh rithe! agus gun tug mi fhein a bho a b'fhearr am buaile m'athar air a son, an uair a bha mi og' (It was not at all the thing that was got for it that grieved my heart so sorely, but the parting with it! the parting with it! and that I myself gave the best cow in my father's fold for it when I was young.) The voice of the old man faltered and a tear fell. He was never again seen to smile. (*CG* I, XXXII)

One wonders how the reformers in Scotland succeeded in destroying a religious system so well integrated with the native culture of the people. While the people were very religious and devout, the organised church must have been extremely weak. It is doubtful if all the Islands had a resident priest to defend the native system.

It does seem that the shortage of priests, however, forced the Christian people to develop prayer formulae, rituals, and devotional practices which, while being completely orthodox, were culturally integrated. If there had been an abundance of priests and if the church had been highly organised, it is doubtful if such a system would ever have evolved.

Mockery too played a part in the disappearance of the old culture. Caitríona Nic Neill, a descendant, no doubt, of the kings of the Island of Barra, remarked:

> There were many curious customs among the old people; but strangers began to come into the country, and they began to mock the people … and the beautiful customs of the country were allowed bit by bit to drop, and some of them to be lost. Cha mhor feadhainn a sheasadh ri magadh feadhainn is fearr ionnsachadh na iad fhein. Cha mhor idir. (There are not many people who would stand to be made fun of by people of more learning than themselves – not many at all.) (*CG*, 3, 8-9)

A short moving account is given by a daughter describing her mother's method of passing on the traditional faith to her children:

> My mother would be asking us to sing our morning song to God – as Mary's lark was singing it up in the clouds, and as Christ's mavis *(smeorach Chriosda)* was singing it yonder in the tree, giving glory to the God of the creatures *(Dia nan dúl)* for the repose of the night, for the light of the day, and for the joy of life. She would tell us that every creature on the earth here below and in the ocean beneath

and in the air above was giving glory to the great God of the creatures and the worlds, of the virtues and the blessings and would we be dumb!

My dear mother reared her children in food and clothing, in love and charity. My heart loves the earth in which my beloved mother rests. (*CG*, 3, 25)

We have seen already the part played by the lark in interpreting the gospel, in the Gaelic folk-prayer tradition. Here, both the lark *(uiseag/fosgag Mhoire/fuiseog)* and the mavis/thrush *(smeorach Chriosda/smólach)* are involved as representatives of all creation giving praise to *Dia na nDúl*, the God of the Elements. These birds encourage humans to join in the cosmic song from the air, the land and the sea. Here we have the familiar Celtic cosmology – the sky above, the land beneath, the sea all around, the formula of the six directions – all expressed simply by the mother to her children: Theireadh i ruinn gun robh gach duil air an talamh a bhos agus anns an fhairge shios agus anns an adhar shuas a' toir gloir do Dhia mor nan dul.'

The same sentiments of thanksgiving for the repose of night, the light of day, the joy of life are expressed in a Morning Prayer from Scotland. We can also notice in it a Neoplatonic echo in the idea of the light of day leading to the light of eternity, as in the *Exultet* the flame of the Easter Candle merges with the Morning Star:

Dhe, thug mis a fois na h-oidhch anraoir
Con solus aoibh an la an diugh,
Bi da mo thoir bho sholus ur an la an diugh,
Chon solus iul na siorruidheachd. (*CG*, 1, 32)

(O God, you brought me from the repose of last night to the joyful light of this day. Bring me from the new light of this day to the guiding light of eternity.)

PART FOUR

The Cycle of the Year

CHAPTER FIFTEEN

The Liturgical Year

Perhaps the simplest way of illustrating the Liturgical Year is to draw a cross and put a circle around it. The four points at which the arms of the cross meet the circle stand for the four Stations of the Sun.

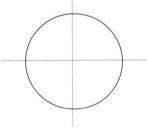

This is the fundamental calendar, based on the four Stations of the Sun – the two solstices and the two equinoxes. On these four occasions the sun behaves in a peculiar manner which can be seen by means of alignments with posts, standing stones and perhaps some feature on a distant hill or mountain. At the solstices, the sun seems to stand still for a while and reverse the direction of it's rising. At the equinoxes the sun rises directly at the east and sets directly at the west, so that at the equinoxes there is equal day and equal night.

It on this solar calendar that the Liturgical Year is based and the four stations of the sun are brought into relation with two central figures of Christianity – Our Lord himself and St John the Baptist.

In the beginning, there was basically only one feast among Christians, the Feast of Easter *(he Eorte)*, celebrated each

Sunday and in a more solemn way once a year on what is now called Easter Sunday. The more developed calendar of Polemius Silvius in the middle of the fifth century mentions Christmas, Epiphany, Passiontide, Easter and several saints as well as pagan festivals such as the Lupercalia, Terminalia, Parilia, etc. (James, 1961, 202-203)

The peculiarities of the solstices – six months apart, increasing, decreasing – were obviously taken into account by the early Christians when they decided that, apart from the passion, death and resurrection of Christ, other episodes of his life should also be celebrated.

There was one major difficulty. There were no documents to tell them the exact date of Christ's birth, no Birth Certificate or anything of that kind. The case of St John the Baptised, that other great figure of the New Testament, is similar, except that we know from the scriptures that St John the Baptist was six months older than Our Lord (Lk 1:23-38). The Christians, however, made good use of the scriptural texts and made the Feast of the Nativity, the Birth of Christ, to coincide with the winter solstice when the sun was on the increase, and made the birthday of St John the Baptist to coincide with the summer solstice (24 June) when the sun was beginning to decrease. In this way, the two great figures of the New Testament are linked to the two great stations of the sun.

Beginning then, with the Birth of Christ at the winter solstice (the few days difference is of no account) we count backwards: three months to the autumn equinox, three further months to the summer solstice and a further three months to the spring equinox, the date of the conception of Our Lord, the Feast of the Annunciation when the angel told Mary that she would have a son.

If we follow a similar course in the case of St John and go back nine months, we find that the conception of St John the Baptist took place at the autumn equinox. This Feast of the

Conception of St John the Baptist is not found in the Tridentine or in the present calendar, but in the great Irish martyrology, *Félire Óengusso Céli Dé*, on 24 September we have the magnificent encomium to St John, based on Our Lord's own description of him:

Compert Iohain uasail

Babtaist, as mó scélaib:

acht Íssu de dóinib

as amram ro génair. (Stokes, 1905, 196)

(The conception of noble John the Baptist, who is greater than can be told, who is the most wondrous that has been born of men, save Jesus.)

The Liturgical Calendar of the Byzantine Rite agrees with *Felire Oengusso:* 23 Sept.: 'Conception of the holy Prophet, Forerunner, and Baptist, John.' (Raya, 1958, 188)

Here then, we have this perfect calendrical balance in which the births of Christ and St John the Baptist occur at the solstices and their conceptions occur at the equinoxes. This is the basic framework of the Liturgical Year.

According to ancient tradition, the death and resurrection of Christ was thought to occur on the anniversary of his conception, in other words Easter was linked to the spring equinox. (F. O. 84)

In practice, this stable solar date, 21 March, is modified by the fact that the calculation of the date of Easter not only involves the sun but the moon also. In the current regulation in the Roman Rite, Easter Sunday is the first Sunday after the first full moon after the spring equinox. This is why the date of Easter is so variable. What a marvellous thing it is that in this age of technology we have to wait for the full moon to celebrate the greatest feast of the Christian year. This makes us aware of the cosmic dimension of the redemption and situates us within the harmonious cycles of the universe.

An early Easter homily discusses the equinox – equal day, equal night – as connected with creation. Balance and harmony among the elements were a mark of nature's primordial passage from chaos to cosmos. (Chupuggco, 1992, 50)

The autumn equinox is connected with the zodiacal sign of Libra, the Scales or Balance, and the spring equinox is linked to Aries, the Ram, reminiscent of the Lamb of God, the Paschal Lamb whose blood was smeared on the Israelite doors so that the destroying angel would pass them by at the Jewish Passover. This is the archetype of the Christian Easter when Christ passed over, through death, from the conditions of this earthly existence to the heavenly world, making it possible for his followers to traverse the same path.

Taking Easter Sunday then as focal point, we move backwards for forty days, the period of Lent. Lent begins on Ash Wednesday in February or the beginning of March, depending on the date of Easter. It is a period of preparation for the feast of our redemption.

Easter itself will fall at the end of March or in April. In the past some great feasts had an octave, that is, they continued to be celebrated for a week, one day being considered too short. This gave the faithful an opportunity of considering the various aspects of the feast. In the case of Easter, however, one week (octave) was thought to be too short and so Easter was given an octave of octaves which brings us to Pentecost Sunday, fifty days after Easter, and this concludes the Easter Season.

Again, taking the other great feast of the year, Christmas, as the starting point, the Season of Advent, beginning in late November or early December and consisting of four Sundays in the Roman Rite, serves as a kind of preparation for Christmas as Lent does for Easter.

Then after Christmas there is a post Christmas Season of short duration, ending at the Feast of the Epiphany on 6

January, or to some extent extending to the Feast of the Presentation in the Temple (2 February), Candlemas. Shortly after this Lent begins.

It can be seen then, that the life of Christ and the various episodes in the work of our redemption are presented in the Liturgical Year in a somewhat historical manner, from the prophecies of his birth (Advent) through his public life, passion, death and resurrection, to the sending of the Holy Spirit on the apostles at Pentecost. It covers roughly the period from late November to early June.

The remaining part of the year can be seen as the 'After Pentecost Period' when we celebrate the working of the Holy Spirit in the world to transform it in accordance with the mind of Christ.

This brings us back to Advent when the cycle begins again.

In Summary

The First Sunday of Advent can occur between 27 November and 3 December.

Christmas Day, 25 December.

Epiphany or Public Manifestation of Our Lord, 6 January.

Ash Wednesday (Beginning of Lent) can occur between 8 February and 7 March.

Easter Sunday can occur between 26 March and 22 April.

Pentecost Sunday can occur between 14 May and 10 June.

The long period then from, say, early June to early December, is the period in which we celebrate the action of the Holy Spirit in the church in an emphatic way.

From Advent to the Ascension of Christ into Heaven, the emphasis is on the work of our redemption as brought about by the birth, public life, passion, death, resurrection and ascension of Our Lord, his life on earth and his transition to heavenly conditions. Then comes Pentecost in which, from his new heavenly home, he sends the Holy Spirit on mankind to transform it to his own likeness and finally transfer it to the otherworld into which he himself has entered. It is the Holy Spirit sent by the Risen Christ who makes the redemption operative in us.

A summary of the Liturgical Year is presented in the admirable Fourth Eucharistic Prayer:

After the call to 'give thanks', the prayer addresses the God who lives in unapproachable light surrounded by praising angels. He is the creator of all things and has given mankind an eternal destiny in the vision of his glory.

Even when mankind rebelled against him he did not abandon them but helped all people to seek and find him 'and through the prophets taught them to hope for salvation' – Advent Season.

'…you sent your only Son to be our Saviour. He was conceived through the power of the Holy Spirit, and born of the Virgin Mary.' – Christmas.

'To the poor he proclaimed the good news of salvation, to prisoners, freedom, and to those in sorrow, joy.' – Public Life, Lenten Period.

'In fulfilment of your will he gave himself up to death; but by rising from the dead, he destroyed death and restored life.' – Eastertide.

'And that we might live no longer for ourselves but for him, he sent the Holy Spirit from you, Father, as his first gift to those who believe.' – Pentecost.

'to complete his (Christ's) work on earth and bring us the fullness of grace.' – Operation of Holy Spirit in the World, Period from Pentecost to Advent.

The work of the Holy Spirit in the church is above all the work of 'transformation', of 'change'. This work of transformation is expressed in two ways, as shown in the double epiclesis. In the first epiclesis it is the transformation of the bread and wine by the power of the Holy Spirit that is requested: 'Father, may this Holy Spirit sanctify these offerings. Let them become the body and blood of Jesus Christ our Lord.' In the second, or postconsecration epiclesis, it is the transformation of ourselves that is requested, by the power of the Holy Spirit, and this transformation will come about by eating and drinking the already transformed bread and wine. In other words, the Holy Spirit is not seen here as transforming us directly into the image of God but indirectly by our contact with the Eucharist – the bread and wine which has already been in vital contact with the power of the Holy Spirit and been themselves changed: '… by your Holy Spirit, gather all who share this bread and wine into the one body of Christ, a living sacrifice of praise.'

Perhaps the idea can be illustrated simply in terms of fire, and indeed it was in the form of tongues of fire that the Holy Spirit descended on the apostles and for this reason red vestments are worn by the celebrant at Pentecost.

In the life of St Ciarán Saighre (Seir, Co Offaly) there is a story of an evil man, Trichemh, who came to Saighir and extinguished the Easter Fire. This fire was lighted at the Easter Vigil and was only extinguished before Easter to be relighted. It was the only fire in Ciarán's monastery. Ciarán said there would be no fire until next Easter except God sent fire from heaven. He prophesied that the culprit would be eaten up by wolves and this actually happened. He was, however, brought back to life again later. Guests arrived cold and hungry. Ciarán raised his arms to heaven and prayed earnestly. A ball of flame fell from heaven to light the fire again and the guests were able to warm themselves and have their supper cooked. (Plummer, 1922, 110-111)

Here fire descends from heaven to transform the cold fuel into flame. By contact with this fire the guests are themselves

warmed, that is, they become partakers in the nature of fire
and are transformed. It will be noticed that, as in the case of
the Eucharist, the guests are not transformed directly by the
flame from the sky but indirectly by means of the transformation of the fuel into an ordinary fire.

The mystique of the divine fire is beautifully expressed in
the magnificent prayer for Ember Saturday after Pentecost in
the Tridentine Missal:

> Illo nos igne, quaesumus, Domine, Spiritus Sanctus inflam-
> met; quem Dominus noster Jesus Christus misit in terram,
> et voluit vehementer accendi.

> (May the Holy Spirit, we beseech Thee, O Lord, kindle in
> us that same fire which our Lord Jesus Christ sent down
> upon earth, earnestly desiring that it should burn mightily.)

In the Celtic Tradition we have a similar prayer, magnificent in its comprehensiveness, relating to fire. It was said in
the Hebrides of Scotland by *bean an tí* (woman of the house)
in the morning as she exposed the fire which had been covered over with ashes the night before, in the ritual known as
Smáladh na Tine:

> Togfaidh mé mo thine inniu
> i láthair aingeal naofa neimhe,
> i láthair Airil is aille cruth,
> i láthair Uiril na n-uile scéimh,
> gan fuath, gan tnúth, gan formad,
> gan eagla, gan uamhan neach faoin ngréin,
> agus Naomh Mhac Dé do m' thearmann.
> A Dhia, adaigh féin i mo chroí istigh
> aibhleog an ghrá
> do m' namhaid, do mo ghaol, do m'chairde,
> don saoi, don daoi, don tráill,
> a Mhic Mhuire mhín ghil,
> ón ní is ísle crannchuire
> go dtí an t-ainm is airde. (ÁPD 161)

(I will build up my fire today in the presence of the holy angels of heaven, in the presence of Airil of most beautiful form, in the presence of Uiril of all beauty, without hate without envy, without rivalry, without fear, without horror of anyone under the sun, for I have the Holy Son of God as my sanctuary.

O God, enkindle in my inmost heart the flaming spark of love for my enemy, for my relative, for my friends, for the wise person, for the foolish person, for the unfortunate person, O Son of gentle, shining, Mary, from the lowest most perverse person to the one of highest fame.)

CHAPTER SIXTEEN

The Celtic Year and the Cycle of Nature

Having given an account of the normal calendar based on the four stations of the sun on which the Liturgical Year is founded we now go on to examine the four great Celtic Feasts or at least those of the Insular Celts.

These are: Samhain (1 November); Imbolg (1 February), Bealtaine (1 May) and Lughnasa (1 August). It will be noticed that a feast begins each of the four seasons of the year, winter, spring. summer and autumn.

These Celtic feasts bisect the quarter periods set by the solstices and equinoxes, so that Samhain is half-way between the autumn equinox and the winter solstice, Imbolg half-way between the winter solstice and the spring equinox; Bealtaine half-way between the spring equinox and the summer solstice and Lughnasa half-way between the summer solstice and the autumn equinox.

In the story, *Tochmarc Emire,* it is explained that the year was divided into two halves, the summer from Bealtaine to Samhain and the winter from Samhain to Bealtaine: 'in samrad ó beltine co samain ocus in gemred ó samain co beltine,' (Van Hamel, 1933, 43)

This division of the year into the bright and dark halves was marked in some places by the custom of the *buaile.* The cows were taken up the mountains and kept there for the summer grazing. The younger people looked after them and made butter and cheese. While there, they lived in little huts erected for the purpose. At Samhain, when winter approached,

the cows were led down again and kept in the byres or in shel-
tered spots on the farm throughout the winter. In parts of the
Alps the custom is still practised and the cows on their way up
the mountains can be seen decorated with garlands, ribbons
and cow-bells. (cf. Danaher, 1972, 86, 206)

The etymology of the terms is somewhat uncertain.
Samhain is said to be *Sam-fuin,* end of summer. *Imbolc/Oi-
melc* is thought to be connected with sheep and milk and so
to that period of the year, the beginning of spring, in which
sheep begin to lactate.

Tochmarc Emire gives a more ritualistic description of the
Feast of Bealtaine:

> Co beltine .i. bil-tine .i. teine soínmech .i. dá tenid do
> gnítis druídh co tincetlaib móraib ocus doléictis na cethrai
> etarru ar tedmannaib cacha bliadnae. Nó co bel-dine .i.
> Bel dano ainm de idail; is and doaiselbthea díne cacha
> cethrae fo selb Beil. Beil-díne iarom beltine.
>
> (Beltine, i.e. biltine, i.e. lucky fire, i.e. two fires which used
> to be made by the druids with great incantations, and they
> used to drive the cattle between them (to guard) against
> the diseases of each year. Or Bel-dine; Bel was the name of
> an idol god. It was on it (that day) that the firstling of
> every kind of cattle used to be exhibited as in the posses-
> sion of Bel. Beil-dine hence beltine).

From this we have the *seanfhocal* (old saying), 'Idir dhá
thine Bhealtaine' (Between two fires of Bealtaine). In parts of
the country the Bealtaine bonfires are still lighted.

The last festival, *Lughnasa,* is also called *Brón Trogain* in
Tochmarc Emire:

> Co bron trogain .i. Lugnasad .i. taite fogamuir .i. is and
> dóbroini trogan .i. talam fo thoirthib. Trogan ainm do
> thalmain. (The beginning of Foghamhar (Autumn). i.e. in
> it Troghan brings forth, i.e. the earth under fruits. Troghan,
> then, is a name for the earth.)

In his introduction to *Leabhar na gCeart,* John O' Donovan gives a useful account of the Celtic Year as it was observed in Ireland:

It might at first sight appear probable that the year of the Pagan Irish began with Oimelc, the spring, when the sheep began to yean and the grass to grow, but this is far from certain; and if there be no error of transcribers in Cormac's Glossary, we must conclude that the last month of *Foghamhar,* i.e. that preceding *Mis Gamh* or November, was the end of their summer, and of their year, *Fogamar .i. don mis déighenaig do h-ainmnigheadh,* i.e. Foghamhar, was given as a name to the last month. Since the conversion of the Irish to Christianity they began the year with the month of January, as is clear from the *Feilire Aenghuis.* Besides the division of the year into the four quarters, of which we have spoken, and into two equal parts called *gamh* or *geimh* (Welsh *gauaf*) and *samh* (Welsh *haf*), it would appear from a gloss on an ancient Irish law tract in H. 3. 18, p. 13, TCD., it was divided into two unequal parts called *Samh-fucht* [*tucht,* i. e. time], or summer-period, and *Gamh-fucht* or *Geimh-fucht,* i. e. winter-period; the first comprising five months, namely, the last month of spring, and the three months of summer, and the first month of autumn; and the other the two last months of autumn, the three months of winter, and the two first months of spring. This division was evidently made to regulate the price of grazing lands. (1847, LV)

The Cycle of Nature

The calendrical tradition of the Catholic Church receives remarkable expression in the marvellous ritual of marking the paschal candle at the beginning of the Easter Vigil. After the blessing of the New Fire, the celebrant takes the large candle and, with a stylus, cuts a cross on the wax. Then he traces the

Greek letter alpha above the cross and the letter omega below it. These letters form the beginning and end of the Greek alphabet. The numerals of the current year are then traced between the arms of the cross. While this is being done, the celebrant recites the formula:

Christ yesterday and today
The beginning and the end,
Alpha,
and Omega:
all times belong to him,
and all the ages;
to him be glory and power,
through every age and for ever. Amen.

While this ancient ritual is being performed in the semi-darkness of the night, with the blazing bonfire in the background, one feels transported into a world of archaic rites and mentality where people felt themselves as part of a great cosmic unity springing from a primary source. Here, the rational is in abeyance; here we are confronted with primeval vision.

The transient nature of time is indicated by the day of the solar month. Today is 1 November, yesterday was 31 October, tomorrow will be 2 November. We are situated precariously within this gushing stream of time.

The days of the week are catered for in the Irish tradition by folk-prayers such as *A Rí an Domhnaigh, tar le cabhair chugham is tóg in am ón bpéin mé ...* (ÁPD 416) and the more elaborate *Tiomna Cholm Cille* (ÁPD 415) of which a shortened, adapted version is provided here:

Cónaigh, a Chríost, i m' chroíse,
a Choimdhe, a Mhic Mhuire;
gach Satharn/ Domhnach/ Luan/ Máirt/ Céadaoin/ Déardaoin/ Aoine,
tar, a Thiarna,
agus cónaigh i mo chroí.

Tar i mo chosa is i mo lámha
Éist a Thiarna, le mo ghuí.
Tar i mo bhéal is i mo shúile,
tar, a Dhúilimh, i mo chroí.
(Come to dwell, O Christ, in my heart, O God, O Son of
Mary; every Saturday/ Sunday/ Monday/ Tuesday/ Wednes-
day/ Thursday/ Friday come, O Lord, and dwell in my
heart.
Come (to dwell) in my feet and in my hands, listen, O
Lord, to my cry; come (to dwell) in my mouth and in my
eyes, come, O Creator (to dwell) in my heart.)

Similarly, for the four seasons of the year, a manuscript of
the Royal Irish Academy (23 C 20) supplies a prayer referring
to the saints of each period:

An Geimhreadh: (Winter)
Naoimh an talaimh is aingil na n-ardreann romham
um Íosa neartmhar mo chara 's mo Shlánaitheoir
ón saog(h)al searbh 's ó chealg-ghoin námhad na n-ord
Sa Gheimhreadh aitim go dtaga do m' ardú leo.
(May the Saints of the earth and the angels of the high
constellations be before me, surrounding powerful Jesus,
my friend and Saviour. From this bitter world and from
the poisonous stings of the enemy of the Christian order, I
ask in the winter that they lift me up to themselves.)

An tEarrach: (Spring)
Naoimh an earraigh dom chabhair gach lá le Pól,
Bríd ar bharr – banaltra an ArdMhic Mhóir,
Saoithe seasaimh is fearr chun namhaid a chló
Is go dtaga dá bhfearta sin m'anam 'bheith sámh i nglóir.
(The saints of springtime may they come to my help each
day, with Paul, Brigid first, the nurse of the great High Son,
superbly competent sages to vanquish the enemy, and as a
result of their great deeds may my soul find rest in glory.)

An Samhradh: (Summer)
Naoimh an tsamhraidh go dtaga i m' dháil go fóill,
Um Íosa an Leanbh a cheannaigh ar ardchíos sló,
Is díobh sin Peadar 's ní fheadair cá bhfágfainn Eoin
dís le leagtar an t-easchara is dána beo.
(Saints of summertime, may they come to meet me now,
surrounding the Child Jesus who redeemed the human
race at a high price. Peter will be among them and John
(the Baptist) without doubt, two well-equipped to destroy
the boldest enemy.)

An Fómhar: (Autumn)
Naoimh na scabal is fearr atá le fáil san fhómhar,
Go dtaga do m' thearman feasta le Parthalón,
Bíodh an tAingeal i m' fharradh is Máire an Ógh,
go ndíona m' anam ó lasair ghoirt ghránna an smóil.
(*An Sagart,* Samhradh 1985, 16-17)
(The best saints of the scapular that belong to autumn,
may they come from this on to protect me with
Bartholomew among them (24 Aug). Let the Angel
(Michael, 29 Sept) be with me and the Virgin Mary (15
Aug, Lá 'le Muire san Fhómhar), may they protect my soul
from the ugly, fiery wound of sin.)

In the account of the creation of the world by God as given
in *Senchus Mór,* the Zodiac receives considerable attention so
that cosmology and calendar are connected:

The same King divided it into twelve divisions, and gave a
name to each division respectively; and the figures of the
divisions are set each in its own place around the firmament, and it is from these figures they are named, i.e.
Aquarius, Pisces, Aries, Taurus, Gemini, Cancer, Leo,
Virgo, Libra, Scorpio, Sagittarius, Capricornus. And these
are the twelve divisions through which the sun and moon
run; and the sun is thirty days ten hours and a half in each
division of these, and on the fifteenth it enters each division.

In the month of January the sun is in Aquarius; in the month of February the sun is in Pisces; in the month of March the sun is in Aries; in the month of April in Taurus; in the month of May it is in Gemini; in the month of June it is in Cancer; in the month of July it is in Leo; in the month of August it is in Virgo; in the month of September it is in Libra; in the month of October it is in Scorpio; in the month of November it is in Sagittarius; in the month of December it is in Capricornus.

These are the twelve divisions through which the sun runs. (O'Donovan and Hancock, 1865, 31)

The Zodiac, while obviously an international rather than a native product, figures again in *Saltair na Rann* and in a remarkable drawing from *Liber S. Isidori* in the library at Basel, Switzerland. In this the picture of Libra is a kind if half-figure with hands outstretched. This is probably St Michael, often shown with a scales in which he weighs souls, as in the Cross of Muiredach at Monasterboice, Co Louth, at the Rock of Cashel and in the Cathedral of Kildare. His feast occurs on 29 September when the sun has just entered the sign of Libra, the Scales. Virgo carries a huge ear of corn most appropriate to the season of harvest (Virgo 23 August-22 September). For Pisces there is only one fish and Sagittarius is a rather odd looking figure. Capricorn is a handsome goat complete with beard. For each Sign there is an Apostle and one of the Twelve Tribes of Israel. (*JRSAI*, 1925, 130-135)

The connection between the doctrines of Christianity and the seasons of the year, with their particular operations in terms of agriculture, can be found in Our Lord's teaching about the sower going out to sow the seed, the enemy who sowed weed seed in the corn field, the harvest and the gathering in of souls at the end of the world, the signs of the seasons, the rapid passing of time denoting the need to prepare for death, the lengthening of the nights denoting the end of the world, and so forth.

In the great medieval churches of France and England especially, the integral tradition in which both creation and redemption are expressed comes gloriously to our attention in the profusion of decoration.

Vegetation in stone often tops the pillars; beasts wild and tame, real and imaginary, stare at one through the leaves and branches, the high groined roof stemming from tall pillars recalls the sacred wood – the 'nemeton' *(neimheadh)* of the Celts. The multicoloured light coming through the stained-glass windows reflects the light of the sun passing through different coloured foliage in a wooded grove.

Within this context a most interesting Norman baptismal font in Brookland Church, Kent, gives the Signs of the Zodiac and under each one the name of the month, in Norman-French, to which the sign belongs with the agricultural operation proper to the month:

Aqvarivs-Janvier: Janus-headed figure, feasting.

Pisces-Fevrier: Hooded figure warming himself at the fire.

Aries-Mars: Hooded figure pruning tree with hook.

Tavrvs-Avril: Female figure holding flower in each hand.

Gemini-Mai: Figure on horseback with hawk.

Cancer-Jvin: Figure with scythe mowing hay.

Leo-Juillet: Figure with rake.

Virgo-Aovt: Figure binding down.

Libra-Septembre: Figure threshing corn.

Scorpio-Octobre: Figure pressing wine.

Sagittarivs-Novembre: Hooded figure feeding pigs.

Capricornvs-Decembre: Figure with uplifted axe, killing pig.

The Four Seasons are sculptured on the Norman font at Thorpe Salvin, Yorkshire, as follows:

Man reaping corn (Autumn).

Man on horseback (Summer).

Man sowing corn (Spring).
Man warming himself at the fire (Winter).
(Allen, 1885, 321)

In all of this, the Zodiac portrayed in the great cathedrals of Europe such as Chartres and Autun, the elaborate sculpture of vegetation, birds, beasts and human activity, evokes the idea of creation and of human life as it was actually experienced by those who frequented the church in the Middle Ages and later.

Possibly, in many cases, the stained-glass windows concentrated on the idea of the Redemption with the life of Christ and the saints portrayed in brilliant colour. In this way, the two great themes of early liturgical piety – creation and redemption – received an architectural and artistic portrayal in the actual church building.

In the various Eucharistic Prayers the work of creation receives relatively little attention, the emphasis being placed on the life of Christ and the work of our redemption accomplished by him.

We have, however, a very fine example from the early period of the church of an *Anaphora* or Eucharistic Prayer which develops the idea of creation to a very high extent indeed and may be seen as the literary counterpart of the adornment of the church building with sculptures and paintings from the world of nature. This is the *Apostolic Constitutions,* Book Eight, and goes back to the fourth century. An extract, from this *Anaphora* will illustrate the importance given to creation:

> You appointed the sun in heaven to begin the day and the moon to begin the night, and you inscribed the chorus of the stars in heaven to the praise of your magnificence.
>
> You made water for drinking and cleansing, life-giving air for breathing in and out, and for the production of sound through the tongue striking the air, and for hearing which is aided by it to receive the speech which falls upon it.

You made fire for comfort in darkness, for supplying our need, that we should be warmed and given light by it.

You divided the ocean from the land, and made the one navigable, the other fit to be trodden by our feet; you filled it with creatures small and great, tame and wild; you wove it a crown of varied plants and herbs, you beautified it with flowers and enriched it with seeds.

You constructed the abyss and set a great covering on it, the piled-up seas of salt water, and surrounded it with gates of finest sand; now you raise it with winds to the height of the mountains, now you level it to a plain; now you drive it to fury with a storm, now you soothe it with a calm, so that it gives an easy journey to travellers in ships.

You girdled the world that was made by you through Christ and flooded it with torrents, you watered it with ever-flowing springs and bound it round with mountains as an unshakeable and most safe seat for the earth.

For you filled the world and adorned it with sweet smelling and healing herbs, with many different living things, strong and weak, for food and for work, tame and wild, with hissing of reptiles, with the cries of varied birds, the cycles of the years, the numbers of months and days, the order of the seasons, the course of rain-bearing clouds for the production of fruits and the creation of living things, a stable for the winds that blow at your command, the multitude of plants and herbs. (Jasper, R., and Cuming, G., 1980, 72)

The *Anaphora* then goes on to explain that God placed man at the head of creation. An eternal destiny was prepared for him but he turned away from God. God, however, did not reject him but sent Christ his Son to bring him back. The theme of redemption then continues in the ordinary way.

Here we have the original cosmic vision of an integrated universe being brought back to its centre in the infinity of God.

This basic theme of creation is of course magnificently presented in Psalm 104 (103) which follows the six days of creation as in the Book of Genesis. On the seventh or Sabbath Day, God rests and the Psalmist proclaims his praise and admiration for what has been accomplished.

The Canticle of the Three Young Men in the Fiery Furnace (Dan 3:57-88) seems to have been of great significance to the Irish, probably for two different reasons. Firstly, the story of the three young men thrown into the fiery furnace and rescued by God in this terrible predicament conforms to the *Lúireach* or 'protection theme' so favoured by the Celts. The scene is depicted on the High Crosses of Monasterboice, Arboe, Kells and Moone. In the Rule of the Céilí Dé, the *Benedicite,* as it was called, was in use in connection with meals where it served its second function as the great song of praise of God for all his works.

In the Tridentine Rite of Mass it was recited by the priest on his way back to the sacristy, after the celebration of the Eucharist. In this canticle those elements which make up the world of our experience are called upon to bless the Lord: sun, moon, rain, dew, heat, cold, night, day, light, darkness, lightning, clouds, earth, sea, mountains, hills, beast, cattle, birds, plants, wells – all are invited to bless the Lord.

Parts of the Canticle also occurred on the Ember Days. These Ember Days were associated with the period of harvesting in Italy which would not correspond exactly with conditions in more northerly countries. The Ember Days of December (Wed., Fri., Sat.) were linked to the Olive Harvest; those of Pentecost Week to the Wheat Harvest and the Ember Days of September to the Vine Harvest. (*IER,* June 1960, 408-409)

These, like the Rogation Processions, have disappeared, leaving technological man with his technology but with no liturgical reminder of his connection with the land and the cycle of the year.

The remarkable figures in the ruined mediaeval church of Killeshin, Co Laois, show vividly the internetted web of life where dragons swallow and regurgitate men, and men, animals and vegetation appear linked together in an ordered pattern expressive of the *neart* or dynamic energy emanating from God in the support of life. The 'Green Man' is enmeshed in new growth and the zig-zag lines suggest the flow of water and the process of nature.

In this matter of the creation, its connection with the *Anaphora* and its expression in the profusion of sculptured vegetation in ancient churches, we must mention here the remarkable poems of Liam Ó Marnáin, who wrote early in the nineteenth century. Two of his poems on the theme of the glories of creation are given by Úna Ní Ógáin in her fine collection, *Dánta Dé* (BÁC, 1928). It would be difficult to find among the Greek and Latin Anaphoras a better or more poetic expression of the idea of thanksgiving to God for the creation of the world with all that it contains:

(1) Míle buíochas leatsa a Fhír-Spioraid naofa.
a cheap na spéartha is neamh ar dtús.
a líon tar éis sin an mhórmhuir bhraonach
le carnaibh éisc inti ag snámh na dtonn.

(2) Chuir cnoic is sléibhte i bpáirt a chéile
'S chuir aibhne a' tsaoilse le fána ár stiúr,
Bánta an fhéir ghlais is gleannta 'on réir sin,
Coillte is craobhacha faoi bhláth gach súrd.

(3) Is glan 's is léir duit gach bláth ag séideadh
Is ag leathadh ar ghéagaibh na dtortha dtiubh
Mil dá réir sin dá fágáil le taoscadh
Tríd chumhachtaibh naofa dá mbarraibh siúd.

(4) Na mílte buíochas arís led' dhaonnacht
's led' chumhachta naofsa, a Rí na nDúl,
Do ghlan na spéartha is do bhreac na réaltaí
Go soilseach gléineach san oíche dhúinn.

(5) Thug meabhair is éifeacht do lán an tsaoghaíl
Chuir maise is méin mhaith 'na dteannta siúd,
Do cheap na héanlaith 's chuir ceol 'na mbéalaibh,
Gan suíomh ar éadach nó ar thigheas 'na gcionn.

(6) Ba pháirt de d'dhaonnacht nuair scaoilis d'AonMhac
Ó d'láimh dheis ghléigil dár dteagascadh,
Le trua do d'thréada bhi ar fán gan aodhaire
Go cásmhar céasta faoi phéin an úill.

(7) Is, a cháirde, géillidh, gurbh úd é an t-aodhaire
Nach raibh riamh taodach nó crua ina chroí,
Do bhí lán de dhaonnacht is le searc dá thréada
Is do bhuaigh gan buíochas ar Phlútó an fhíll (feall).

(1. A thousand thanks to you, O Holy True-Spirit, who created the skies and heaven at the beginning, who filled up, after that, the great liquid sea with heaps of fish swimming in the waves.

2. You put up hills and mountains together and put the rivers of the world to flow down the slopes from them. You created plains of green grass as well as glens, woods and branches with every type of flower.

3. You are clearly aware of every flower blown on by the wind and spread out on the branches of thick fruit. Honey, accordingly, is to be obtained and extracted from these blooms through your sacred power.

4. A thousand thanks to you, again for your kindness and for your holy power, O King of the Elements; you cleaned the sky and painted on the stars brightly, shiningly at night for us.

5. You gave understanding and force to the whole of life as well as artistry and good disposition. You created the birds and put music in their mouths without need for clothes or a roof above them.

6. It was a part of your kindness when you sent your Only

Son from your bright right hand to instruct us. You did this out of pity for your flock that had gone astray without a shepherd, troubled, tormented through the apple-transgression.

7. And, O Friends, concede, that this was the shepherd that was not arrogant or hard of heart. He was full of kindness and love for his flock and he triumphed over 'Pluto of the Deception' (the Devil).

8. He paid, without further claim, our debts all together and took multitudes with him from the gloomy Underworld, and he returned as a triumphant warrior without hurt or harm from the tomb again.)

What an extraordinary thing that a *file seachránach* (wandering poet) in the early nineteenth century could produce a composition that reflects so accurately the thanksgiving for creation and redemption theme of the early church.

Although addressed as 'Holy True-Spirit' *(a Fhír-Spioraid Naofa)* at the beginning, it is God the Father who is meant, as is clear from the reference to his only Son.

The word *daonnacht,* 'humanity/kindness/clemency', occurs three times and is certainly a key-word in the composition. It is implied that it is God's *daonnacht* which is responsible for his creating the world and all that is in it in the first place, and then this same *daonnacht* inspires God to send his Only Son to teach erring mankind, give the straying sheep a shepherd and reverse the consequences of original sin. This idea of *daonnacht* then provides the point of transition from creation to redemption.

Christ is the Shepherd, in accordance with biblical symbolism and country living, and this shepherd is *lán de dhaonnacht,* full of clemency.

In the last stanzas an elaborate Easter theme is developed. Satan, who deceived our first parents in urging them to eat the forbidden fruit is described as 'Pluto an Fhill'. Pluto in classical mythology is the god of the underworld. Christ defeats him and rescues from the gloomy underworld, Adam and Eve and the saints of the Old Testament such as the prophets, King David, King Solomon and countless others. This is the *Argain Ifrinn* or plundering of hell, a doctrine of the early church much loved by the Irish in accordance with the heroic tradition of heroes such as Fionn Mac Cumhaill, Cú Chulainn and Conall Cearnach.

With the rising sun of Easter morning, he rises from the tomb. If a Celtic liturgy were ever to be developed the material is here for a Eucharistic Anaphora.

Do dhíol gan éileamh ar bhfiacha in éineacht
Is thug táinte saor leis ó ghruaim aníos,
Agus d'fhill le laochas gan cneá gan créachta
Mar shoilse gréine ón dtuamba arís. (Uimh. 46)

The Composite Calendar
(Solstices, Equinoxes and Celtic Feasts)
Calendrical Associations:

Samhain: (1 Nov) Feast of All Saints. All Souls. Beginning of dark half of year. Breaking down of barriers between worlds. 'Samhaintide', from 1 Nov to mid-Dec, theme of Last Judgement. Reward and Punishment.
Advent: Preparation for Birth of Christ. Winter solstice (21 Dec). Entrance of ray of light from rising sun to New Grange. 'O Antiphon': 'O Oriens'. Birth of Christ. 'Wren Boys'. Epiphany, 6 January. 12 days of Christmas.

Imbolg (1 Feb). Naomh Bríd. Beginning of spring and agricultural year.
Presentation of Christ in the Temple (2 Feb).
Season of Lent.

Spring Equinox. (21 March). Ancient start of year.
Conception of Christ (Annunciation). The Paschal Mystery,
death and resurrection of Our Lord.

Bealtaine (1 May). Beginning of bright-half of year – bonfires,
dragon fighting, fertility.
Easter Season.
Pentecost – descent of Holy Spirit on the apostles.
Pentecost Season – work of Holy Spirit in church.
Summer Solstice (21 June): Birth of St John the Baptist.
'Bonfire Night'.

Lughnasa (1 Aug). Domhnach Chrom Dubh; First-fruits of
harvest – wheat, oats, barley and wild-fruits – 'Fraocháin'.
Pilgrimage time: Loch Dearg, Croagh Patrick, Cnoc Bhréan-
nainn, etc.
Transfiguration of Christ (6 Aug). Glory of Risen Christ
shown, first fruits of redemption, the rest of the faithful will
follow with Blessed Virgin Mary leading the way into heaven
at the Feast of the Assumption (15 Aug). Parthalán an
Fhómhair (24 Aug). The Beheading of St John the Baptist (29
Aug.). Connection with Irish through druid Mogh Roith.
'Scuab as Fanaid'.
Autumn Equinox (21 Sept). Feast of St Michael (29 Sept).
Defeat of rebel angels in war in heaven. Psychopomp. Dragon
fighter. Sites of cult. First-fruits festival in Hebrides.

CHAPTER SEVENTEEN

Samhain, All Saints and All Souls

In the present form of the liturgical year we can distinguish a complete season running from the Feast of All Saints and All Souls, first and second of November, up to about the middle of December.

This six-week period has an explicitly dominant theme which is found particularly in the gospel pericopes. A glance at these will show the preoccupation with the irruption of the divine on the human scene, the coming of God into the world, the judgement scene, the violence and disruption following on the encounter of the divine and human worlds. From the texts it is clear that the meeting between the two dimensions of reality is not without discomfort and danger. There is a very deliberate use of texts which stress the irruption of the otherworld into this world and the passing over of the dead from this world to the world beyond. In other words, this is a period in which the barriers between the two worlds have crumbled.

For convenience we will call this period the 'Season of Samhain' or 'Samhaintide', *Samhain* being the Celtic Feast for the First of November with which the season begins.

A considerable obscurity lies over the selection of 1 November as the Feast of All Saints and it is difficult to discount the view that it was in some way influenced by Celtic custom, which gave such an enormous importance to the Feast of Samhain. In the ninth-century Irish martyrology, *Félire Óengusso Céli Dé* (Ed. Stokes, W., London 1905), one of the manuscript readings for 1 November gives *'noaib in domain dálaigh, sóerait samain síanaig'* (the saints of the teeming world ennoble stormy Samhain). This may denote that the Feast of All Saints was celebrated in Ireland at an early date and it has been argued that the feast spread from here to the continent by way of Northumbria. (Hennig, J. 'The Meaning of All the Saints', *MedSt.* 10 (1948) 147-161)

Our season, then, has something of the character of a prolongation of Samhain over a six-week period.

Now, while it is biblical texts which are used in the Roman liturgy to describe the meeting of the two worlds and the breaking down of barriers fraught with danger, nevertheless it is remarkable that the particular period of the year in which these texts are used corresponds to some extent to the period of Samhain in the old Gaelic Calendar. The year was divided into two equal parts, the dark half, from Samhain to Bealtaine, that is from 1 November to 1 May, and the bright half from Bealtaine to Samhain, from 1 May to 1 November. Samhain and Bealtaine (Halloween and May Eve) are the sacred points of the Celtic year, the threshold periods of 'in between periods' in which order collapses and chaos predominates. At Samhain (Halloween) the summer isn't quite over and the winter hasn't yet begun, so this evening is *Tráth na Táirsí,* the threshold period, neither within or without.

Samhain is traditionally the beginning of the Celtic year. The dark half of the year comes first, giving place to the bright part, winter giving place to summer, death giving way to life. It is the Celtic New Year's Eve and predictions are made regarding the year to come. Whoever finds the ring in the *Báirín Breac,* for instance, will be married soon. Bonfires are lighted to assist the sun to keep on shining and to destroy the evils of the past six-month period.

Oíche Shamhna is called *Oíche na gCleas,* the night of the tricks, and one of the tricks is to remove gates. While the children who do this are generally not aware of its meaning, it is a significant act. The removal of the gate means that the recognised barrier between my property and yours has been removed and people and animals wander freely between the areas which were once distinct. In other words, what we have here is a symbol of the disappearance of the normal barriers which separate this world from the world of the *Sí* or the Tuatha Dé Danann.

The Tuatha Dé Danann had power over the fertility of the land. They could cause good harvests or bad, they had power over cattle and could cause disease or prosperity. The human population had to acknowledge their power. They made offerings by pouring a little milk on the ground, placing a specially baked cake outside at the four feasts – Imbolc, Bealtaine, Lúnasa, Samhain.

At Samhain (Halloween), groups of people in masks, straw suits and various other types of disguise, went from house to house to make a collection of money, eggs, loaves of bread, etc., or whatever the householders may have had. If the people of the house gave generously, they would prosper throughout the year; if they proved mean or stingy they could expect misfortune in the future.

There was a particularly clear indication of this at the Hogmanay Rite in parts of Scotland. The fire was in the centre of the kitchen and if the Hogmanay Men or Guisers had been well treated they performed the *iompú deiseal* around the fire – that is they walked around the fire in procession, one after another, keeping the fire at their right-hand side, that is, following the course of the sun. This is the recognised Celtic ritual for blessing and good fortune. On the other hand, if contributions had been less than generous, the Guisers marched around the fire *tuathal*, against the sun (anti-clockwise) – a certain sign of evil and ill-luck. (cf. Carmichael, 1972, 156-157)

Fundamentally, it seems to be that these strange, rather weird processions of masked figures, sometimes playing musical instruments, blowing horns, and performing dances or dramas, and sometimes accompanied by the *Láir Bhán/Mari Lwyd* – an artificial horse with snapping jaws – were meant to represent the Tuatha Dé Danann and the Fomóirí coming back to collect their taxes.

Taxes had to be paid and offerings made to the underground race in recognition of their control over the production of corn and milk. Even after the Fomóirí had been defeated at the Battle of Maige Tuired it was recognised that the defeated King Bres had power over milk and corn and he was even able to promise four harvests per year if the victors agreed not to kill him.

He was not spared on this account, however; traditional laziness asserted itself and he was told that one sowing and one harvest per year was quite enough. (But think what it would have meant if they had accepted his offer and the country were able to produce corn, milk and fruit out of season and sell the produce abroad at enormous profit!) He was allowed to live on telling them that ploughing, sowing and reaping should all the done on a Tuesday. (Gray, E., 1982, 67-69.)

Moreover, three of the Fomóirí had been brought out of the lands of the Fomóirí by Mac Céacht and kept as hostages in Conaire's house as a guarantee that the Fomóirí would not spoil grain or milk in Éire beyond their lawful allowance: *i ngiallna nar choillet ith ná blicht i nHérind tara cháin téchtae.* – Knott, E., (Ed), *Tógail Bruidne Da Derga,* (Dublin 1936) Lines 916-921.

One of the great tales of the Irish mythological system of which the scene is set at Samhain is *Echtra Nerai* (Nera's Adventure). From the Bible and the Catholic liturgy we are familiar with the apocalyptic treatment of the invasion of this world by the world beyond. *Eachtra Nera,* while treating of the same subject – the meeting of the two worlds at Samhain – shows how the subject is treated in the Celtic manner. The parallel accounts should serve to focus the attention of the reader on the otherworld, which after all, is a central feature of both the Catholic faith and the *creideamh sí*. ('Echtra Nerai – The Adventures of Nera', *Revue Celtiques* x (1889), 214ff; Rees, A. and B., *Celtic Heritage*, (London 1976) 298ff; Joynt, M., *The Golden Legends of the Gael*, (Dublin) Part 1, 62ff.)

Eachtra Nera: Summary
It was Samhain and at the palace of Aileall and Méabh, King and Queen of Connacht, at Ráth Cruachan in present day Co Roscommon, the fires blazed as supper was being prepared. Two men had been hanged that day and King Aileall offered a prize to whoever was daring enough to go out into the darkness of the night and tie a withe around one of the dead mens' legs. Several of those present went out one by one into the darkness to attempt the task but came in again hurriedly as the night was full of spectres and demons.

Then Nera, one of the bravest, went out and tried to tie a twig around the dead man's leg. The dead man spoke and told him how to do it properly. Then the dead man asked Nera to carry him on his back to a house where he would get a drink of water as he had been very thirsty when he was hanged. There was a ring of fire around the first house they came to and so they couldn't enter. The hanged man explained that the people of that house had been careful to practice *Smáladh na Tine,* that is covering the fire with ashes at night, and this served to protect the house against the otherworld attack.

The next house had a ring of water around it and they could not enter there. The hanged man explained that the people had been careful to throw out any dirty water before going to bed.

Nera took the hanged man on his back to the third house

which had neither fire or water around it and there they entered. There was plenty of dirty water inside in a tub. The hanged man drank some of it and squirted the rest of it on the faces of those in the house and killed them all. Then Nera took the dead man back to the gallows and hung him up again.

Nera then set out to return to Ráth Cruachan to collect his prize from the king but as he approached he saw a fearful sight. The dún or fort was on fire and the Tuatha Dé Danann had come out from their *Sí* or fairy dwelling inside the cave of Cruachan and had cut off the heads of his friends.

The Tuatha Dé Danann were just then returning inside the *Sí* and Nera slipped in after them. He was of course discovered and brought before the King of the *Sí* who treated him kindly. He was given the daily task of bringing firewood for the fire and he was given a beautiful *Bean Sí* for his wife, so things were looking up for Nera.

He noticed a well in the *Sí* and every morning a blind man came carrying a lame man on his back. When they arrived at the well the blind man would ask, 'Is it there?' and the lame man on his back would answer 'It is there.' Then they would go home again.

Nera asked his wife what they were doing and she told him that they were the official guardians for the king's very precious crown which was kept in the well. The blind man couldn't see it to steal it and the lame man could see it but he was too lame to run away with it.

His wife also told him that the king and queen and his friends in Ráth Cruachan had not been killed at all – that it was an illusion, but that the Tuatha Dé Danann had planned to kill them next Samhain. She said that he should go and warn them of this and to come and attack the *Sí* before the *Sí* attacked them.

Nera went out and passed on this message, bringing the

summer flowers of the *Sí* with him to convince them, as of course it was the heart of winter in the human world.

Nera, his wife and family went out while the humans attacked the *Sí* and confiscated its treasure. Then Nera, his wife and family with all their cattle took up residence in the *Sí* once more and they have never been seen again.

A folklore version of *Eachtra Nera* puts the devil in the place of the hanged man and shows how the forces of the underworld are finally outwitted. (Rees, A. and B., *Celtic Heritage,* (London, 1976) 301ff.)

A boy is sent by his father to collect a slasher which he had left in a graveyard where he had been cutting down bushes. It was Samhain and the boy made his way as quickly as he could to where his father had left the slasher leaning against the gate. He found it without any difficulty and was turning round to go home before it became completely dark when a voice spoke beside him. It was a tall handsome man in dark clothes. 'Don't be afraid, boy,' said he, 'and no harm will come to you. I am the devil and I have need of you. You must take me on your back to that house yonder where the light is.'

The boy began to tremble but had no option but to take the devil on his back and strangely enough he had no great difficulty in walking, as the devil was not heavy. When they arrived at the house there was a ring of fire around it for the fire had been covered over with ashes with the ritual prayer said by the *bean a' tí:*

Coiglím an tine seo
mar a choiglíonn Críost cách,
Muire ar mhullach an tí
is Bríd ina lár.
An t-ochtar aingeal is aoirde
i gCathair na nGrás
ag cosaint an tí seo
is a mhuintir go lá.

(I preserve this fire as Christ preserves everybody; Mary at the top of the house and Brigid at its centre. The eight highest angels in the City of Grace guarding this house and its people until the coming of day)

The devil could not enter here and he told the boy to move on to the next house. The next house had a ring of water around it for holy water had been sprinkled in the house and once more the devil instructed the boy to move to the next house.

At the third house there was neither fire nor water to be seen and the devil descended from the boy's back and prepared to enter. 'You may go home now,' he said, 'for this house suits me well. Here there is a quarrelling couple and they will have a son. It will be my son but they will not know that. He will become a priest and before his first Mass he will sprinkle the congregation with holy water. All those on whom a drop of the water will fall will be damned, they will belong to me and come to my domain.'

The boy ran home with the slasher and said nothing of his adventures. Nor did it seem that any extra time had passed than would be required to go to the churchyard. The boy soon forgot the incident but it returned to his memory again on hearing that a son had been born to the couple in the house he and the devil has visited.

The years passed and this couple's son began to study for the priesthood. The time for his ordination came and the boy knew that it was up to him to thwart the devil's plan and save the people from damnation.

The day came when the priest, the devil's son, was to say his first Mass in the church. A large congregation had gathered in the church for the occasion and among them was the boy now grown up to be a man. Under his coat he had concealed the slasher which he had brought back from the graveyard on the night of Samhain long ago.

The priest came on the altar, dipped the sprinkler in the vase of holy water and lifted his right arm to sprinkle the people. At that moment, the man sprang forward and with a deft stroke of the slasher severed the priest's arm from his body. At that moment there was a mighty burst of flame and the priest disappeared in it. All knew then that this had been the devil's son and that in the nick of time they had been saved from hell.

Another tale of Samhain comes from the Fiannaíocht Cycle and describes how Fionn Mac Cumhail overcame the machinations of Ailléan Mac Midhna from the fairy mound of Sí Fhionnachaidh at Sliabh gCuillinn, Co Armagh. (*Agallamh na Seanórach,* Stokes, W., und Windisch, E., *Irische Texte,* (Leipzig 1900) 1655ff; Ó Cadhlaigh, C., *An Fhiannuidheacht,* (Baile Átha Cliath 1947) 40-42; Carbery, E., *In the Celtic Past,* (Dublin) 35ff.)

It was the night of Samhain and a great feast was in progress in the palace of the Ard Rí, Conn Céadchathach, in Tara. The joy of the feasting was overcast, however, for every year, at Samhain, one of the Tuatha Dé Danann, Ailléan Mac Midhna used to come from Sí Fhionnachaidh in Ulster to burn down the wooden buildings of Tara. He came each Samhain, playing magic music which put even the bravest warriors to sleep and when they awoke in the morning the Palace of Tara lay in ashes around them.

During the feast the king announced that he would give a large prize to anybody who could save Tara from being burned down that night and keep the place safe until morning. Fionn Mac Cumhail agreed to try.

He first procured a poisonous spear from Fiacha Mac Congha and Fiacha showed him how to use it. 'When you see Ailléan coming playing the harp and fire coming from his mouth, put the point of the spear to your forehead and the pain and poison from the spear will enable you to keep awake.' Fionn wrapped his large mantle around him and, taking the spear, went to guard the gates of Tara.

Soon the first notes of the fairy music were heard and Fionn applied the sharp point of the spear to his forehead. Inside Tara, the boisterous sounds of drunken feasting began to grow still as the music reached them and one by one the guests sank down in sleep. As the music drew nearer, the weapons fell from the sentries' hands and they too lay down to sleep.

Then Fionn saw Ailléan approaching with fire issuing from his mouth as he played his harp. Fionn felt his attention wavering with the power of the fairy music and he sank the spear deep in his forehead until the blood flowed down his face. As the flame spurted from Ailléan's mouth Fionn threw up his cloak to prevent it reaching the thatched buildings of Tara and seeing that he was opposed, Ailléan turned and ran.

Fionn pursued him, holding the spear in his hand ready for the cast. Over hill and dale they went, over mountain and glen until at last the otherworld mound of Sí Fhionnachaidh appeared in view. It was then that Fionn made the cast and with a deadly accurate aim the spear pierced Ailléan Mac Midhna to the heart, at the very entrance to the *Sí*.

Fionn drew near and cut off his head. He brought the head back to Tara and there it was raised on a pole for all to see.

It was in recognition of his saving of Tara that Fionn Mac Cumhaill was promoted to be leader of the Fianna Éireann.

In these stories of Samhain from the Celtic culture, we see the incursion of the otherworld in the affairs of men, an incursion that is sometimes hostile and dangerous and needs the hero's skill and courage to overthrow its destructive power. The hero must be alert and in readiness to act decisively when the time comes.

While the Celtic and Judaeo-Christian cultures are poles

apart, nevertheless, it is useful to see what they have in common, and what they have in common in their celebration of winter and the dying year is a heightening awareness of the invasion of this world by the supernatural world and of the necessity of being ready to deal with the event.

All Souls' Day

On All Souls' Day, 2 November, the dead are especially remembered. Masses for the Dead are celebrated, prayers said, churches visited, graves cleaned. People are very conscious of the otherworld at this time of Samhain.

A widespread belief was that dead members of the family returned to their old home for this one night. Care was taken to show that they were welcome. In some places a good fire was put down, a bowl of spring water laid on the table, candles lighted and the door left unlocked while the family retired early to leave the place free for the returned souls. (Danaher, 1972, 228-229)

In Wales and Brittany it was the custom for a group of people to go from house to house on All Souls' Eve looking for alms, sometimes in the form of 'Soul-Cakes'. They exhorted the people in the house to remember their dead and on receiving alms promised to pray for the dead of the family. (Whitlock, 1978, 147; de La Villemarqué, 1981, 507-509)

In Ireland the connection of the megaliths with death was shown in the custom of walking three times *deiseal* (sunwise) around a megalithic tomb or tumulus and then placing a stone on the cairn with the formula:

> Síocháin, ar d'anam agus cloch ar do charn. (Peace to your soul and a stone on your tomb.) (*Ireland of the Welcomes*, April 1995)

In Scotland, Samhain was associated with megaliths where it was the custom to light the bonfire on a tumulus or barrow. An example cited is that of Fortingall, Perthshire, where the bonfire was built on the 'Mound of the Dead' (a Bronze Age tumulus), by communal effort and was lit by the older men of the community. The people danced around it while it blazed and ran around with flaming brands taken from it. In other areas the flaming sticks were carried around the boundaries of farms for protection and to encourage the fertility of the earth. (Whitlock, 1978, 146-147)

Marian McNeill discusses the situation in Scotland:

In folk-belief, the spirits of he dead haunted the megalithic monuments that marked the ancient burial grounds and these were the main sites of the festival. Offerings and sacrifices were made to ancestral spirits, to whom great power was attributed.

In many of the Celtic territories there are traces of the ancient horse races and of the funeral games and dances. The latter lingered into the nineteenth century.

In accordance with the policy of the Christian Church to graft a Christian festival upon each pagan one, Samhainn in due course became Hallowmas, or the Feast of All Saints. Whilst the Feast of All Saints commemorated the blessed dead who had been canonised, the Feast of all Souls (November 2nd), which was established in 998, was consecrated to the faithful dead and to prayer for the eternal repose of their souls.

In Roman Catholic countries, people visit the graves of those dear to them on the *jour des morts* and, kneeling, sprinkle them with holy water. In modern Brittany, as in ancient Egypt, people left food on the table before retiring for the night, and it is questionable if the old belief has even yet entirely died out in Scotland. (1961, 3, 12)

To summarise, then, the Catholic celebration of the Feasts of All Saints and All Souls: what is most obvious during these days of the darkening period of the year is the irruption of the divine on the human scene, multitudes of the saints surrounding the throne of God in heaven as described in the Reading at Mass and then, on the following day, the preoccupation with the dead, another department of the otherworld. Perhaps there is no time in the whole of the liturgical year that we are so obsessed with the otherworld than on those two days – and this was the time in which the pagan Celts were most obsessed with the otherworld also. Even for the Catholics, if the barriers separating the two worlds weren't entirely removed, they have to some extent crumbled.

This brings me to a further point. I have always found the last Sundays of the Year and the fist couple of Sundays of Advent a most difficult and incomprehensible part of the liturgical year. They are full of the idea of God returning to reward the good and punish the wicked. There is a series of contrasts in the gospel pericopes – the wise virgins and the foolish virgins, the sheep and the goats, the prepared and the unprepared, the really holy and the seemingly holy, the generous and the ungenerous. But again, this is precisely the kind of thinking which we have encountered in the celebration of Samhain. My own view is that a whole liturgical season can be distinguished running from All Saints to half way through December which contains these ideas. This I would term Samhaintide. Advent, in this personal view, would begin about mid-December as an immediate preparation for the Birth of Christ.

CHAPTER EIGHTEEN

Advent and Fír Flatha

The Season of Advent is a period of time leading up to the feast of Christmas. As such it directs our attention to the notion of the birth of a child. And the birth of a child directs our attention further still to the destiny of that child – what kind of life will it have, what will be its role in life, what effect will this child have on the world and on humankind. In short, will this particular child to be born at Christmas have a special destiny; will he bring about a profound and radical change in the world?

Perhaps it was with a thought such as this in mind that the great artist Gauguin produced his famous painting of the South Sea Islands. The picture goes from right to left and the large canvas shows first a baby, then various groups of people of different ages going about their business, and then, on the extreme left-hand side there is an old woman with her face in her hands as she contemplates death. On the corner of the picture there are three questions written in French: 'Where do we come from?', 'Where are we going?', 'What are we?'

These three questions express the enigma of human existence, and down through the centuries people have wrestled with them, trying to find an answer to the mystery of life as best they could.

The various texts which we hear in church during Advent express a longing for a saviour and an enlightener, for somebody who will rescue us from our predicament and who will give direction to our lives.

Over and over again we hear such phrases as:

'Come and show us the way of truth.'

'Come and set the captive free from his prison home.'

'Come and enlighten those who are in darkness and in the shadow of death.'

In these phrases two things are asserted: firstly, that we are people who feel that we are trapped in some impossible situation, and secondly that in this predicament we have to call on external help to liberate us and set us free. And the person we call upon is Christ the Son of God, in his character of Liberator.

While the liturgy presents us with a cosmic vision, in which God becomes man to liberate the human race from sin and death, each of us singly feels part of this human condition in a personal way. For each of us in our own way feels trapped in some situation from which we cannot escape. However liberated we may be, the ties of circumstance, of convention, heredity or neurosis, bind us in chains of steel.

When the liturgy then addresses Our Lord as the Liberator and says, 'Come and rescue us from prison,' it is only expressing a deeply-felt need of the human condition. And it is precisely to this that Our Lord addressed himself in that passage of scripture in which he said that God the Father had sent him into the world to bring good news to the poor, to proclaim liberty to captives, to give new sight to the blind and to set the downtrodden free.

In an ancient Irish collection of manuscripts called *Leabhar na hUidhre,* there is the story of Mongán, King of Ulster which illustrates a situation similar to our own. In the story, a row broke out between the king and his *file* or court poet. The king had contradicted the poet by saying that a former king of Ulster had been buried in Ulster while the poet had said that he was buried in Leinster. The *file* was furious at this contradiction and said that he would use his magical power to blight the crops and cause famine on the land unless the king could prove his assertion within three days.

Messengers were sent out in all directions looking for information but no information was forthcoming. The evening of the third day came and the king was desperate, for the time would be up at the setting of the sun. At this point, the queen began to cry. But just then, the king had a kind of vision and he said, 'Don't cry, for I see a rescuer at hand. I see him passing over the Lakes of Killarney on his way to Ulster. He brings the information which will save us.'

Some time passed, and again the queen began to cry and the king spoke again, 'Don't cry,' he said, 'for now I see him coming nearer. He is now crossing the Morning Star river in Limerick.' There was another delay and again the queen began to cry. And again the king said, 'Don't cry, for now he is crossing the Boyne and he will reach us before the setting of the sun.'

As the sun was about to sink into the western horizon the warrior stood before the king and queen dressed in the apparel of an earlier age and in his hand he held the shaft of a spear. He explained that it was he who had killed the king and that the missing spearpoint had passed through the king's body. The king was buried near where he had fallen in his native Ulster and so Mongán's assertion was vindicated and the king and queen were set free, by the aid of a visitor from the otherworld, from the terrible entanglement into which they had fallen.

The liturgy of Advent is like this story. It presents us with people who are trapped and who must depend on a liberator from outside. Like Caoilte Mac Rónáin crossing the rivers of Ireland one after the other as he approaches Ulster, so the readings of Advent present Our Lord as drawing progressively nearer, just as the number of candles lighted on the Advent Wreath increase as we approach Christmas. And over and over again, the liturgy of Advent utters the cry: 'Come Lord and rescue us, come and make no delay.'

One feature of the Advent liturgy are the marvellous 'O-Antiphons', sung during the immediate preparation for Christmas in the liturgy of the Roman Rite.

The origin of these Antiphons is obscure, but they may date from the eighth or ninth century. They may have had some connection by way of Christian response to the Roman celebration of the Saturnalia from 17 to 23 December, in association with the winter solstice.

There are 7 antiphons in all and traditionally they are sung in Benedictine monasteries with great solemnity at Vespers on these days. The celebrant, vested in violet cope, intones the opening address, e.g. 'O Sapientia'. Then the choir continues the antiphon with its elaborate plain chant melody. The celebrant incenses the altar during the singing of the *Magnificat* and the bells are rung. At the end of the *Magnificat* the antiphon is repeated. These 7 O-Antiphons follow a fixed pattern.

Briefly, each antiphon begins with an address to Our Lord under a specific title. Then there may follow an elaboration of this title, as for instance in the first Antiphon which elaborates on the idea of Wisdom as coming forth from the mouth of the Most High, reaching the outposts of the universe and holding all things together in harmony, or, other titles may be added to the opening one. Finally, each antiphon closes with a plea to Christ to come *(Veni)* to teach us the way of prudence, to save us, to enlighten us.

The O-Antiphons contain a number of leading ideas. One among them is the idea of Wisdom contained especially in the Antiphon *O Sapientia* for 17 December. Here, Christ is addressed as the Wisdom who came forth from the Most High God. He orders and arranges the universe from end to end, strongly and gently. We ask the personified Wisdom to come and teach us the way of prudence. Here Wisdom is associated with the creation of the world – the mapping out, the planning, the dividing and ordering of the universe.

When we turn to Celtia, can we find anything approaching this biblical concept of Wisdom upon which such an emphasis is laid in the Christmas liturgy? I believe that a certain similarity is discernible in the Gaelic idea of *fír* associated with kingship.

It can be said that from the Irish king four qualities were required:

1. He must be free from physical blemish – if he lost a hand in battle, for instance, as in the case of Nuada in the First Battle of Maigh Tuireadh between the Tuatha Dé Danann and the Fir Bolg, he had to resign.

2. Similarly, he had to observe certain *geasa* or taboos. The violation of these would lead to doom as in the case of Conaire Mór violating his *geasa* in the story *Togail Bruidne Da Derga*.

3. Then there was 'fial' – generosity, the giving of gifts, lavish entertainment, hospitality. This was one of the true marks of a *flaith* (prince) and even in English the word *flaithiúil* is used to denote generosity. It was the absence of this quality of *féile* in King Bres that led to his deposition. Visitors to his *dún* complained that their knives were not greased with meat and they came away without smelling of beer. It is significant that in the eighth century poems of Bláthmac, Christ is portrayed in typically Irish fashion as a great chieftain giving lavish feasts and bestowing largesse.

4. Finally, there was *fír* – *fír flathemon/fírinne flatha* – the prince's truth.

In *fír flathemon* is contained the notion of truth, justice, prudence, wisdom, order. The king in Ireland was required to have the quality of *fírinne flatha* for the just and wise ordering of his kingdom. The lack of this quality, in not inflicting a sufficiently just sentence on his former companions for their misdeeds, led to the tragedy of Conaire Mór as well as the breaking of his *geasa*. *(Tógail Bruidne Da Derga)*

There is also the story of Lughaidh Mac Con, king of Tara. A case was brought to him for judgement by a woman. She had a herb garden, a very valuable possession in those days when herbs were used for medicine and the dying of fabrics. She claimed that another woman's sheep had jumped over the fence and eaten up all her herbs. The king gave as his judgement that the sheep should be given to the owner of the garden in compensation. It might well be thought that this was a reasonably fair judgement but it was not to be left unchallenged.

The young Cormac Mac Airt was present and he objected to the decision of the court. He pointed out that both the herbs and the wool of the sheep would grow again and that it was sufficient that the sheep be shorn and the wool given in compensation. 'That is a true judgement,' said the assembled people, 'it is the son of a true prince who has given judgement.' At this moment, the part of the building where the false judgement had been given fell down. Lughaidh Mac Con was deposed and Cormac Mac Airt became king in his place. It is from this episode that the part of Tara known as *Claonfhearta Teamhrach* (the sloping mounds of Tara) derives its name. (O' Grady, 1892, 255)

Justice and wise government belong to the king who is held to be divine or has divine prerogatives in ancient tradition. (Rees, 1961, 129) In the O-Antiphon for 22 December Christ is addressed as King *(O Rex Gentium)* and the special characteristics of kingship are attributed to his reign in the Preface for the Mass of Christ the King:

As king he claims dominion over all creation,

that he may present you, his almighty Father,
an eternal and universal kingdom:
kingdom of truth and life,
kingdom of holiness and grace,
kingdom of justice, love and peace.

In the Irish mythological tradition great emphasis is laid on the king's truth *(fír flathemon)*. This is essential for a successful reign. An ancient instruction for rulership declares:

By the prince's truth great peoples are ruled,
by the prince's truth great mortality is warded off from men,
By the prince's truth great battles are driven off into the enemy's country,
by the prince's truth every right prevails and every vessel is full in his reign ...
by the prince's truth fair weather comes in each fitting season, winter fine and frosty, spring dry and windy, summer warm with showers of rain, autumn with heavy dews and fruitful. For it is the prince's falsehood that brings perverse weather upon wicked peoples, and dries up the fruit. (Rees, 1961, 129)

A particularly illuminating account of this is given in the case of Cairbre Cinncait, so-called according to legend after his catlike ears. The *Aitheach-Thuatha* or plebians, probably of Fir Bholg stock, rebelled against the Milesian aristocracy and massacred them at a feast at Magh Cró, near Knockmaa, Co Galway. Three pregnant queens escaped the massacre and fled overseas and it was their three sons who at a later stage returned to take up the kingship in Ireland after the collapse of the *Aitheach-Thuatha* kingship.

After Cairbre's death, the kingship was offered to his son Morann but he, being a truly intelligent and just man (as we shall see later), refused the kingship and said that the famine would cease only on the return of the rightful heirs to the throne. 'The nobles were afterwards sent for, and the *Aitheach-Thuatha* swore by heaven and earth, the sun, moon and all the elements, that they would be obedient to them and their descendants, as long as the sea should surround Ireland. They then came to Ireland and settled, each in his hereditary region, namely *Tipraide Tíreach,* in the east of Ulster, *Corb Olum* in the south, over Munster, and *Fearadhach Finnfeachtnach,* at Teamhair of the Kings. (O' Donovan, 1856, 1, 95)

The *Annals of the Four Masters* record the change from famine to prosperity during the reign of *Feardhach:*

Maith trá ro boi Éire fria linnsiomh. Robdar certa suaimnech na siona. Tuismis an talamh a toradh. Iascmhar na hinbhiora, blichtmhara na buair, ceanntrom na collte. (Good was Ireland during his time. The seasons were right tranquil. The earth brought forth its fruit; fishful its rivermouths; milkful the kine; heavy-headed the woods.) (O' Donovan, 1856, 1, 96-97)

Of all the kings of Ireland perhaps none was so renowned for his wisdom as Cormac Mac Airt, although the darker, more sinister side of his character is apparent in the story *Forbuis Droma Damgháire* from the *Book of Lismore.* By means of a magic cup given him by Manannán Mac Lir of the Tuatha Dé Danann, he could distinguish truth from falsehood.

On the morning of Bealtaine, Cormac received a visit from a warrior from Tír na nÓg, a land where there was nothing but truth, a land without age nor decay nor jealousy nor hatred. He gave Cormac a silver branch with three golden apples on it. When shaken, the branch would produce soothing music which put the sick and wounded and women in childbed to sleep. In return for the branch, Cormac had to grant the otherworldly visitor three wishes. Firstly, he took Cormac's daughter with him as his first wish, then his son and finally his wife. After this Cormac set out in pursuit and through a thick mist arrived at the wonderful land of Tír na nÓg. Here he met Manannán who restored his wife, son and daughter and gave him in addition a golden cup. When three lies were told in its presence it would break into three pieces but when three truths were spoken it became whole again. This enabled him, once he had returned to Ireland to distinguish truth from falsehood in all his judgements. (Rees, 1961, 310-312)

We next encounter the idea of wisdom, prudence and just judgement in an native context in the story of Morann's Collar *(Íodh Mhorainn)*.

Morann was the son of Cairbre Cinnchait and had refused the kingship as we have seen. He was born with a caul on his head and Cairbre had him thrown into the sea. However, a large wave arose which partly broke the caul, freeing the child's head. He spoke saying: 'Rough is the wave'. He was rescued and given to the smith Maon and his wife to be reared. While the smith was examining the child by candlelight the child exclaimed, 'Bright is the candle.' Finally, Cairbre recognised him as his son and he was made chief justice. He gave many instructions as to the proper way to rule a kingdom and these form the basis for later wisdom texts of this kind. The remnant of the caul which remained around his neck was the *Íodh Mhorainn*. If he began to give an unjust judgement the *Íodh* tightened around his neck and began to choke him and so forced him to reverse his decision. Similarly, it could be removed and put around the neck of a witness and tightened if he began to tell a lie. (Ó hÓgáin, 1991, 306-307)

Morann was also said to have gone to see St Paul and to have obtained a letter from him. He wore this letter around his neck and it prevented him from giving a false judgement, as in the case of the caul. Here we have a Christianised version of the story and of course it is pre-patrician.

According to legend, Morann believed in the Christian God through the *Reacht Aigeanta* or Natural Law, 'through examination of the elements and through his own clear understanding'.

Another story which touches Morann's personal life illustrates his wisdom and tolerance. He discovered his wife making love to his servant. He turned the servant into a speckled calf. His wife said she was sick and wanted to eat the meat of the calf. Morann took his sword and approached the calf. He asked the calf what the sword feared. The calf answered 'stone'. Then a question and answer scene took place between Morann and the calf:

The sword feared stone;
The stone feared fire;
The fire feared water;
The water feared wind;
The wind feared hills;
The hills feared boars;
The boars feared hounds;
The hounds feared bad women.

When asked what women feared, the calf said that he did not know. Morann then said that he would not kill his wife as other men did not kill their unfaithful wives. Perhaps the implication was that women's psychology was beyond men's understanding and that wisdom demanded that this be recognised.

There seems to be an echo here of the case of Partholón, one of the early invaders of Ireland according to *Lebor Gabála Érenn*.

As in the case of Morann, Partholón's wife was having sex with his servant while he was away. When Partholón got to know of it he was furious but when he confronted his wife Dealgnat he got little satisfaction. She accused him of neglecting her as he was continually off fishing. 'If you leave food before a child,' she said, 'he will inevitably eat it. If you leave milk before a cat he will inevitably drink it, and if you leave a man and a woman alone together nature will take its course.' Faced with this type of argument, and unable to answer it, Partholón lost his temper. He gave the dog a vicious kick which killed him on the spot. The name of the dog was Saimhéar and the little island now called 'Fish Island' on the Erne, two hundred yards downstream from the Falls of Assaroe, Ballyshannon, Co Donegal, was called Inis Saimhéir as a result of the episode. Michael Dames surmises that this may be the remnant of a seasonal myth in which the old god is abandoned by the goddess in favour of the new and younger god, as winter must make way for summer. (1992, 178ff.)

Perhaps a certain parallel could be drawn between these incidents in the native tradition and the story in the gospel concerning Our Lord's pardon of the woman caught in the act of adultery and about to be stoned to death. (John 8:3-11)

The O-Antiphon for 23 December calls Christ *Rex et legifer noster*, a title derived from Isaiah 33:22: 'For Yahweh is our judge, Yahweh our lawgiver.'

Keating pays tribute not only to the scrupulous impartiality of pagan rulers and judges in Ireland but also to the truth of the *seanchaithe* who communicated the historical records to future generations:

Now, in pagan times in Ireland no professor of *seanchus* could rank as an *ollamh* or author in *seanchus* who had been known once to falsify historical truth. Moreover, no one could hold the rank of *breitheamh* who had given a partial judgement; and besides some of them were bound by *geasa* in the pagan times. First, when Sean, son of Áighe, delivered a partial judgement *(claoinbhreath)*, blisters grew on his right cheek, and when he delivered a just judgement they did not grow.

Connla Caoinbhriathrach never delivered an unjust judgement, for he was a virtuous truly upright man according to the light of nature *(ba duine iodhan fírionnraic do réir sholuis na nádúire é);* Seancha son of Cúl Claon never gave judgement without having fasted the night before. When Fachtna, his son, delivered an unjust judgement, if it was in the autumn he delivered it, the fruit fell to the ground that night in the country in which he was. But when he delivered a just judgement, the fruit remained in full on the trees; or if in the spring he delivered an unjust judgement, the cattle forsook their young in that country ... And so it was with several pagan authors, they were subject to *geasa,* preventing them from partiality in history or judgement *(do bhídís geasa ortha dá dtoirmeasc ó chlaonadh seanchusa nó breitheamhhnais do dhéanamh).* From what we have said, the Irish records are to be believed like the records of any other country, seeing that they are borne witness to by the writings of old pagan authors and by their having been approved by the holy clerics and prelates of the Irish church. (Dinneen, 1908, 3, 35-37)

It can be seen then, that the ideas of wisdom, prudence, judgement, truth, are given high emphasis in the Advent-Christmas liturgy. This wisdom belongs primarily to Christ who is addressed as 'Wisdom' *(O Sapientia).* It is bound up with the idea of the creation of the world and with a linking in harmony of the various elements which go to form the universe.

In the native Irish context the parallel concept of *fír* receives the same high recognition with a corresponding emphasis on the cosmic connotations of the 'king's truth'.

The Post Communion Prayer for the Second Sunday of Advent in the Roman Missal asks for this gift of Wisdom and discernment:

Father, you give us food from heaven. By sharing in this

mystery, teach us to judge wisely the things of earth and to love the things of heaven.

The Collect carries a similar message:

God of power and mercy, open our hearts in welcome. Remove the things that hinder us from receiving Christ with joy, so that we may share his wisdom and become one with him when he comes in glory.

While still on this subject of 'Wisdom', some consideration should be given to the mysterious fount of wisdom – *Tobar Segais* – the Well of Segais or the Well of Connla. This well of knowledge could be either the source of the rivers Boyne or Shannon, or the seven chief rivers of Ireland. It had its counterpart in Tír Tairngire, the Land of Promise, where five rivers flow from it. Manannán Mac Lir explained to Cormac Mac Airt during his visit to the otherworld that the five streams are the five senses by which knowledge is obtained. (Rees, 1961, 310-312)

Nobody is allowed to visit *Tobar Segais* except Nechtan of Brú na Bóinne and his three cupbearers Flesc, Lam and Luam.

Bóann, Nechtan's wife, however, defies the prohibition and circumambulates the well three times *tuathal,* that is in the unlucky direction – lefthandwise against the course of the sun. The well bursts forth dismembering and drowning her to form the sacred river of the Boyne, *An Bhó Fhinn (Bóinn),* 'the White Cow'.

Over the well grew hazels of wisdom. The nuts fell into the river and the salmon ate them and so imbibed the wisdom or *fíos*. This was communicated to Fionn Mac Cumhaill, who, as described in *Macgnímartha Find,* having been ordered to boil the *Eo fis* or Salmon of Knowledge caught by his master, Fionn Éces burned his thumb in the process. He put his thumb in his mouth to reduce the pain, and in doing so, swallowed a little of the salmon which adhered to it. From that on, he had only to chew his thumb to acquire hidden knowledge and illumination.

It is significant that in some texts Christ is referred to as: *in t-eo sénta cas corcra* (the blessed curly violet salmon) and *eo na dtrí dtobar* (salmon of the three wells), (*DIL*, 275)

In traditional Christian iconography, the fish is a well-known symbol of Christ. This is based on the Greek word for 'fish', *ichthus,* the initials of which stand for: 'Jesus Christ, Son of God, Saviour'. It is difficult to know if the image of Christ as a salmon in the native texts is derived ultimately from the tradition of the early church, but the very precision with which a transfer is made from a fish to a specific type of fish argues for a background knowledge of the *Eo fis.* The fish as a symbol of Christ can be seen in innumerable books, paintings and ecclesiastical decorations. While retaining its basic traditional connotation as 'Jesus Christ, Son of God, Saviour', it can be extended to cover the Celtic sense of the fish being a salmon and embracing the idea of Christ, being not only Son of God and Saviour but also Wisdom, 'a Christ who is both the power of God and the wisdom of God'. (1 Cor 1:24)

We can consider also the idea of *fios* or supernatural knowledge being acquired by drinking the water of the otherworldly well directly. One day, as Fionn Mac Cumhaill and two companions, Diorraing and Mac Reithe, were on the top of Carn Feradaig (Cahernarry, near Limerick), they found the door of the *Sí* open. The daughters of Bec Mac Buain, the owner of the wisdom-bestowing well, tried to close the door to prevent them from entering. In the struggle, some of the water from a bucket which Céibhfhionn, one of the Mná Sí, held spattered into mouths of the three. Immediately they acquired knowledge.

Perhaps it is possible to find a parallel for the peculiar phrase, *eo na dtrí dtobar.* In Ireland, there is a tradition of particular power attaching to *uisce na dtrí teorann* – the water of the three boundaries, that is a well or stream at a centre where three farms or three townlands meet. (Danaher, 1972, 110) Or, as in the tradition of Gaelic Scotland, it can refer to the meeting of three streams.

Alexander Carmichael gives a particularly striking example of the use of a rite involving the sanctuary formed by the meeting of three streams. (1972, 1, 52ff.)

In a period of Scotland's history when the administration of justice in the courts of law tended to be untrustworthy, it was customary for a person summoned to court to perform this particular ritual. The person went at dawn to a place where three streams met and, forming a cup with his palms, filled it with water. He bathed his face while saying a prayer and then went off to plead his case in court with renewed confidence:

I will wash my face,
in the nine rays of the sun,
as Mary washed her Son
in the rich fermented milk.

Love be in my countenance,
benevolence in my mind,
Dew of honey in my tongue,
my breath as the incense.

I will travel in the name of God,
in likeness of deer, in likeness of horse,
in likeness of serpent, in likeness of king:
stronger will it be with me than with all persons.

(Falbhaidh mi an ainme Dhé,
an riochd feidh, an riochd each,
an riochd nathrach, an riochd righ:
is treasa liom fin na le gach neach.)

In this rite for procuring a share of the divine wisdom and prudence in a particularly trying situation, that closeness to nature which is such a feature of the Celtic way of life is exploited to the full.

The bathing represents purification, or, in this case, primarily perhaps, contact with the sacred water of wisdom emanating from the Nemeton or sanctuary formed by three streams. Three is the sacred number and in the Christian context we immediately think of the Trinity. It occurs again as a multiple in the prayer: 'in the nine rays of the sun' *('s na naodh gatha gréine)*. The three streams coming together symbolise the Trinity, Father, Son and Holy Spirit, Three Persons in One God. *Eo na dtrí dtobar* is Christ the Incarnate Word of God, the salmon inhabiting the *Cumar na dTrí nUisce,* the meeting-point of the three waters.

The animals mentioned in the formula are particularly appropriate. The deer is characterised by his wariness; the serpent is symbolic of wisdom and the horse has strength and speed. The king has dignity. This combination of qualities should prove of immense value to the defendant. It may be noted that, while the king has obvious associations with the otherworld in Celtic mythology, so have the animals mentioned – deer, serpent and horse.

From the concept of the fish as associated with Christ and then associated with wisdom and knowledge, we arrive at another instance of the fish linked to *fios* in a Christian context in Ireland.

This is in connection with the holy wells. It is thought that at one time there were as many as 3000 holy wells in the country but now this number is greatly reduced. Nevertheless, there are still a considerable number at which the rites are performed. In some of these, there is a tradition that a fish, often a trout, or sometimes an eel, inhabits the holy well. Again, in many cases, tradition asserts, that if the pilgrim or devotee sees the fish, then his or her cure is assured. In other words, the appearance of the fish to the devotee while the rite is being performed is an act of revelation. The ancient tradition of *fios* or supernatural knowledge through the fish is being continued. In this case, knowledge is much more limited than in the case of Fionn Mac Cumhaill.

As we have already remarked, Eochaidh Mac Eirc was the ideal king whose reign was marked by good weather and abundant foods:

> Eochaid mac Eircc ba ri Herenn in tan sin. Ni bai fleochadh acht drucht frissin re sin, ocus ni bai bliadain cen mess. Ro cuirthi ga sa Herind re lind, ocus is leis do righnedh in recht coir in Herind ar tus.
>
> (Eochu son of Erc was king of Ireland at that time. There was no wetting save only dew in that time, and there was no year without harvest. Falsehood was expelled in Ireland in his time, and by him was executed the law of justice in Ireland at the first) (*Lebor Gabhála,* IV, 20-21)

A remarkable tribute is paid to him in a poem-version (52-53):

> Eochu mac Eirc, boí dia bríg
> ferr cach ríg acht Crist cáid.
>
> (Eochu son of Erc, who was sufficient in virtue better than every king save stainless Christ.)

Here a connection is made, as in many other places, between the *fír flatha,* the integrity of the king, and cosmic order. If the *Bainis Rí/hieros gamos,* the marriage of the king to the goddess of the land. is successful there will be peace and prosperity in the kingdom.

A plentiful supply of food depends on the good marriage relations between the Sky Father and the Earth Mother. Perhaps the archetype for this is in the mating of An Daghdha and An MhórRíon as related in Cath Maighe Tuireadh.

If there is a good marriage relationship the rain will fall at the appropriate seasons and the sun will shine to give adequate but not excessive heat and so the Earth Mother will be fertilised to produce and abundant harvest.

It may well be that the Bainis Rí was a ritual mimesis, or imitation of the marriage between sky and earth to produce food.

The O Antiphon which concerns us most directly is that given in the Breviary for 21 December, the day of the winter solstice, when the sun enters Newgrange:

O Oriens, splendor lucis aeternae, et sol justitiae; veni et illumina sedentes in tenebris, et umbra mortis. (O Rising Sun/Dawn of the East; brightness of everlasting light and sun of justice, come and enlighten those who sit in darkness and in the shadow of death.)

During the dark cold days of winter when the sun was seen to be in retreat before his enemies, the Earth Mother was barren, the growth of vegetation was now in sad decline. Unlike the moon, which suffers a monthly decline in which it almost disappears, the sun goes down in the west each evening, successfully negotiates the underworld realm of death and rises again the following morning – albeit on winter mornings somewhat the worst for wear. But it has survived death.

After it has reached the most dire state of harassment, at the winter solstice, it rises victorious, to the relief of all. It is the *Sol Invictus,* the 'Unconquered sun'. This 'Unconquered Sun' becomes available once again to fertilise the Earth Mother so that she can provide a supply of food to tide the community over the following year. For the megalithic people this must have been the meaning of 'salvation'.

An analysis of the Blessing of the Baptismal Font at the Easter Vigil (Tridentine Missal) reveals a similar type of thinking but of course, 'salvation' in this case means union with God, a loving relationship with him, a created sharing in the life of the Trinity even in this world.

The priest dipped the lighted paschal candle into the water

of the font three times, saying: 'May the power of the Holy Spirit descend into the water of this font', and then added, 'And make the whole substance of this water fruitful for re-birth.'

The Neophytes, or newly baptised, emerge from the font-womb as people reborn – that is born for the second time, but this time they are born into a new type of existence in which they are related to God in a new particular way. Their first birth from their mother's womb gave them a natural, this worldly existence. This second birth from the font-womb brings them into a spiritual world where their life is hidden away with Christ in God.

The Return of the Hero

In the work of our redemption we can distinguish three different comings or visitations of Our Lord.

There is his First Coming to earth as man in the incarnation. This is coming in history 2000 years ago.

Then there will be his coming in judgement at the end of the world at the *Parousia* or Second Coming.

Between Pasch and Parousia, Christ comes in mystery – under the disguise of bread and wine, food for the journey through this earthly life of ours to bridge the gap between time and eternity and gradually acclimatise us to life in heaven. This triple visitation is expressed in the Opening Prayer for the Vigil Mass of Christmas:

> God our Father, every year we rejoice as we look forward to this feast of our salvation. May we welcome Christ as our Redeemer, and meet him with confidence when he comes to be our judge, who lives and reigns with you and the Holy Spirit, one God, for ever and ever.

We have seen in the story of Mongán and his liberation from disaster, a parallel in a minor key, to the liberation of the human race from eternal damnation by the coming of Christ.

The coming of Christ in the Eucharist, as the sacred food of the otherworld which gradually breaks the bonds which binds us to this life and draws us into the next world, may have a parallel in another story from Celtic mythology – the story of Connla, son of King Conn Céadchathach of Tara. The story is found in *Leabhar na hUidhre*.

According to the story, the king, Connla, his son and a druid were standing on the great hill of Uisneach (Co Westmeath) in the very centre of Ireland. Suddenly a beautiful woman in rich garments appeared before them and recited a long poem in which she explained that she belonged to Avalon *(Tír na nÓg)* – the otherworld where there was no ageing or death or decay but a land of untold happiness. From Avalon she had fallen in love with Connla and she asked him to return with her to this land of perpetual summer.

Connla in his turn fell hopelessly in love with the woman from the *Sí* and wanted with all his heart to go away with her. But then certain doubts began to assail him. He began to re-alise that he had a problem. All his friends were in this world, his work was here in this world, he was involved in politics which he could not hand over to somebody else. Above all there was the strong possibility that when his father died he would be king. He wanted with all his heart to go away with the woman but his mind was torn with internal conflict. Finally he arrived at a decision. He told the woman sadly that despite his love for her he could not accompany her to *Tír na nÓg.*

She went away but, as she was leaving, him she gave him an apple. The apple was the sacred food of the otherworld for Avalon was the land of apples.

For a whole month Connla ate the apple. And although he was eating it the apple never diminished. He noticed that the apple was affecting him strangely. He began to lose interest in his normal activities. Things and policies, which up to then had been of great importance to him, ceased to interest him to the same extent. His ambitions dwindled. Gradually his mentality was changing.

A month later Connla stood on the same hill of Uisneach. Suddenly the same woman was standing before him. This time there was no doubt or hesitation. Connla sprang into her crystal boat, a magic mist descended and they sailed away to Avalon and they were never seen again.

The story of Connla is our story too, for the Eucharist we receive between Pasch and Parousia is the food of the other-world – the Bread of Angels, as St Thomas Aquinas calls it. By eating this food we are gradually weaned away from our attachments to this world and drawn into the world of eternity.

The third visitation or coming of Christ in glory receives considerable emphasis in new *Roman Missal,* being mentioned in the Memorial Acclamations:

> 'Christ has died, Christ is risen, *(Pasch),* Christ will come again *(Parousia)*'; 'Lord Jesus, come in glory'; '– until you come in glory'.

The Embolism is particularly strong in the concept of our life in this world being eschatologically orientated. We are poised in a somewhat uncomfortable temporal space between the first and second coming of Christ. During this interval we need protection from sin, evil, anxiety, as we wait in hope:

> Deliver us Lord, from every evil, and grant us peace in our day. In your mercy keep us free from sin and protect us from all anxiety as we wait in joyful hope for the coming of our Saviour, Jesus Christ.

Undoubtedly one of the most powerful of all symbols of the glorious return of the Saviour at the end of time to gather his people into the sunny landscape of heaven was the *Etimasia* – the empty throne pictured in the mosaics of Rome and Ravenna in which the elect wait for the Saviour to come and occupy the throne.

A similar theme of the Return of the Hero occurs in some folktales from Ireland and elsewhere.

In Ireland we have a number of tales relating to local champions who are not dead but live on in an enchanted sleep waiting for the day of destiny. When the day of destiny arrives they will wake up from their enchanted sleep for the final deliverance of their people from all that oppresses them. Among these are historical and legendary characters such as Aodh Ó Neill, Aodh Rua Ó Domhnaill, Balldearg Ó Domhnaill, Fionn Mac Cumhaill, Dónall na nGeimleach Ó Donnchú and, in Lough Gur, Co Limerick, the highly Gaelicised Norman, Gearóid Iarla Mac Gearailt.

According to the legend, Gearóid Iarla sleeps an enchanted sleep under the lake at Loch Gur and every seven years, when the moon is full and the lake is bathed in moonlight, he can be seen riding round the lake on a white horse. The horse has silver shoes and when the shoes are worn out, that will be the day of destiny and he will rise up from his enchanted sleep and bring final liberation to his people.

In Wales, there is the great King Arthur of the Arthurian legends. His grave is still pointed out in the ruins of the mediaeval Benedictine Abbey of Glastonbury. Glastonbury in Somerset is one of the most famous religious sites of the British Isles revered both by pagans and Christians. There is a Christian legend that Our Lord spent the hidden years of his life in Glastonbury accompanied by Joseph of Arimathea who was involved in the tin mines in Cornwall.

In Celtic terms, Glastonbury is on two levels – it is a geographical site and it is a supernatural dwelling place of the Celtic Pantheon, the Tuatha Dé Danann. As such it is the Isle of Avalon. And it was to this site that three queens veiled in black carried the body of Arthur in a boat after his last battle. And in the earthly Glastonbury a grave opened of itself to receive his body. The archbishop came and said the prayers of the dead over the grave. And the enchantress Morgan Ia Fée explained to the archbishop that it was only the dense matter of his body that was buried there and that his spirit lived on in the Isle of Avalon, and 'King Arthur,' she said, 'will return one day when the world shall have need of him.' And a tombstone appeared miraculously above the grave and on it was written: 'Hic jacet Arthurus Rex, quondam rex et futurus', 'Here lies Arthur the King. He was once a king and he will be king again.'

CHAPTER NINETEEN

Imbolc and St Brigid's Day

In the folk tradition of Ireland, the first day of February is the beginning of spring and the beginning of the agricultural year of the farmer. It is the ancient Celtic Feast of Imbolc. Little is known, however, about the pre-Christian feast of Imbolc and the day is known as *Lá Fhéile Bríde,* the feast day of Brigid, Ireland's much-loved and venerated second patron saint.

Apart from St Patrick himself, perhaps no other Irish saint has attained such prominence at home and abroad as St Brigid. Countless people bear her name, churches, convents and holy wells are called after her, not only here but in many other countries as well. Her name features in ancient litanies and martyrologies and an old text speaks of her as *Muire na nGael,* Mary of the Irish. From an early period she has been linked with the church of Kildare where she is reputed to have founded a monastery and, as abbess, ruled over priests and nuns.

Some scholars believe that Kildare itself had originally been a pagan sanctuary of the great Celtic Goddess Brigid. Then when Christianity came along a saintly woman bearing the same name as the goddess took over the pagan sanctuary and turned it into a convent. If this happened it would explain why some of the characteristics of the goddess came to be attributed to the Christian saint Brigid, for instance, her feast being on the ancient Celtic Feast of Imbolc, which marked the beginning of spring, as well as her close association with agriculture, especially with cows and corn.

Now, while some elements of the cult of the goddess may have come down to St Brigid, nevertheless, the various accounts of her life show her as a great Christian saint whose life reflected the gospel to a heroic degree. She stands unchallenged as the supreme example of charity to those in need.

St Brigid was born shortly after the time of St Patrick but, in folk tradition, they are often regarded as living at the same time and of being great friends.

Possibly the earliest *Life of St Brigid* that we have is that of Cogitosus, from the seventh century. He insists that there were two fundamental ideas running through her life: these were that she was first of all a woman of great faith and, secondly, that she was a woman of the most extraordinary charity. He insists that her many miracles were worked as a result of her faith. We are constantly reminded of Our Lord's words: 'All things are possible to him who believes.' (Mt 9:22)

Cogitosus tells us that 'she founded her monastery on the firm foundation of faith'. (Prol. 4) In one of her miracles she changes water into beer and she does this 'by blessing it with the power of faith. For he who changed water into wine at Cana in Galilee, also changed water into ale through the faith of this most blessed woman.' Again in imitation of Our Lord she once gave sight to a man born blind (11, 3) and this is attributed to her wonderful faith. And her miracles, which she works through faith, are manifestations of God's power. On one occasion while her workmen were reaping corn, it began to rain. But by a miracle she stopped the rain over that particular field while it continued to fall heavily all around. In another occasion she hung up her cloak on a sunbeam coming through the window.

As well as this deep faith which characterised Brigid, there was also her remarkable charity. No fewer than 23 of the 32 chapters contained in the earliest book of her life have to do with her concern for the poor, the oppressed or the embarrassed or simply her guests, whether friends or strangers. She never allowed the poor to go away empty-handed and there were occasions that this habit of hers of giving things away to beggars got her into a lot of trouble. Difficult as it must have been to see Christ in these people, this is what she did, and she, as it were, ritualised this idea everyday by dividing the butter into twelve parts and one larger part. This was meant to remind her that when people came to the door looking for food, or when she was entertaining guests, she was entertaining Our Lord and his apostles.

Much of her life story is concerned with domestic life and running a house, and her miracles deal largely with the multiplication of food and drink and with healing.

Nevertheless, there were occasions when she performed miracles of a different kind. A young man came to her asking for her help. His wife, he said, didn't love him any more. She wouldn't eat with him and she wouldn't sleep with him and she was threatening to divorce him. St Brigid blessed a bucket of water for him and told him to take it home and when his wife wasn't about to sprinkle the water all over the house. He did this and immediately his wife fell hopelessly in love with him all over again and this time it was permanent.

In the year 1185 Giraldus Cambrensis came to Ireland. He was very impressed by St Brigid's perpetual fire:

At Kildare, in Leinster, celebrated for the glorious Brigit, many miracles have been wrought worthy of memory. Among these, the first that occurs is the fire of St Brigit, which is reported never to go out. Not that it cannot be extinguished, but the nuns and holy women tend and feed it, adding fuel with such watchful and diligent care that, from the time of the Virgin, it has continued burning through a long course of years; and although such heaps of wood have been consumed during this long period, there has been no accumulation of ashes.'

As in the time of St Brigit twenty nuns were here engaged in the Lord's warfare, she herself being the twentieth, after her glorious departure, nineteen have always formed the society, the number having never been increased. Each of them has the care of the fire for a single night, the last nun, having heaped wood upon the fire, says, 'Brigit take charge of your own fire, for this night belongs to you.' She then leaves the fire, and in the morning it is found that the fire has not gone out, and that the usual quantity of fuel has been used.

This fire is surrounded by a hedge, made of stakes and brushwood, and forming a circle, within which no male can enter; and if any one should presume to enter, which has been sometimes attempted by rash men, he will not escape the divine vengeance. Moreover, it is only lawful for women to blow the fire, fanning it or using bellows only, and not with their breath. (Wright, 1887, 96-97)

St Brigid then, was characterised by her great faith, her charity and her continual awareness of God's presence. She was a woman whose life was spent among the ordinary things of life. But her early biographers recognised that this rather humdrum domestic scene was transformed by her outstanding holiness. One of those who wrote her life summed it up in this way:

She it is that helpeth every one who is in straits and in danger. She it is that abateth the pestilences. She it is that quelleth the wave-voice and the wrath of the great sea. This is the prophesied woman of Christ. She is the Queen of the South. She is the Mary of the Gael.

Now, when Brigit came to the ending-days, after founding churches and churchbuildings in plenty, after miracles and wondrous deeds in number (like) sand of sea or stars of heaven, after charity and mercy, she received communion and sacrifice from Ninnid the Pure-handed, when he had returned from Rome of Latium, and sent her spirit thereafter to heaven. But her remains and her relics are on earth with great honour and with primacy and pre-eminence, with miracles and marvels. Her soul is like the sun in the heavenly city among quires of angels and archangels, in union with cherubim and seraphim, in union with Mary's Son, to wit, in the union with all the Holy Trinity, Father and Son and Holy Ghost.

I beseech the Lord's mercy, through Saint Brigit's intercession. May we all attain that union *in saecula saeculorum*. Amen. (Stokes, 1877, 85-87)

According to Seán Ó Súilleabháin of the Irish Folklore Commission:

The main significance of the Feast of St Brigid would seem to be that it was a christianisation of one of the focal points of the agricultural year in Ireland, the starting-point of preparations for the spring sowing. Every manifestation of the cult of the saint (or of the deity she replaced) is closely bound up in some way with food-production and this must be the chief line of approach to a study of the spring festival. (*JRSAI*, 1945, 164 footnote)

As in the case of the other three feasts, a large body of custom and ritual has grown up around the feast of St Brigid and remnants of this can be found here and there even to the present day. The bulk of material relating to the observance of the feast, however, comes from the Irish Folklore Commission which carried out an extensive survey of the material then remaining (1942) and of what was remembered by the older people to have once been observed in their district.

As the beginning of the season of spring, the feast of Brigid was looked upon as a time when a forecast could be made regarding the weather.

Gach 're lá go maith
Ó 'm lá-sa amach
agus leath mo lae féinigh.
(Every second day to be fine from my own (feast) day on
and half my own day also) – this was a saying attributed to
Brigid. (Danaher, 1972, 13)

St Brigid was very generous and her feastday is an omen of
good times to come. She ushers in a more plentiful season,
for when her day comes the *Dubhluachair,* or the darkest,
severest part of the year is gone. The *Dubhluachair* is between Christmas and February 1st. In this severe weather
the rushes turn black. (Department of Irish Folklore,
UCD, manuscript (henceforth IFC), 900: 138)

In some areas the feast was kept as a holiday, or certain
types of work were forbidden such as those involving the
turning of wheels. People visited the holy well dedicated to St
Brigid if such existed in their locality. A festive supper was
generally part of the celebration and, as it was believed that
the saint performed a circuit of the country on the eve of the
feast (last night of January), certain actions were performed to
invoke her blessing as she passed by. A special cake, a sheaf of
corn, the *Brat Bhríde* or piece of cloth, might be left outside
the door or a meal left ready on the table inside as for a guest.
(Danaher, 1972, 14-15)

Here, however, we are concerned with four major items
which are features of the celebration of the feast and remnants
of these once widespread practices remain to the present day.
These major items are: *Crois Bhríde* (St Brigid's Cross), *Brat
Bhríde* (St Brigid's Cloak), the *Brídeog,* a procession from
house to house in which a doll or a figure representing Brigid
was carried, and *Gnás na Tairsí* or Threshold Rite.

St Brigid's Cross

The distinctive type of cross known as St Brigid's Cross may be seen over the door in many houses today and is also a popular item in shops catering for the tourist industry. These crosses are made of straw, rushes or stiff grasses or osiers, and the type usually seen today is the four-legged type, though this is not necessarily the most widespread type in terms of tradition. As a very comprehensive study of these crosses has been made by John O'Sullivan, with photographs of the various types collected throughout the country, it will only be necessary here to give a short account of this particular aspect of the cult of Brigid. (*Folklife*, 1973, 60-81)

The four-legged irregular cross type, often referred to as the 'Swastika' type, had a wide distribution throughout the country. It has no wooden foundation as in other types but is made by doubling rushes over each other to form an overlapping cross. The number of rushes may be as small as four or over twenty. Usually the projecting rushes are tied with a cord at the ends. While rushes are the normal material used in this type of cross, straw is also known to have been used in a few localities. It was more widely distributed in Ulster and Leinster than in Connacht and Munster. (Danaher, 1972, 17)

Not only is the diamond or lozenge shaped straw cross the most widespread throughout the country but its peculiar shape must be compared with a similar design on objects going back to remote antiquity. The design is found on statuettes of the Fertility Goddess from Old Europe depicted on the figure's belly. A figurine with a dotted lozenge incised on the belly comes from Gladnice near Pristine, southern Yugoslavia, c. 6000 BC. (Gimbutas, 1989, pl. 203)

Marija Gimbutas, interprets the diamond/lozenge figure quite clearly as being intimately associated with the goddess's chief function – the fertility of the earth:

The dot, representing seed, and the lozenge, symbolising

the sown field, appear on sculptures of an enthroned, pregnant goddess and are also incised or painted on totally schematised figurines. A lozenge with a dot or dash in its centre or in the corners must have been the symbolic invocation to secure fertility.

The lozenge figure may also be seen incised on stone at Newgrange, Co Meath, and in his interesting photographs P. A. Ó Síocháin has compared Neolithic diamond engraving on stone with the diamond design on the traditional Aran Sweater showing that this archaic motif may well have continued into folk-craftsmanship up to the present day. (1967, 179, 181)

The diamond figure is also found in ecclesiastical art in Ireland. It is found on Donaghmore Cross, Co Tyrone; on the portal to the round tower of St Brigid's Cathedral, Kildare; Killaloe Cathedral, Co Clare; Killeshin, Co Laois; St Saviour's Church, Glendalough, Co Wicklow, and on the doorway of the Nuns' Church in Clonmacnoise, Co Offaly. The magnificent High Cross of Dysert O'Dea, Co Clare, has an example of the multiple diamond cross consisting of five diamonds.

Thus it is seen that this particular design is found in a variety of areas and materials extending far beyond the Christian period. All that can be said is that some of the shapes which St Brigid's Cross assumes resemble those found in various forms of art, some from a very archaic period. Evidence is lacking, however, for the derivation of one from the other.

Another type of cross, resembling the 'Swastika' type somewhat, but having only three legs and made of straw or rushes, is not widely distributed. It is found only in Ulster, in the Counties Antrim, Armagh, Donegal, Down and the four-legged type is also found in these areas. (Danaher, 1972, 17)

A curious type of cross, which might be called the 'Sheaf Cross', comes from the Galway, South Roscommon area and consists of two small sheaves of unthreshed corn, plaited and tied at the ends. The sheaves are joined at the centre by a wooden peg or scallop on which a potato is skewered. The peg fixes the sheaves to the thatch.

A small sheaf of oats and a potato used to be left on the doorstep until bedtime and stuck on a 'scolb' and put up behind a rafter at bedtime on St Brigid's Eve. When the spring came, the oats would be rubbed between the hands and the seed would be put with the oats for sowing. The potato used to be cut and sown with the rest of the 'slits'. While this was being done St Brigid was invoked to protect the crops from all diseases. (IFC 902: 182)

This is a particularly clear instance of the St Brigid's connection with the fertility of the land. The grain from the sheaves consecrated to Brigid was mixed with the seed being sown in the field. Brigid's power of fertility was transferred to the seed to guarantee an abundant harvest. The potato is obviously a modernisation but following the old pattern of the corn. It too was mixed with the seed potatoes to secure a good crop.

From the Portumna area, Co Galway, comes a comprehensive account of the materials from which the cross is made, where it is put, its connection with the fertility of the land and protection of the household from disease and sickness:

Sa dúiche seo, déantar an chros d'adhmad, de thuí, de luachair, agus cuirtear os cionn an dorais é , nó sa tsionáil, nó ar na frathacha. Nuair a dhéantar cros nó dhó cuirtear práta ar bharr na croise agus cúpla gráinín de choirce nó cruithneacht a cheangailt léi, agus chuirfidís an práta sin agus an coirce an chéad lá a thosóidís le obair an Earraigh i riocht is go mbeadh rath is beannacht Bríde ar na barra an bhliain sin. Cuirtear suas na croiseanna go mór mór chun breoiteacht is aicídí a choinneáil i bhfad uathu. (IFC 902: 216-7)

(In this district, the cross is made of wood, of straw, of rushes, and it is placed above the door or on the ceiling or on the rafters. When one or two crosses are made, a potato is placed on top of the cross and a couple of grains of oats or wheat is tied to it and this potato and the oats is sown on the first day on which the work of spring is begun so that Brigid's blessing may be on the crops that year. The crosses are put up especially to keep sickness and disease far away from them.)

An account from Oileán Chléire (Cape Clear Island), Co Cork, tells of how the cross was used on the island in the treatment of sickness:

Do chuirtí anuas ar ucht dhuine thinn nó bhreoite í. Do dheintí é sin gach lá chomh maith le Lá le Bríde ach mar sin féin do b'í Cros Bhríde í. (IFC 900: 37) (It used to be put down on the breast of a sick person. This used to be done every day as well as St Brigid's Day, nevertheless, it was St Brigid's Cross.)

The cross was also considered as a protective agent against storms, thunder, etc., and along the sea-coast they were placed on the thatch and made of the white straw which grows on the sandhills. *Rabhtaí,* or severe storms, are often connected with this time of the year: *Rabhtaí Rua na hInide,* (around the beginning of Lent and St Brigid's Day), *Rabhtaí Lá 'le Pádraig* (St Patrick's Day Storm), and *Rabhtaí Lá 'le Muire* (25 March). These were the worst and stormiest periods of the year and *Rabhtaí Rua na hInide* was considered to be the worst of all. The crosses were needed to give protection against these spring storms. (IFC 900: 136)

St Brigid's Cross was a preservative against fire and this was particularly important at a time when many houses had thatched roofs which were highly inflammable. This account comes from the Grange Area of Co Sligo: 'On St Brigid's

Night (the night before the feast), crosses of dried rushes or
cíb chasach (sedge) are made and put up in the roofs of the
dwelling houses and cowhouses. It was said that the house
they were in would never be burned and would be preserved
from ill luck.' (IFC, 903: 223)

Origin Stories: How St Brigid's Cross began

As the historical reason for the custom of making St Brigid's
Cross was unknown to the people, they naturally invented
stories to account for it. One of the most widely distributed
origin stories is that of 'The Dying Pagan'. The following
short is version from Glenamaddy, Co Galway:

> St Brigid was passing by the road one day when she heard
> somebody moaning inside the fence. She went in, and
> there was an old man dying; on enquiring, she found that
> he was a pagan. She wanted to convert him. To do so she
> was at a loss to show him what the cross was like. She went
> out, and pulled rushes from which she made a cross as
> quickly as she knew how. From this saintly act, we now
> have the custom of making St Brigid's Cross. She baptised
> him and he became a Christian. (IFC 902: 158-9)

Another story illustrating the origin of St Brigid's Cross is
that of 'The Poisoned Milk'. This is quite different from the
account of the pagan's conversion and places greater emphasis
on the cross as a means of protection against danger of various
kinds.

According to the version of the story from Co Clare, a certain woman disliked Brigid and wanted to kill her. Her
chance came when Brigid visited her house. She bade Brigid
sit down and offered her a drink of milk into which she had
introduced some poison. Brigid, however, got a little straw and
made the sign of the cross over the milk. She drank the milk
and remained unharmed. The people heard of this miracle

and began the custom of making crosses in honour of St Brigid and hanging them up in their houses. (IFC 901: 61-2)

In the Cork version of this story it is a *brobh luachra* (rush) which St Brigid uses to bless the milk. In this case the basin bursts asunder and the poisoned milk is spilled. The woman confesses her crime and said that she planned to kill Brigid as she coveted the golden cross which Brigid wore. After this episode St Brigid always wore a silver cross. 'The story of St Brigid's escape from death spread through the country and, as a protection from danger, on St Brigid's Eve, a cross was made from rushes or straw and put in the inside of the roof in the kitchen as a protection from all danger for the year.' (IFC 900: 187-9)

A story from Co Derry relates how Brigid had no food left in the house for her father's meal as she had given everything to the poor. She prayed earnestly and made crosses from rushes and placed them in the cheese-presses. When her father returned he found the presses full of cheese. This episode occurred around 1 February. (IFC 904: 255-6)

This story places the emphasis not so much on protection from danger but rather on the plentiful supply of food for the household which St Brigid guarantees to those who hang up her cross in their homes.

While the origin stories vary considerably from each other, the cumulative effect is to encourage the use of St Brigid's Cross by laying stress on its power to bring prosperity to the household, to cure their ills and to safeguard them from evil.

Brat Bhríde – St Brigid's Cloak

We have already mentioned the *Brat Bhríde* or piece of cloth left outside the house on St Brigid's Eve and brought in next morning. It was believed that St Brigid blessed it as she passed by on her journey through the country on the holy night. Through this encounter with Brigid on her return from the otherworld, this piece of cloth acquired the ability to cure certain diseases such as headache, toothache, etc., and was carefully preserved against such an eventuality.

A clear and succinct account of the custom comes from the Nohoval area of Co Cork:

> On the eve of the feast a linen cloth was put out on the hedge and left there all night. St Brigid was said to pass by 'to the west' during the night and she either touched the cloth or left her blessing on it. It was called 'Brat Bhríde' and was used in cases of illness among people and animals. This custom survives still. (1942) (IFC 900: 125)

Another account from Co Cork refers again to Brigid passing by and leaving her blessing on the cloth and gives a general description of the custom as it was practised in the Kilworth area:

> Cuirtear blúire éadaigh in ait éigin lasmuigh den tigh, ar thor nó ar an gclaí, nó ceangaltar de laiste an dorais ar an dtaobh amuigh é, oíche 'le Bríde. Rud éigin bán is mó úsáidtear, blúire síoda más féidir é.
>
> Deirtear go bhfágann Bríd Naofa a beannacht air agus í ag gabháil na slí, agus go mbíonn leigheas ann 'na dhiaidh san. 'Brat Bríd' a tugtar ar an éadach sin.
>
> Bhí mná i Cill Úird fadó agus aon uair a bhíodh tinneas cinn orthu do cheangailidís an 'Brat Bríde' timpeall an chinn chun a phian a leigheas. (IFC 900: 179)
>
> (A piece of cloth is put in some place outside the house, in a bush or on the wall or tied to the latch of the door on the outside, on St Brigid's Eve. Something white is mostly used, a piece of silk if available. It is said that Blessed Brigid leaves her blessing on it as she passes by and that after that there is a cure in it. It is called 'Brat Bríd'. There were women in Kilworth long ago and they used to tie the 'Brat Bríd' around the head to cure headache.)

The placing of the *brat* on a bush, wall, door latch or win-
dowsill was sometimes accompanied by prayer and a fine ex-
ample of a *Rann* of this kind comes from Co Cork:
Bríd agus a brat,
An Mhaighdean Mhuire agus a Mac,
Micheál agus a sciath,
Éist amháin le Dia.
(on hanging)
Cas orainn aniar anocht,
Agus bliain ó anocht,
agus anocht amháin le Dia.
(IFC 900; 82-83)
(Brigid and her cloak; the Virgin Mary and her Son;
Micheal and his shield; listen to God only. Come hither to
us tonight, and in a year from tonight and on tonight itself
with God.)
The Brat was also used in connection with lambs:
'Dá mbeadh uan ann ná tógfhadh leis an gcaoire, an brat a
chur timpeall orthu, (agus) thógfhaidís lena chéile.' (IFC
899: 54) (If there were a lamb that would not take to the
sheep, if the *brat* were put around them they would take to
each other.)

The Brídeog
The Brídeog was a very popular custom in many parts of the
southern half of Ireland until perhaps the beginning of the
twentieth century and indeed much later in some places. It
can still be seen (1991) in the area of Kilgobnet, near Killarney,
Co Kerry. The custom resembles somewhat the procession of
the 'Wren Boys' from house to house on St Stephen's Day (26
December). A very clear account of the Brídeog as it was performed on St Brigid's Eve in the area, comes from the parish
of Killorglin, Co Kerry:
A figure was carried in procession from house to house.

Boys and girls dressed up and wore masks. The men usually wore women's clothes and tall hats made of straw. They carried a horn which they blew on approaching every house. They were made very welcome. The usual phrase was 'Welcome Brigid'. They danced in every house and before they left the woman of the house stuck a pin in the Brídeog (doll) and left it there.

The Brídeog was made from a churn staff and the body stuffed with straw. People who were not 'dressed up' usually followed the Brídeog. It was customary to 'break up' at the house where the 'Biddy' (doll) was made and to dance the remainder of the night.

There were no songs and no hymns used on the occasion. There is no local explanation of the origin of the custom. (IFC 899: 26-8)

In another account from Kerry the Brídeog group danced in each house and collected some money:

At the present time (1942), the Biddy (Brídeog) is taken round from house to house by a number of boys and girls dressed up in all sorts of garments. They are all disguised with masks. There is a short dance in each house and some money is given to the man who carries the Biddy.

With this money a dance is held some time afterwards. This is called a 'Biddy Ball' and is attended by all the neighbours. (IFC 899: 38)

In the Brídeog Procession from house to house we have doubtless the ritualisation of the return of Brigid in spring-time after her winter sleep. With the re-awakening of nature shown by the lengthening days, the buds on the trees, the greening of the fields, the lambing and calving season, the nesting of birds, Brigid returns to visit her people and reassure them that life has come back to the earth and that she will provide food and protection for them for the coming year.

Gnás na Tairsí – The Threshold Rite

While the making of the cross on St Brigid's Eve was a comparatively simple matter in many places, particularly in Munster, it was surrounded by much ceremony in other parts of the country and particularly so in some areas of the north and west. Since perhaps the most spectacular part of the activity took place at the threshold or entrance to the house, we use the term *Gnás na Tairsí* or 'Threshold Rite' as a general description of what took place from the preparation of the materials for the crosses on the evening of 31 January to their erection on the roof on St Brigid's Day, 1 February. There were considerable local variations; nevertheless, the rite is basically the same wherever it is found.

A particularly clear description of the procedure comes from the Parish of Kilcommon, Erris, Co Mayo, which combines the custom of the *Brat Bhríde* (Brigid's Cloak) with the making of the cross. This particular aspect of the celebration of St Brigid's Feast is generally kept apart. This parish account has the advantage of combining many aspects of the feast:

> Before nightfall, usually the man of the house procured a garment for a *Brat Bhríde.* The article of clothing selected was one which would be in greatest use by the member of the house whose occupation was the most dangerous. As the head of the family was generally a fisherman and exposed to the dangers of the deep for the current year, and the one most in need of the saint's protection, a coat or waist-coat of his was used for the *Brat.* Frequently the man's muffler – one of the large homemade mufflers which covered nearly the whole head and worn on night fishing – became the *Brat.* The man took out this article of clothing into the haggard, drew a good long sheaf of straw out of the stack, and wrapped the garment around the sheaf in a manner giving it as far as possible the rough outline in appearance of a human body. He then reverently

carried the object between his arms, in the manner one carries a child, and deposits it outside at the back door. He leaves it there and comes into the house. The preparation for the supper is proceeded with, the fire on the hearth is kept well stoked and burning brightly, and radiating cheer and happiness. Then when supper is laid on the table and the inmates are ready to sit in, the man of the house announces that he is now going out to bring in Brighid, as she too must be present at the festive board.

The man goes out and around to the back door, where he kneels, and then in a loud voice says to the people inside who are expectant and waiting for the coming request:

Téigí ar bhur nglúine agus osclaigí bhur súile
agus ligigí isteach Bríd.
Response from within: 'Sé beatha, Sé beatha, Sé beatha'
'Téigí ar bhur nglúine agus osclaigí bhur súile
agus ligigí isteach Bríd.'
Do: 'Sé beatha, Sé beatha, Sé beatha'

'Téigí ar bhur nglúine agus osclaigí bhur súile
agus ligigí isteach Bríd'.
Do: 'Sé beatha, Sé beatha, Sé beatha'
(Go on your knees and open your eyes and let Brigid enter; she is welcome, she is welcome, she is welcome.)

The people within continue repeating the third response, 'Sé beatha…'

On the third response 'Sé beatha', from the people within, he takes a up the bundle, gets up off his knees and comes around to the open door, while the people within continue repeating the 'Sé beatha' as he is coming round (to the front door), and when he enters the door they finish the response with 'Muise, Sé beatha agus a sláinte'.

Then the object (the sheaf of straw and *brat*) is laid carefully and respectfully leaning against the leg or rail of the table and under the table. The family then sit down to the supper preceded by a short prayer or invocation such as:

'A Bhríd Bheannaithe, go gcuire tú an teach seo thar anachain na bliana.' (O Blessed Brigid, may you deliver this house from the troubles of the year.)

When supper is finished there was the ejaculatory prayer – the usual one – of: 'Dia graisias le Dia, agus cumhdach Dé ar lucht shaothrú na beatha.' (Deo gratias to God and the protection of God on those going through life.)

Then when the supper vessels are removed and the table cleared, and things put in order, the *brat* is stowed away in a secure place. In addition to the article or garment used for *brat* previously referred to, frequently a piece of new cloth was used to supplement the garment. Strips of this cloth were subsequently used for cures in cases of headache or as they used to say 'bad heads' such as dizziness, etc.

The next operation was the making of St Brigid's Cross from this particular sheaf of straw. Some people went to great pains in making the cross and I have seen some very large and artistic ones made and it certainly looked a nice emblem when it was stuck or secured to the ceiling or rather to the scraw (thatch), usually above the kitchen window, in line with the kitchen bed. The cross was supposed to be a safeguard against storm or the blowing away of the roof of the house during the coming twelve months. It was supposed this danger of the winter's storm or its crisis had passed on St Brigid's Eve when provision was made for protection against the next winter by exhibiting of Brigid's Cross in the manner described. (IFC 903: 50-4)

The same account goes on to say that the whole family

took part in making the crosses and what was left of the sheaf was used to make the *Buaracha*. These were straw collars for the cows to preserve them from disease and evil for the coming year.

An equally interesting and elaborate form of *Gnás na Tairsí* comes from an area at the opposite extreme of the country, Rathnure, Co Wexford. Here it is rushes which are used to make the cross.

> After sunset, the man of the house used to cut a bundle of rushes with a reaping hook unawares of the people inside and hides it outside the house until the time for the feast arrives. He again leaves the house and, walking round it in the direction of the sun, picks up the bundle and completes one circuit. When he reaches the open door all inside kneel down and listen attentively to his petition: 'Go down on your knees, open your eyes and let St Brigid in.' They all answer: 'She is welcome, she is welcome.'
>
> He makes a second circuit and a third circuit of the house, always with the same petition at the door, and the same answer is given.
>
> At the end of the third petition, the man of the house enters, lays the bundle of rushes under the table, says grace and invites all to partake of the meal.
>
> After the feast, the rushes used to be placed in the middle of the room and all the family used to weave the crosses of St Brigid. Next day, the crosses used to be blessed and hung up in each room and every outhouse. (IFC 907: 175-6)

CHAPTER TWENTY

The Christianisation of Lughnasa

The Celtic feast of Lughnasa was one of the high points of the Celtic calendar and was celebrated throughout Ireland around the first of August. It was often called *Domhnach Chrom Dubh*.

As the name indicates, the festival was connected with Lugh Lámhfhada, leader of the Tuatha Dé Danann, who defeated Balar of the Evil Eye, leader of the Fomhóraigh. Lugh Lámhfhada won this decisive victory over the Fomhóraigh at the Battle of Maigh Tuireadh *(Cath Maighe Tuireadh na bhFomhórach)*. The site of the battle is still pointed out at Maigh Tuireadh (Moytirra) east of Lough Arrow in Co Sligo, but of course, the battle was really a supernatural one in which the bright, progressive, generous deities defeated the dark divinities who seek to enchain and prevent the evolutionary process. It is a tale full of magic and fantasy which we cannot describe here for we are concerned with the bare essentials, which consists of the conflict between the Tuatha Dé Danann led by Lugh Lámhfhada and the Fomhóraigh led by Balar.

The Tuatha Dé Danann are the gods of light, of plenty, of prosperity and they are being harassed by the stingy, rentracking, malevolent sea-pirates, the Fomhóraigh, who demand exorbitant rents from the Tuatha Dé Danann. Even the great gods of the Tuatha Dé Danann, the Daghda, Ogma, were subjected to servile labour and semi-starvation under the regime of the Fomorian oriented king, Breas.

At last, the Tuatha Dé Danann could bear the situation no longer and led by the great god Lugh (known in Europe, Lugdunum, Lyons, etc.) the two mighty forces met at Samhain at Má Tuireadh (Co Sligo).

After a lot of slaughter on both sides, the battle is finally resolved by single combat between two champions, Lugh representing the Tuatha Dé Danann King, Nuadha, and Balar of the Evil Eye representing the Fomorian King Breas. Balar has a death-dealing eye which is normally covered and it has to be opened by four men with a hook. He turned this venom-filled eye on Lugh but Lugh let fly a stone from his sling which took the evil eye with it through the back of Balar's head and killed twenty-seven of his followers behind. Thus the battle ended with victory for the Tuatha Dé Danann as the Fomhóraigh collapsed at the downfall of their leader.

And now comes the curious part of the narrative which is the key to its religious significance. The Tuatha Dé Danann are tempted to kill the Fomorian King, Breas, but they refrain from doing so for the Fomhóraigh possess the secrets of agriculture. The druids of the Tuatha Dé Danann declare themselves perfectly happy with the work of the seasons as it is: errach fria har ocus sílad, ocus tossach samhraid fri foircend ocus sonairti n-etha, ocus tossach (n-aipchi) foghamair fri forcend aipchi n-etha ocus fria buain. Gaimred fria tomalta. (*Revue Celtique*, XII, 157) (The spring for ploughing and sowing and the beginning of summer for the end of the strength of corn and the beginning of autumn for the end of ripeness of corn and for reaping it, winter for consuming it.)

But Breas was allowed live when he gave the information: Mairt a n-ar, Mairt hi corad síl a ngurt, Mairt a n-imbochdt. (I. 160) (Their plowing (should) be on a Tuesday, their casting of seed into the field on a Tuesday, their reaping on a Tuesday.)

Here it is recognised that the Fomhóraigh, evil as they are, have a part to play and they are allowed continue but kept in their rightful place. This is explained in the story of King Conaire Mór as recorded in *Tógail Bruidne Da Derga* (Knott, E., (Ed), Dublin 1936) where three Fomorians are kept as hostages as a guarantee that they will not spoil milk or grain in Éire beyond their lawful allowance.

What we have here is the conflict of opposites – the god of light, fruitfulness, generosity, fighting against the god of blight, of darkness, of greed. This is the dragon fight of mythology.

Sts Patrick, Seanán, Éanna, Colmán, Kevin and various other Irish saints all indulge in the *peistchomhrac* or dragon fight, and generally the *péist* is banished to a place where he can do no harm. Similarly in Europe, Sts Vigor of Baioc, St Veran de Vavaillon, Julian of Mans, Romanus of Rouen, Beatus of Vendome, St Hilary, St Samson of Dol – all are engrossed in dragon fights. What usually happens is that the dragon or *péist* emerges from a lake, eats up the cows of the local farmers, endangers life an limb, and the dragon is also connected with flooding. The local people then apply to the Christian bishop for help. He leads a procession of the people singing psalms and reciting prayers to the edge of the lake and overpowers the dragon by the power of God. Sometimes he gives the dragon a blow of this crozier.

The French Scholar Cerquand has done an enormous amount of research into this motif of the dragon fight and his conclusions are that the Celtic hero and the Christian saint, in areas with a Celtic tradition, were the heirs of the Celtic God Tarannis who went out accompanied with his people and with his mallet struck the great sea-serpent and subdued him and so prevented the flooding and destruction of the land. (*Rev. Celt.*, VI, 422-441)

After the battle, the victory of the Tuatha Dé Danann was proclaimed all over the land by the MórRíon, the Celtic War Goddess, and Lugh and his followers made a victory march to Tailteann in Co Meath *(Tochmarc Emire).*

Lugh's victory march must have passed through the south of modern Co Leitrim and north Longford to reach Tailteann. Here, in some place not identified, called *Toinge Ech nDea,* the Tuatha Dé Danann washed their horses and it is significant that swimming horses in rivers and lakes became a feature of the Festival of Lughnasa in some areas as, for instance, at Lough Owel, Co Westmeath. (Danaher, 1972, 173)

On arriving at Tailteann, Lugh is declared king. Nuadha, the former king of the Tuatha Dé Danann, has been killed in the battle. The *Bainis Rí* takes place in which Lugh is married to Baoi, the goddess of fertility. The place-name *Cnogba* (Knowth) near Newgrange, may have got its name from her – *Cnoc Baoi.*

The ritual marriage of god and goddess takes place at Samhain and nine months later, at Lughnasa, a child is born to them – their child is the new corn harvest.

It is significant that one of the most important elements of the Rite of Lughnasa was the offering of a sheaf of the newly ripened corn on the Lughnasa hill. It could be placed on the site or buried in the ground. In any case, it resembles the act in which the nurse places his newly born child in the arms of the father.

The Festival of Lughnasa then, can be seen as the ritual commemoration of the Battle of Maigh Tuireadh in which the Fomhóraigh were defeated by the Tuatha Dé Danann and forced to end their tyranny, cease demanding exorbitant taxes, cease causing blight and devastation to the crops and release a plentiful harvest.

At any rate, literary tradition states that Lugh instituted the great *Aonach Tailteann* in honour of his foster mother Tailte, who had died after clearing the Plain of Breagha and making it suitable for agriculture. She was the wife of the great Fir Bholg king, Eochaidh Mac Eirc. She was buried at Tailteann and funeral games were held at the beginning of the harvest. As we have seen, the *aonach* was a highly important institution at which nobles and people gathered together not only for amusements such as horseracing, athletic events, storytelling, etc., and for the sale of livestock and goods but for the promulgation of new laws. Ancient assembly places seem to have associations with the graves of the ancestors and on these sacred occasions the barriers between the living and the dead were broken down. Perhaps it was envisaged that for such important things as the introduction of new laws affecting the tribe as a whole, the advice of the dead was as valued as that of the living. According to *Annála Ríoghachta Éireann,* the last official *Aonach Tailteann* took place in 1169 under the last Ard Rí, Ruairí Ó Conchúir, on the eve of the Norman invasion. Kings were exhorted to attend the *aonach* to ensure the fertility of the land. The *aonach* lasted on in Teltown (Tailteann) in a reduced form into modern times and O'Donovan in his account of the area, furnished a detailed map of the site. Further information is supplied by Máire Mac Néill.

Celebrating Lughnasa

The Festival of Lughnasa was celebrated at about 200 sites throughout the country and a mountain site existed for each Province: Croagh Patrick, Co Mayo, for Connacht; Slieve Donard, Co Down, for Ulster; Church Mountain, Co Wicklow, for Leinster, and Mount Brandon, Co Kerry, for Munster. As well as these there were numerous Lughnasa Hills, as for instance Beltany Hill, Co Donegal; Benaghlin, Co Fermanagh; Ardagh Hill, Co Longford; Knockfeerina, Co Limerick.

Then there were Lughnasa assemblies at numerous holy wells: Struel Wells, Co Down; Dabhach Fharannáin, Co Sligo; St Mullin's, Co Carlow; Dabhach Bhríde, Co Clare.

Lughnasa fairs were also common: Lammas Fair, Bally-

Castle, Co Antrim (last Tuesday in August); Aonach na Ceardchan, Connemara, Co Galway (July 26); Fair of the Furze, Curragh, Co Kildare (July 26); Aonach Chrom Dubh, Ennistymon, Co Clare (Saturday before Garland Sunday).

The most notable ancient Lughnasa assemblies are those of Tailteann, Co Meath; Carman, probably at the Curragh, Co Kildare, and Lough Gur, Co Limerick.

The Festival of Lughnasa, celebrated so widely throughout the land, was the celebration of the victory of light over darkness, of the forces of health and plenty over the powers of want and decay. The miserly, stingy, destructive god, Balar of the Evil Eye, has been overcome by the generous god of light, Lugh Lámhfhada.

The observances of the feast included climbing the Lughnasa Hill, eating the *fraocháin* (whortleberries), laying gifts at the sacred site, games, amusements, feasting, flirting, bonfires. The difference may be noted between Lughnasa and the Anglican Harvest Festival, which comes at the end of the harvest as a thanksgiving to God. The Festival of Lughnasa, on the contrary, was celebrated at the beginning of the harvest to stimulate the forces of nature to produce an abundant crop. *Cath Maighe Tuireadh* may be seen as the myth behind the ritual. At many sites it must have been a great social occasion which brought together young people from fairly distant areas that wouldn't otherwise have met in the ordinary course of events. These meetings sometimes resulted in marriage six months later just before Lent, around the Feast of Imbolc – St Brigid's Day – thus linking together two great festivals of the Celtic year.

At a period when travel outside one's own small area was difficult, with a consequent tendency to marry within one's own community, the possibility of marrying somebody from outside the local area as a result of the Festival of Lughnasa must have introduced a very welcome and healthy factor into society.

Croagh Patrick

There is little doubt but that the Christian pilgrimage to Croagh Patrick replaces the pagan festival of Lughnasa. The dates coincide – the last days of summer and the beginning of autumn with the ripening of the corn. Moreover, there is a tradition that the proper day for performing the pilgrimage is *Aoine Chrom Dubh,* the Friday of Crom Dubh. Crom Dubh is the name of the stingy harvest god who, according to tradition, is defeated by St Patrick. Undoubtedly this is another name for Crom Cruaich of Magh Sléacht near Ballymagauran, Co Cavan, described in the *Vita Tripartita* and in the *Dinnseanchas of Maigh Sléacht:*

> At Maigh Sleacht the king-idol of Ireland stood and twelve idols of stone about him. He was of gold and he was the god of every party who took Ireland until the coming of Patrick. It is to him that they used to offer the first-born of every beast and the first-born of every human. It was to worship him that Tigernmas Mac Fellaich, king of Ireland, used to come at Samhain, along with the men and women of Ireland. They used to prostrate before him so that they destroyed the tops of their foreheads and noses and elbows and knees. Three quarters of the men of Ireland died as a result of these prostrations. Whence 'Maigh Sléacht – the Plain of the Prostrations'. *(Dinnseanchas)*

> Milk and corn they used to ask of him speedily in return for a third of their whole progeny: Great was the horror and outcry about him. *(Dinnseanchas)*

The *Vita Tripartita* gives an account of St Patrick's confrontation with Cend Cruaich (Crom Cruaich):

> After that (i.e. after his labours in North Teathha), Patrick went over the water to Maigh Sléacht, the place in which was the chief idol of Ireland, viz. Cend Cruaich, covered with gold and silver, and twelve other idols covered around

him. When Patrick saw the idol from the water whose name is Guth Ard (probably Garadice Lake, *Guth Ard Theas*) and when he approached the idol, he raised his hand to place the 'Staff of Jesus' *(Bachall Íosa)* on it. And he did not touch it, but the idol leaned over towards the sunset on its right side, for it is southwards its face was, i.e. to Tara. And the mark of the staff still remains in its left side, and yet the staff did not leave Patrick's hand. And the earth swallowed the twelve other idols up to their heads, and they are in that state as a sign of the miracle. And he cursed the demon and expelled him into hell.

According to legend, St Patrick confronted the demons in the form of black birds on what was then known as *Cruachán Aigle,* now Croagh Patrick. He hurled his bell, the Clog Dubh, at them as Lugh had hurled a missile from his sling at Balar, and dispersed them. This bell continued to be used as part of the pilgrimage ritual down to the nineteenth century. It was passed *deiseal* (sunwise) round the body of each pilgrim three times and the cross on the bell was kissed by him or her three times. (MacNéill, 1982, 72-73; 81)

St Patrick had had a conflict also on the mountaintop with the Caorthanach, a dragon who was the devil's mother. He succeeded in confining her to a lake on the mountain side. She escaped, however, and he finally defeated her at Loch Dearg. (MacNéill, 1982, 400)

The last Sunday of July, *Domhnach Chrom Dubh,* is the popular day for the pilgrimage to Croagh Patrick when perhaps 30,000 people make the arduous ascent. At the foot of the mountain they hire pilgrims' staffs to support them over the rough terrain. Only a small number now follow the age-old tradition of starting off on the three-hour journey at midnight, having only a lamp or candle and making the ascent barefoot.

Normally, the pilgrimage begins near the old Augustinian abbey of Murrisk and the pilgrims turn their backs to the north (the area of darkness) to proceed southwards for a while before heading eastwards up the final slope to the summit.

On the way they come to the first station, Leacht Mionnáin. This is a low carn or heap of stones, St Benén's Bed, which the pilgrim goes round *deiseal* seven times repeating the customary prayers, 7 Paters, 7 Aves and one Creed. Then, with a touch of the hand from carn to head, the pilgrim imparts the power of the stones to himself.

Having completed the 7 rounds at Leacht Mionnáin, the pilgrim ascends by the steep path called Cosán Phádraig to the summit and recites 7 Paters, 7 Aves, and one Creed.

Only the merest trace of the previous chapel remains but the pilgrim kneels at the ruin and says 15 Paters, 15 Aves and one Creed. (Before the present chapel was built these prayers were said kneeling before the altar of the old church and an offering of a piece of cloth or a nail or some other token gift was left in the crevices of the stones, as at holy wells.)

The popularity of the pilgrimage in the Middle Ages necessitated various hostels on the route and several monasteries, whose ruins can still be seen, must have served this purpose. Perhaps the best known of these today is the restored Ballintubber Abbey, about fifteen miles east of Aghagower, and the pilgrim path, Tóchar Phádraig, passed between them. Kilmaine and Kilbannon must also have been used by pilgrims from the south-eastern route while the abbey of Murrisk would have served the same purpose on the western side near Clew Bay. Hubert Knox comments:

> The Tóchar Phátraic is a very ancient road which seems to be the ancient pilgrims' road from the east to Croagh Patrick. It can be very well traced from Croagh Patrick back to Drum; it passed from church to church, thus, Balla to Loona Church, where it is well marked, and

thence by Gweeshadan Church to Drum Church, where it is well marked. Thence it is well ascertained to Ballintubber and from thence to Aghagower, passing in the way a small church marked on the map as Temple Shanenagawna near Bellaburke. From Aghagower it went by Lankill and Cloghpatrick to Patrick's Chair and so up the hill.

I have not been able to trace the course east of Balla, but feel sure it must have passed by Kiltimagh and Cloonpatrick and Patrick's Well to Balla. The latter Well, a Bullaun in the earth, was once a place of some importance, where stations were held at an old fort called Lis na Grus close to it. The heap of stones about it seems to be the remnant of such a cairn and alcove as is about the Bullaun called Patrick's Well at Tully in the parish of Kilcorkey in Co Roscommon. (1904, 140)

Historically and in modern times the pilgrimage to Croagh Patrick occupies a very important position in Celtic piety and, in performing it, the pilgrim joins with thousands of others in prayer and asceticism. Using these as weapons he attacks the forces of darkness on the very site on which the great spiritual hero Patrick had confronted the powers of evil and triumphed over them.

In this, Patrick was putting into effect on a local level the Easter victory of Christ over Satan. The whole process was, however, Celticised by connecting it with Lugh and his triumph over Balar at Cath Maighe Tuireadh.

The pilgrim next walks fifteen times around the path which encircles the summit of the hill. Attending Mass in the modern chapel is now generally a part of the pilgrimage.

The next station is within the encircling path and is known as Leaba Phádraig. The pilgrim kneels inside the cavity and says 7 Paters, 7 Aves and one Creed. He then makes 7 rounds of the Leaba proceeding *deiseal* or sunwise as usual.

This part of the rite is performed by the pilgrims in general nowadays but formerly it was only performed by those who wished to have a child. It was usual for them to spend the night on the mountain and sleep on the Bed. This custom resembles the well known practice of sleeping at a megalithic tomb known as Leaba Dhiarmada agus Ghráinne for the same purpose – to stimulate fertility.

On the way down on the southwest side is a triangular area with three cairns of stone known as Reilig Mhuire. The pilgrim goes round each of these 7 times saying the customary prayers and finally round the complete area (Garraí Mór) 7 times.

This completes the pilgrimage although some pilgrims go on to do the rounds at the holy well of Kilgeever.

At the foot of the mountain there is field at Murrisk called 'the Old Patron Field' and a road called Bóthar na Miasa, both indicating the area where the pilgrims regaled themselves with food and drink, dance and song after their strenuous and prolonged exertions.

Lughnasa: a third Easter?

As has been said already, it became the custom in monastic circles in the early Irish church to have, in addition to the ordinary Lent of forty days preceding Easter (Carghas Íosa san Earrach), two other Lents of forty days each, one preceding Christmas, more or less corresponding to our Advent, called Geimhcharghas Éilí (Winter Lent of Elias) and Samhcharghas Mhaoise (Summer Lent of Moses) beginning about three weeks after Pentecost Sunday. (*Leabhar Breac*, 90. cf. *Codex Pal. Vat.* 830, p. 384)

Now, if there were three Lents, there must have been three Easters and indeed the *Leabhar Breac* mentions Domhnach Samh-chásca. On the modern calculation of Easter, the Feast of Pentecost falls between 14 May and 10 June. The average date then would be about 27 May. Add about three weeks to this and we arrive at 24 June, the feast of St John the Baptist, bonfire night, and the summer solstice. If the Summer Lent began after this and went an for forty days, then it culminated around the beginning of August, the festival of Lughnasa, making Lughnasa a kind of third Easter.

Now, the ecclesiastical Feast of the Transfiguration occurs at about this time, on 6 August in the modern calendar and on 26 July in *Féilire Aonghusa*. This makes a curious coincidence between the traditional Celtic feast of Lugh and the appearance of Christ in glory to Peter, James and John on the mountain. (Mk 9:2-10)

Féilire Aonghusa describes the transfiguration scene:
tarmchruthud iar ndedóil Íssu i Sléib Thabóir.

(Transfiguration after twilight of Jesus on Mount Thabor.) It speaks of the five witnesses, Peter, James, John, Moses and Elias, and it is from Jesus, Moses and Elias that the three Fasts are named.

The Transfiguration is the great otherworldly scene in which we get a preview of the glorified Christ in heaven, surrounded by the saints. This feast is an outstanding manifestation of life in heaven after the resurrection of the body and, while the three apostles are still on earth, they are filled with ecstasy from which they do not want to be awakened.

In an age of materialism, the Feast of the Transfiguration or 'Lughnasa Easter' could play a large part in focusing the attention of the faithful on the Risen Life of Christ after his resurrection. Just when the first of the corn is ripe in the fields we can celebrate the resurrection of Christ, the first-born from the dead.

The Transfiguration as a feast deserves far more attention than it usually gets and one wonders if would benefit by being transferred to the nearest Sunday. If every Sunday is a celebration of Easter then a 'Transfiguration Sunday' which highlights the risen life of Our Lord in heaven could be quite appropriate.

It would also be fitting that the nearby Feast of the

Assumption of the Virgin Mary into Heaven (15 August) be associated with the Transfiguration. Mary is the first-fruits of the spiritual harvest, the early ripened corn containing the promise that the rest will follow.

It is clear that the Festival of Lughnasa holds considerable potential in focusing attention on first-fruits, corn, victory over enemy attacks, attainment of object, arrival at a new state of peace and prosperity – ideas that are already present in the liturgy of this calendrical period.

It would appear then, that St Patrick's great fast on Croagh Patrick was in preparation for the third Easter, the Lughnasa Easter or Feast of the Transfiguration as interpreted by monastic writers of a period later than that of St Patrick himself. It was then that he triumphed over the black demon-birds and ever since, on Domhnach Chrom Dubh, his faithful followers climb that sacred mountain to participate in his fight and victory over the forces of evil which still remain to afflict mankind.

The struggle and eventual victory is described in parallel lines with the pre-Christian celebration of Lughnasa among the Celts by Professor Rhys in the *Proceedings of the British Academy* (1910, 35):

The month of August is dominated by Lug and the festivities at the beginning of Autumn were meant to mark the successful close of the prolonged struggle between the sun-god and the Fomóirí whose spells and evil magic produced the blasts and blights that were harmful to the growing crops and to the dairy. The first event in the Coligny Calendar for the month of Rivros was the carrying of the firstfruits to the hill, otherwise to the house: the statements combined favour the idea that the house was on the hill. In Ireland and in Wales the hill was represented by an earthen mound of imposing dimensions and associated with it was a woman who was a fostering mother. This suggests a somewhat subtle question: Was she supposed to be buried periodically in the mound when vegetation, after the harvest, seemed to languish and fall asleep, or was the mound simply and frankly a symbol of the great Mother? In either case ,on the top of the earthen mound may have been a hut of some rude kind, a circle open to the sky or a temenos of some description, in which the firstfruits were deposited and from which the god could be supposed to watch the games, and especially the racing in his honour on the plain below. Should this supposition hold good, we have an intelligible explanation to offer of such remains of antiquity as Silbury Hill overlooking the avenues of Avebury as the racing ground for a Lugnassad on a grand scale.

From what has already been said, one may state without fear of contradiction that the divinity, whether styled Rivos or Lugus, or both, was the god of an agricultural people. He was regarded as the farmers' protector.

I give now, in summary form, a set of parallels between the Cath Maighe Tuireadh Cycle, with its idea of liberation from oppression, and the work of our redemption as performed by Our Lord.

Cath Maighe Tuireadh agus Féile Lughnasa
(The Cath Maighe Tuireadh Cycle)

Gray, E., *Cath Maige Tuired,* (Dublin, 1982); Ó Cuív, B., *Cath Muighe Tuireadh,* (Dublin, 1945); Stokes, W., 'The second battle of Moytura', *Revue Celtique* xii, 52-129. *Éigse* 7 (1954), 191-198.

1. *(Mythological):* Tuatha Dé Danann are oppressed (heavy taxes, etc.) by Balar of the Evil Eye & Fomhóraigh (dark gods of the engulfing sea). cf. *CMT* & *Oidhe Clainne Tuireann.*

1. *(Christian):* Angels and Human Race oppressed by dragon (Satan) and rebellious angels. *Apocalypse* 12.

2. Tuatha Dé Danann (gods of light, evolved) cry out for Liberator. cf. *CMT* & *Oidhe Clainne Tuireann.*

2. Jews (Human Race) cry out for Liberator. cf. Advent Liturgy 'Pour down you heavens and let the earth bring forth a Saviour.' *(Rorate Coeli)*

3. Lugh Lámhfhada arrives as Liberator. (CMT & OCT)

3. Incarnation. Christ comes to set his people free from domination of Satan and Powers of Evil: 'He (God) has sent me to proclaim liberty to captives ... to set the downtrodden free.' (cf. Lk 4:16-19)

4. Lugh Lámhfhada collects *meitheal* – co-operators, armaments, etc. – for forthcoming battle against Fomhóraigh.

4. Christ collects *meitheal* – 12 Apostles to assist him in forthcoming battle against Powers of Evil. cf. Lk 6:12-16.

5. Cath Maighe Tuireadh takes place; Mythic battle but sited near Lough Arrow, Co Sligo: Lugh & TDD versus Balar & Fomhóraigh – Light v Dark; Summer v Winter; Freedom v Slavery, Evolution towards light (sun) v Non-evolution (sea), etc. Battle of the gods at Samhain. Dragon fight.

5. Christ confronts Satan, death, forces of underworld: Temptation in Desert (Mt 4:1-11; First Sun. Lent). *Argain Ifrinn,* Plundering of Hell, at Easter and release of Adam and Eve and Old Testament captives. *(Apoc. Gospel of Nicodemus)* 'It is I who destroyed death, who triumphed over the enemy, who trampled the Underworld underfoot, who bound up the strong one, and snatched man away to the heights of heaven; I am the Christ.' *(Breviary* 2, 367-368). Dragon fight. Easter.

6. Great victory of Lugh & TDD over Balar & Fomhóraigh. Control obtained over Fomhóraigh, though not exterminated.

6. Great victory of Risen Christ over death and underworld. Control obtained over forces of evil though not exterminated. 'Where there is no opposition, there is no fight, and where there is no fight there is no victory', St Columbanus.

7. Victory of Lugh & Tuatha Dé Danann proclaimed by MórRíon to royal heights of Éire, to the *Aos Sí,* to the chief waters and rivermouths.

7. Victor of Christ proclaimed by angels: 'He has risen.' Lk 24:5.

8. Victory Procession of Lugh from Maigh Tuireadh to Tailteann /Sliabh na Caillí (Co Meath). *(Tochmarc Emire)*

8. Victory Procession of Risen Christ – Ascension into heaven – proclaimed by angels. Acts 1:9-11.

9. Lugh declared king in place of Nuadha who was killed in battle.

9. Risen Christ becomes king of heaven and earth. cf. Mt 28:18.

10. *Bainis Rí:* Wedding of Lugh to Baoi (Loughcrew = Loch Chnoc / chroch Baoi?), goddess of the land (Bandia an tSonasa) at Tailteann (Sliabh na Caillí – Cailleach Bhéarra). Samhain.

10. Symbolic marriage of Christ to church (ecclesia).
   Hodie caelesti sponso juncta est Ecclesia, quoniam in Jordane lavit Christus ejus crimina; currunt cum muner-ibus Magi ad regales nuptias,et ex aqua facto vino laetan-tur convivae, alleluja. (Ant. Ben. Epiphany)
   (Today, Ecclesia (the church) is joined to her heavenly bridegroom, since Christ has purified her of her sins in the river Jordan; the Magi hasten to the royal wedding and offer gifts: the wedding guests rejoice as they drink the wine which was made from water.)

It is noticeable that in this Benedictus Antiphon for the Feast of the Epiphany the mystical marriage of Christ with his church is proclaimed. In the Old Testament Israel was considered to be the Bride of Yahweh. In countless Christmas cards the Epiphany scene is shown as the three kings presenting their gifts to the child Jesus in his mother's arms. Here, however, the scenario is quite different. It is not a birthday scene and the Magi are not bringing birthday gifts. It is a wedding ceremony in which Christ and his church (ecclesia) are being married. The three kings come running to present their wedding presents.

11. At Lughnasa child born to Lugh and goddess Baoi – the child is the newly-ripened corn, the harvest. At Rites of Lughnasa sheaf of new corn laid on Lughnasa Hill, presentation of child to Lugh. (cf. *MacNeill*, 1982, 1, 462)
We have a parallel to this in a remarkable Greek vase painting in the Museum at Constantinople dating to the 5th–4th century BC discussed by Jane Harrison. The scene is at Eleusis and shows the birth of a divine child:

> The child rises out of a cornucopia, symbol of fertility. He is the fruits of the earth. He is solemnly presented to Athene because Eleusis gave to Athens her corn and her mysteries. Art could speak no plainer. (1962, 525)

11. Neophyte – newly baptised – newly born of Christ and church. Blessing of Baptismal Font at Easter Vigil:

> 'Respice, Domine, in faciem Ecclesiae tuae, et multiplica in ea regenerationes tuas, qui gratiae tuae affluentis impetu laetificas civitatem tuam' … 'Qui hanc aquam regenerandis hominibus praeparatam, arcana sui numinis admixtione foecundet; ut sanctificatione concepta, ab immaculato divini fontis utero, in novam renata creaturam. progenies caelestis emergat' … 'Descendat in hanc plenitudinem fontis, virtus Spiritus Sancti. (3). Totamque hujus aquae substantiam, regenerandi foecundet effectu.'

(Graciously look upon the face of your Church, O Lord, and increase in it the number of those reborn to you. By the force of your abundantly flowing grace you make your city joyful … May he by an arcane mixture of his divine power make this water fruitful for the rebirth of men. May a heavenly offspring, conceived in holiness and reborn as a new creature, emerge from the stainless womb of the divine font … May the power of the Holy Spirit descend into all the water of this font. And make the whole substance of this water fertile so that it can give birth.)

First fruits ritual
In Gaelic Scotland a first-fruits ritual was performed on the Feast of the Assumption, 15 August. Early in the morning, people went to their fields to pluck ears of ripe corn to make the *Moilean Moire* or Mary's Loaf.

These ears were laid on a rock exposed to the sun to dry. When dry, they were winnowed, made into flour and baked. For the baking or toasting a type of wood sacred to the Celts was used, as for instance, the *caorthann* or rowan wood. The *caorthann* shows its magnificent clusters of scarlet berries at Lughnasa, as the holly indicates the approach of Christmas.

The father of the family broke the loaf into pieces, giving a portion to the mother and each of their children. Then the family, one after the other, the father leading, processed *deiseal* (sunwise) around the fire in the centre of the room singing the *Iolach Mhoire Mhathar*, the triumphal song of Mary the Mother:

Chaidh mi deiseil m'ardrach,
An ainm Mhoire Mhathar,
A gheall mo ghleidheadh,
A rinn mo ghleidheadh,
A ni mo ghleidheadh,
Ann an sith, ann an ni,

Ann am fireantas cridh,
Ann an gnionih, ann an gradh,
Ann am brigh, ann am baigh,
Air sgath do Phais.
A Chriosd a ghrais
Gu la mo bhais
Gu brath nach treig mi!
O gu la mo bhais
Gu brath nach treig mi!
(I went sunways round my dwelling,
In name of the Mary Mother,
Who promised to preserve me,
Who did preserve me,
And who will preserve me,
In peace, in flocks,
In righteousness of heart,
In labour, in love,
In wisdom, in mercy,
For the sake of Thy Passion.
Thou Christ of grace
Who till the day of my death
Wilt never forsake me!
Oh, till the day of my death
Wilt never forsake me!)
(*CG*, 1, 194-197)

(Gaeilge na hÉireann)
Chuaigh mé deiseal mo bhaile,
In ainm Mhuire Mháthar,
A gheall mo chumhdach,
A rinne mo chumhdach,
A dhéanfaidh mo chumhdach
Sa tsíth, sa ní,
San fhíreantas croí.

Sa ghníomh, sa ghrá ,
Sa bhrí, sa bhá,
Ar scáth do Pháis
A Chríost an ghráis,
Go lá mo bháis,
Go brách ná tréig mé.
Ó go lá mo bháis,
Go brách ná tréig mé.

Burning embers are then put into a pot along with pieces
of iron and carried around the outside of the dwelling with
the same type of sunwise procession for the protection of the
farm against disease, ill-luck and the attacks of evil spirits.
Iron is a well-known protective device against the Tuatha Dé
Danann. This explains the Scian Choise Duibhe (black-handled knife) carried by people at Samhain and Bealtaine, the
thongs placed in the cradle to protect the child, and the
horseshoe on the door.

The circumambulation of the altar at Mass with fire in the
censer is another example of archaic ritual to delineate a sacred
space free from the incursion of hostile forces. One can easily
see that the usage may have developed from a ring of fire
made by campers to keep away wolves at night.

In this comprehensive ritual, the reaping of the first corn
of the year is performed with gracious ceremonial. Sun and
rock, sacred wood and sheep-skin, are employed in the
preparation of the first loaf of the new harvest. The baked loaf
is shared ritually among the family. Homage is paid to the
hearth as the very centre of family life. Protection is sought
for the family possessions as well as the inner life of virtue and
wisdom.

Stemming from Israel's worship, the liturgy of the
Firstfruits of the corn harvest was found in the Friday and
Saturday Ember Days of Pentecost in the Roman (Tridentine)

Missal. These would correspond to the ripening of the corn
in Italy in May, over two months earlier than in Ireland due to
climatic conditions. The second Lesson for Ember Saturday
from Leviticus 23 describes the usage:

> In those days the Lord spoke to Moses, saying: Speak to
> the children of Israel, and thou shalt say to them: 'When
> you shall have entered into the land which I will give you,
> and shall reap your corn, you shall bring sheaves of ears,
> the first-fruits of your harvest, to the priest: who shall lift
> up the sheaf before the Lord.'

The festival of Lughnasa, however, had a less sedate character
and there was the question of wresting the means of survival
from the earth against the opposition of reluctant and hostile
forces. The god Lugh was the farmer's ally in this struggle for
food and prosperity, while St Patrick adopted a similar role
and became the great ally of the Irish people in their struggle
with the powers of darkness excluding them from eternal
salvation.

Brittany is a Celtic country rich in 'Pardons' – local
colourful pilgrimages in honour of St Anne, Patroness of
Brittany, the Virgin Mary and numerous local saints. It is surprising how many of these occur during the strictly Lughnasa
period – from the third Sunday in July to the first Sunday of
August – the *Domhnach Chrom Dubh* period in Irish terms.
These include Ste-Anne-d'Auray, St Nicodéme, Pont-Aven,
Fouesnant, Douarnenez, Huelgoat, and many others (Melia,
1978, 530 footnote). The Pardon of St Anne d'Auray takes
place around her feastday on 26 July while that of Ste-Anne-la
Palud takes place later on the last Sunday of August.

It is thought that both places were probably pre-Christian
cult centres of the Celtic goddess Anu – the Anu/Ana of *Dhá
Chíoch Anann* near Killarney – who was assimilated to the
figure of St Anne by early Christian missionaries. The Ste-

Anne-la Palud cult legend maintains that St Anne was a Breton princess who had a cruel husband. An angel carried her to Palestine where she married St Joachim and gave birth to the Virgin Mary. Later she returned to Brittany where Jesus visited her and caused a fountain to spring up. She is 'Mamm Goz ar Vretoned' (Grandmother of the Bretons) and has an exalted position parallel to the grandmother in a Breton family.

The laity play an important part in these regional pilgrimages. Men and women, often in regional costume, carry the crosses, banners, statues and relics of the saints in procession (Doan, 1980, 27-31).

Daniel F. Melia has published a penetrating study of what is perhaps the greatest of all the Breton Pardons, the *Grande Troménie* at Locronan (Finistere), in the *Journal of American Folklore*, vol 91 (1978), 528ff. He compares it to the Pilgrimage to Croagh Patrick. Both occur at about the same time, the *Troménie* procession taking place on the second and third Sundays in July. The *Grande Troménie* (its elaborate form) takes place only once every six years (Melia, 1978, 528-529).

As in the case of Croach Patrick. the *Grande Troménie* involves climbing a hill and stops at certain stations, the distance covered being about 12 kilometres. St Ronan was an Irish saint and his legend is recited in the form of a drama at the beginning of the procession.

Three parishes are involved and a considerable number of people play an active part in the actual performance of the rite. As well as carrying crosses, banners, and St Ronan's bell, 44 minor stations are set up and maintained by local families. These consist of little huts made of branches and foliage, each of which contains a statue of a local saint and a dish for offerings. These are small token offerings but giving a donation seems to be an integral part of the ritual. These little shrines remain there for the week. Their origin is uncertain; they may be connected to the Jewish 'Feast of Booths' or to the Greek

Thesmophoria. Perhaps there is an echo here of pre-Christian veneration of deities at trees, wells and rocks (Melia, 1978, 532-533).

At nine am on Sunday, the representatives of the three parishes, through which the procession will pass, foregather outside the church of Locronan where the saint is buried. They touch the top of the poles of their banners together in greeting and then march into the church for High Mass. At around 2.00 pm the procession gets under way. The clergy go first, then the banners carried by young men and women in traditional Breton dress, the relics of the saint in a wooden reliquary, the saint's bell hanging in a small wooden tower, and then the general public.

The young men who carry the relics and bell wear small unsheared goatskin bags in which are bottles of locally-made cider. Along the route the local farmers replenish their supplies and certain families provide pancakes for the pilgrims.

On the route there are twelve permanent stations. Some of these are marked by a stone cross. There is the healing well of St Eutrope at the First Station, where pilgrims drink the water, and near the Twelfth Station a great megalith, Kazeg vaen, used to be circumambulated *deiseal* three times. It was believed that female infertility was cured by lying on the stone, as at *Leaba Phádraig* on Croagh Patrick.

At the Tenth Station, at the ruined chapel of St Ronan on top of the mountain of Locronan (Menez Lokorn), there is a long stop and a sermon is preached.

At each station a priest reads a portion of the gospel, the Our Father is said, as well as a short litany, and the procession moves on to the next station. The twelve readings try to give a summary of the gospels and a set order is observed, going from Jn 1:1-18 at the first station to Mt 19:27-29 at the twelfth or last station.

The procession returns to the town square, where before the

church of Locronan a huge bonfire is lighted when darkness falls.

Melia points out the many similarities between the Locronan 'Pardon' and the pilgrimage to Croagh Patrick: the same Lughnasa date; a sacred hill; a token offering (rag or nail at Croagh Patrick), a holy well; a structure with fertility connotations; distribution of food (*Bóthar na Miasa* at Croagh Patrick); *Leacht Mionnáin* at Croagh Patrick is the traditional grave of St Bennén. According to the legend he had been killed by the fleeing demon birds and brought back to life by St Patrick. At Locronan, the witch Keben kills King Gradlon's daughter. St Ronan, however, restores her to life and banishes Keben. The use of a saint's bell as a device for banishing demons is a common feature of both sites (Melia, 1978, 536-539).

Conclusion

Much research remains to be done on the interweaving threads of religion and culture in the Celtic lands. Sacred monumemts from different periods appear on the landscape and pose questions as to their use and purpose. Above all, the important question is if ancient customs, backed by an archaic philosophy or worldview, can be of help to citizens of the consumer society today, in their frenetic search for meaning in the world.

I have already said something of the idea of the divine presence in the world, moving people onwards towards spiritualisation and final vision in God. The concepts of unity of being, of final harmony and integration, of conflicting forces moving towards a synthesis have been considered. The Gaelic folk-prayer tradition has been dealt with, and the great liturgical periods of Advent-Christmas and Easter have been examined, with special emphasis on the Gaelic understanding of these feasts. We have seen the four calendrical festivals of the insular Celts – Samhain, Imbolc, Bealtaine and Lughnasa

– in their Christianised forms.

In the background lay the powerful mystique prevailing in the land of Éire in which the mystic race of the Tuatha Dé Danann occupied the consciousness of the people, and from the ancient monuments and hollow hills controlled the fertility of the land and dictated the destiny of kings.

Bibliography

Adam, A., *The Liturgical Year* (New York 1981)

Allen, J., *Norman Sculpture and the Mediaeval Bestiaries* (London 1887)

Atkinson, R., *The Passions and the Homilies of the Leabhar Breac* (Dublin 1887)

Bailey, A., *The Caves of the Sun* (London 1998)

Barclay, W., *The Acts of the Apostles* (Glasgow 1955)

Berger, P., *The Goddess Obscured* (London 1988)

Berry, T., 'The Dynamics of the future Reflections of the Earth Process', *Monastic Studies,* 12 (1976)

Best, R., and Bergin, O., *Lebor na hUidre* (Galway 1970)

Bord, J. and C., *Sacred Waters* (London 1985)

Britt, M., *The Hymns of the Breviary and Missal* (London 1922)

Brock, S., *The Harp of the Spirit* (Fellowship of St Alban and St Sergius 1983)

Byrne, L., *Ancient Stories of Ireland* (Luton 1996)

Budge, E. A. Wallis, *The Egyptian Book of the Dead* (New York 1967)

Burl, A., *Prehistoric Stone Circles* (Aylesbury 1983)

Campbell, J., *Occidental Mythology* (London 1976)

Carbery, E., *In the Celtic Past* (Dublin)

Carpenter, E., *The Origins of Pagan and Christian Beliefs* (London 1996)

Carney, J., *The Poems of Blathmac Son of Cú Brettan* (Dublin 1964)

Carmichael, A., *Carmina Gadelica* (Edinburgh 1900)

Cawley, A., (Ed.), *Everyman and Medieval Miracle Plays* (London 1981)

Chupungco, A., *Shaping the Easter Feast* (Washington, DC, 1992)

Cohn, N., *Cosmos, Chaos and the World to Come* (Yale University Press 1993)

Cunliffe, B., *The Celtic World* (London 1992)

Dames, M., *Mythic Ireland* (London 1992)

De La Villemarque, T. H., *Le Barzaz Breiz* (Paris 1981)

Danaher, D., *The Year in Ireland* (Cork 1972)

Denzinger, H., *Ritus Orientalium in Administrandis Sacramentis* (Graz 1961)

DIL = *Dictionary of the Irish Language,* (Royal Irish Academy, Dublin 1983)

Dinneen, P., *Foclóir Gaedhilge agus Béarla* (Dublin 1927)

Dinneen, P., *Foras Feasa ar Éirinn; The History of Ireland by Geoffrey Keating DD.* (London 1908)

Doan, J., 'Five Breton Cantiques from Pardons', *Folklore* 91 (1980)

Durandus, G., *Rationale Divinorum Officiorum* (Lugduni MDCV)

Durrwell, F., *La Résurrection de Jesus Mystére de Salut* (Paris 1954)

Eliade, M., *The Myth of the Eternal Return* (Bollingen 1954)

Eluere, C., *The Celts First Masters of Europe* (London 1993)

Ford, P., (Ed.), *Celtic Folklore and Christianity* (Los Angeles 1983)

Frazer, J., *The Golden Bough* (London 1923)

Fraser, J., Grosjean, S., O'Keefe, J., *Irish Texts* (London 1931)

Gassner, J., *Medieval and Tudor Drama* (New York 1971)

Gillies, W., 'An Early Modern Irish "Harrowing of Hell"' *Celtica* 13 (1980)

Gimbutas, M., *The Goddesses and Gods of Old Europe* (London 1989)

Gray, E., *Cath Muige Tuired* (Dublin 1982)

Green, M., *Dictionary of Celtic Myth and Legend* (London 1992)

Gregory, Lady, *Cuchulainn of Muirthemne,* (Gerrards Cross 1970)

Guerber, H., *Greece and Rome: Myths and Legends* (New York 1986)

Gwynn, E., 'The Rule of Tallaght', (*Hermathena*, XLIV, 1927)

Gwynn, E., and Purton, W., 'The Monastery of Tallaght', (*PRIA*, Dublin 1911)

Gwynn, E., *The Metrical Dindshenchas* (Dublin 1906)

Haight, R., 'Jesus and Salvation, an Essay in Interpretation', *Theological Studies,* vol. 55, no. 2 (1994)

Harbison, P., *Pilgrimage in Ireland* (London 1991)

Harrison, J., *Prolegomena to the Study of Greek Religion* (London 1962)

Harrison, J., *Themis* (London 1963)

Henry, P., *Saoithiúlacht na Sean-Ghaeilge* (Baile Átha Cliath 1978)

Hitchcook, G., *The Epistle to the Ephesians* (London 1913)

Horn, W., White Marshall, J., Rourke, G., *The Forgotten Hermitage of Skellig Michael* (Oxford 1990)

Hole, C., *A Dictionary of British Folk Customs* (1978)

Huxley, F., *The Way of the Sacred* (London 1989)

Hyde, D., *Legends of Saints and Sinners* (Dublin 1915)

James, E., *Seasonal Feasts and Festivals* (London 1961)

James, M., *The Apocryphal New Testament* (Oxford 1924)

Jasper, R., and Cuming, F., *Prayers of the Eucharist, Early and Reformed* (New York 1980)

JCHAS = *Journal of the Cork Historical and Archeological Society*

JRSAI = *Journal of the Royal Society of Antiquaries of Ireland*

Kendrick, T., *The Druids* (London 1927)

King, A., *Liturgies of the Primatial Sees* (London 1957)

Knox, H. T., *Notes on the Early History of the Dioceses of Tuam, Killala and Achonry* (Dublin 1904)

Lash, J., *The Hero* (London 1995)

Lattey, C., *The New Testament, Vol II The Acts of the Apostles* (London 1936)

Lewis, D. G., 'A Short Latin Gospel of Nicodemus written in Ireland', *Peritia,* vol. 5, 1986, 263-275.

Logan, P., *The Old Gods* (Belfast 1981)

Macalister, R., *Lebor Gabála Érenn* (Dublin 1938-)

MacCana, P., *Celtic Mythology* (London 1970)

MacCarthy, B., 'On the Stowe Missal', *RIA. Transactions* vol. XXVII (1885)

MacCulloch, J., *The Religion of the Ancient Celts* (London 1911)

MacGregor, A., *Fire and Light in the Western Triduum* (Collegeville 1992)

MacKenzie, W., *Gaelic Incantations* (Inverness 1895)

MacKillop, J., *A Dictionary of Celtic Mythology* (Oxford 1998)

Mac Neill, E., *Duanaire Finn* (London 1908)

MacNeill, M., *The Festival of Lughnasa* (Dublin 1982)

Macquarrie, J., *Paths in Spirituality* (Oxford 1972)

Markale, J., *Le Christianisme Celtique et ses Survivances Populaires* (Paris 1983)

Martene, E., *De Antiquis Ecclesiae Ritibus* (Rotomagi 1700)

McNeill, M., *The Silver Bough* (Glasgow 1961)

Melia, D., 'The Grande Tromenie at Locronan – a major Breton Lughnasa celebration', *Journal of American Folklore,* vol. 91 (Jan-March 1978), 528ff.

Miles, C., *Christmas Customs and Traditions* (New York 1976)

Muller-Lisowski, K., 'Contributions to a Study in Irish Folklore; Traditions about Donn', *Béaloideas* 18 (1948) 142-199.

Murphy, G., *Early Irish Lyrics* (Dublin 1956)

Ní Bhrolcháin, M., *Maol Íosa Ó Brolcháin* (Maigh Nuad 1986)

Ní Ógain, R., *Duanaire Gaedhilge,* Iml. II (Baile Átha Cliath)

Ó Cadhlaigh, C., *An Rúraíocht* (Baile Átha Cliath 1956)

O'Curry, E., *On the Manners and Customs of the Ancient Irish* (Dublin 1873)

O'Donovan, J., *Leabhar na gCeart* (Dublin 1847)

O'Donovan, J., *Annála Ríoghachta Éireann: Annals of the Kingdom of Ireland* (Dublin 1856)

O'Donovan, J., and Hancock, W., *Seanchus Mór,* vol. 1 (Dublin 1865)

Ó Duinn, S., *Forbhais Droma Dámhgháire: The Siege of Knocklong* (Cork 1992)

Ó Duinn, S., *Orthaí Cosanta sa Chráifeacht Cheilteach* (Maigh Nuad 1990)

O'Dwyer, P., *Célí Dé* (Dublin 1981)

O'Grady, S., *Silva Gadelica* (London 1892)

Ó hOgain, D., *Myth, Legend and Romance: An Encyclopaedia of the Irish Folk Tradition* (New York 1991)

Ó Laoghaire, D., *Ár bPaidreacha Dúchais* (Baile Átha Claith 1975)

Ó Nualláin, S., *A Survey of Stone Circles in Cork and Kerry* (Dublin 1984)

O' Rahilly, C., *Five Seventeenth-Century Political Poems* (Dublin 1977)

O' Rahilly, C., (Ed), *Táin Bó Cuailgne* (Dublin 1967)

Ó Riordain, S., *Tara* (Dundalk 1994)

Ó Síocháin, P., Ireland: *A Journey into Lost Time* (Dubhlinn 1967)

Ó Súilleabháin, S., *Irish Wake Amusements* (Cork, 1979)

Ó Tuama, S., *Caoineadh Airt Uí Laoghaire* (Baile Átha Cliath 1963)

Ó Tuama, S., and Kinsella, T., *An Duanaire, 1600-1900; Poems of the Dispossessed* (Mountrath 1981)

Ogilvie, R., *The Romans and their Gods* (London 1969)

Opie, I., and P., *The Singing Game* (Oxford 1988)

Opie, I., and Tatem, M., *A Dictionary of Superstitions* (Oxford 1992)

Partridge, A., *Caoineadh na dTrí Muire* (Baile Átha Cliath 1983)

Plummer, C., Bethada Naem nErenn 1 (Oxford 1922)

Plummer, C., (Ed), *Irish Litanies* (HBS 1925)

Plummer, C., *Miscellanea Hagiographica Hibernica* (Bruxelles 1925)

Plummer, C., (Ed), *Vitae Sanctorum Hiberniae,* Tomus Primus (Oxford 1910)

Power, D., *Unsearchable Riches: The Symbolic Nature of the Liturgy* (New York 1984)

PRIA = *Proceedings of the Royal Irish Academy*

Raya, J., *Byzantine Missal* (Birmingham Alabama 1958)

Rees, A., and B., *Celtic Heritage* (London 1976)

Ross, A., *Everyday Life of the Pagan Celts* (London 1972)

Rundle Clarke, R., *Myth and Symbol in Ancient Egypt* (London 1959)

Ryan, J., *Irish Monasticism* (Dublin 1931)

Sanderson, J., *The Story of St Patrick* (Boston 1895)

Schuster, I., *The Sacramentary* (London 1925)

The Scottish Council for Research in Education, *Aithris is Oideas*
    (Edinburgh 1964)

Smith, W., *A Smaller Classical Dictionary* (London 1854)

Stokes, W., *The Tripartite Life of Patrick,* Part I (London 1887)

Stokes, W., *Three Middle Irish Homilies on the Lives of Saints Patrick,
    Brigid and Columba* (Calcutta 1877)

Stokes, W., *The Martyrology of Oengus the Culdee* (London 1905)

Stokes, W. and Strachan, J., *Thesaurus Palaeohibernicus,* II (Cambridge 1903)

Taylor, D., *Singing Rhymes* (Ladybird Books 1979)

Thurian, M., and Wainswright, G., *Baptism and Eucharist: Ecumenical
    Convergence in Celebration* (Geneva 1983)

Tierney, J., *The Celtic Ethnography of Poseidonius* (Dublin 1960)
    (Reprinted 1985)

Tolhurst, J., *The Ordinale and Customary of the Benedictine Nuns of
    Barking Abbey* (HBS London 1927)

Tyrer, J., *Historical Survey of Holy Week* (OUP 1932)

Ua Duinnín, P., *Amhráin Thaidhg Ghaedhealaigh Uí Shúilleabháin* (Baile
    Átha Cliath 1903)

Vaillant, G., *The Aztecs of Mexico* (Penguin 1953)

Van Hamel, A.G., (Ed), *Compert Conculainn and Other Stories* (Dublin
    1933)

Vendryes, J., (Ed.), *Airne Fíngein* (Dublin 1953)

Watts, A., *Myth and Ritual in Christianity* (London 1983)

West, R.C., *Western Liturgies* (London 1938)

Whitlock, R., *A Calendar of Country Customs* (London 1978)

Wormaid, F., *English Calendars before AD 1100* (London 1934)

Wright, T., *The Historical Works of Geraldus Cambrensis* (London 1887)

Zaehner, R., *Hindu Scriptures* (London 1978)

ZCP = *Zeitschrift fur Celtische Philologie*

Index